START YOUR OWN
BUSINESS
AND HIRE YOURSELF

Insider Tips for Successful
Self-Employment in Any Economy

Suzanne Caplan

JIST Works
America's Career Publisher

Start Your Own Business and Hire Yourself

© 2010 by Suzanne Caplan
Published by JIST Works, an imprint of JIST Publishing
7321 Shadeland Station, Suite 200
Indianapolis, IN 46256-3923
Phone: 800-648-JIST   Fax: 877-454-7839   E-mail: info@jist.com

Visit our Web site at **www.jist.com** for information on JIST, free job search tips, tables of contents, sample pages, and ordering instructions for our many products!

Quantity discounts are available for JIST books. Please call our Sales Department at 800-648-5478 for a free catalog and more information.

Trade Product Manager: Lori Cates Hand
Interior Designer and Page Layout: Toi Davis
Cover Designer: Honeymoon Image + Design, Inc.
Proofreaders: Charles Hutchinson, Jeanne Clark
Indexer: Jeanne Clark

Printed in the United States of America

14 13 12 11 10 09   9 8 7 6 5 4 3 2

Library of Congress Cataloging-in-Publication Data
Caplan, Suzanne.
    Start your own business and hire yourself : insider tips for successful self-employment in any economy / Suzanne Caplan.
       p. cm.
    Includes index.
    ISBN 978-1-59357-744-5 (alk. paper)
 1. New business enterprises--Management. 2. Small business--Management. 3. Self-employed.
 I. Title.
    HD62.5.C3667 2010
    658.1'141--dc22
                                    2009031878

ISBN 978-1-59357-744-5

CONTENTS

Chapter 6: Knowing the Market and Hiring the Best

Chapter 7: Smart Marketing: Don't Spend Thousands

Chapter 8: Making a Profit 105

INTRODUCTION

I am a lifelong entrepreneur. My first small venture began when I was 10 years old. Living on a winding dead-end street, I determined that there was the need for a local newspaper. I collected the information (gossip and observation), hand-printed each copy, and sold them door to door for a quarter. Almost all the homeowners bought one because they admired my ingenuity (and they wanted to know what everyone else knew about them).

We (my partner—another young neighbor—and I) considered every dollar as profit, so we ended up with more spending money than most of our peers. Now I realize that we did not have a very good business model; however, then I was thrilled and motivated by the jingle in my pockets. That entrepreneurial spirit hasn't gone away. I still love to put my ideas out in the market, work hard, display them in front of potential buyers, and make a sale.

What the American people want to buy—and what people continue to think that they need—is in a state of constant change. Some goods and services are continually needed; food, clothing and housing are always basic. But there have been times when discount bulk foods are high on the list and others when organic and specialty foods drive the market. Home-improvement projects vary from do-it-yourself, to getting basic help with the more complex aspects such as electrical work, to fully kicked-up design ventures. All along these lines, there are entrepreneurs: individuals who market what they can provide to or do for the customers looking to hire them. The best ones will follow the trends of the times. When new things come along, these entrepreneurs will incorporate them into their businesses. In this way, we've seen business go from the horse and buggy (the way my grandfather started his business before the last century) to the Internet, which is where my current business venture is housed.

Perhaps you were an HR specialist at a company that downsized. Think about whether you can provide those services to several smaller customers who cannot afford a separate HR department. You were in the IT department in a business that was merged and your group was consolidated. Are there businesses that cannot afford a full-time

IT person but still need advice and ongoing services? It is almost impossible to think of a job that does not translate into a service that you could provide for many different companies.

My entrepreneurial life has included selling products (which I manufactured), books (which I wrote and promoted), and services (such as consulting, and designing and presenting seminars). The businesses were driven by circumstance and by passion. Some were a way to earn a living and others were designed to follow work that I loved.

My newspaper grew up to be a continuing service business in which I was organized with others to do yard work, snow removal, and delivery of the actual papers. As a teenager, I was invited to work with my father in his businesses—one was a manufacturing company and the other a wholesale distributor. The invitation had a salary attached, so I accepted. I worked everywhere in the company, from the office to the factory floor. This was my on-and-off mode until I was out of college and married. A few years later, I ended up as CEO of the entire operation when my dad passed away suddenly. This was my job for more than 20 years.

The Increasing Importance of Independent Contractors

I am an independent contractor and I use them frequently. In the construction of this book, a number of services will be required. Publishing has become a freelance business in substantial ways. Initially I wrote this book in longhand on a yellow legal pad because that is the way I think the best. Then I went to a secretarial service and had my scribbles transcribed into a Microsoft Word document that was e-mailed back to me. Then I enlarged and edited the chapters and finally sent them to my publishing company's editor. She put the final touches on the effort, although on occasion she uses the help of a freelance editor herself. You would surprised to know how many of the companies involved in producing this book are almost completely virtual.

But using the secretarial service is not the only instance in which this book will be touched by a self-employed or entrepreneurial venture. Most publishers these days outsource a good bit of their work, including graphic design, proofreading, indexing, and of course the printing itself. Books are distributed and sold by other various outside entities.

My additional advisors include my personal PR agent and an independent marketing advisor. We will work on a strategy to promote the book as well as my other work. I can see the value in those people who are self-employed and I bet my personal money on them. There will always be some clients who may be interested in working with only a larger company in a building with a great lobby and expensive offices, but I would rather not pay higher fees just to help someone pay for the higher rent. A growing number of potential clients share these values. We are living in changing times in which less is often viewed as better. And many professional firms are downsizing as well as becoming almost virtual. This provides opportunities for the newly self-employed.

Starting a Business Is Not a Get-Rich-Quick Scheme

What new business owners need to realize (and what many who have been around for some time already know) is that self-employment is a creative way to make a living, but it's not necessarily a winning lottery ticket. Businesses that start with a good concept and are operated by hard workers can indeed be very profitable. Give customers more than they expect and they will return your efforts with fair value and loyalty.

The same may not be true if you are selling a commodity product or selling to a non-relationship customer (in which the buyer and user of the product are not the same person). These are far more price-sensitive transactions. The only way to triumph in this environment is to sell quantity and keep cost very low. I know people who are perfectly happy selling consumable goods day in and day out. They make a steady living.

Intangible Reasons for Entrepreneurship

The reality is that some businesses may be more fun than profitable. Or they may be more satisfying than profitable. These are reasonable choices for a self-employed person: having the hope that you are making a difference creating value in your work while earning a living; or making a difference in the larger world while taking care of your own needs. Money is one of the factors that drives people toward starting their own business, but it is not the only one.

If you need to make a big financial hit, choose your industry for its growth and profitability and be prepared to invest capital. More often than not, it takes money to make money.

Are you seeing a theme here? Being self-employed is a great shot at work freedom. You can design your life the way you hope it will be and then go out and make it happen. All of those things that you didn't like about working for someone else need not be a part of your own venture.

Taking Care of the Day-to-Day Aspects

You also may find out that some of the mundane duties are necessary, required by government (particularly those related to taxes), or an important tool in business management. This fact has been a surprise to me in every venture. I wanted my business to be more informal and collaborative, but that didn't always help with getting tasks done when they should be done; deadlines are required.

There are few types of businesses that I have not been a part of in my decades of entrepreneurship. I have worked with manufacturers, retailers, distributors, restaurants, and professional services. They have different structures but have to follow the same basic business rules.

After taking over my father's company, I went into the community and started programs that encouraged new entrepreneurs. We worked with street vendors, a beauty salon, a small painting company, and a home-repair shop. Each owner was very different; they brought their own reasons and skills into their business. The ones who succeeded were the ones who loved what they did and found experts to help them where they needed it.

I have been a consultant for several restaurants and several printing companies. They all had something in common, aside from the fact that they were having problems and needed outside turnaround consultation. The restaurant owners loved to cook; and, with the exception of one, the owners enjoyed their guests. Printers are almost always unique—part artist and part manufacturer. Few of the small business owners possessed the discipline or the interest to learn the cost accounting to keep watch on the bottom line. The successful ones found an employee or outside advisor they trusted and would listen to. I made these contributors a full member of the team.

Recently, I had the pleasure of interviewing a local beauty-salon owner for a business radio show. He built a talent and his drive into a successful chain with 14 locations, a number of product lines that are sold in other salons, and a major fashion hair gallery in one of the most interesting areas of Manhattan. From a single shop in Pittsburgh, Philip Pelusi has grown into a force in the beauty business. He describes one of his assets as his brother, who possesses great management and financial knowledge. Henry and Philip have built an empire of shops and products and image.

What Do You Do and What Do You Want?

What have you liked and disliked about your job in the past? If the answer is that you like the 9-to-5 world where someone else is responsible for generating work for you and taking care of the details, my suggestion is that you keep on looking. If you love what you do or are particularly good at some skill and are willing to put yourself out there for a vote by each potential customer, read on. I am pleased to walk you through all that you need to know to make your venture as successful for your ego as it is for your pocketbook. I will cover all that you need to know on every aspect of business operations and give you the resources to either learn what you don't already know or outsource the services you do not like or feel confidence in doing.

Where Do You Begin?

A great place to start is the Small Business Development Centers, which you will find housed at the universities in your state. They provide training as well as consulting, all of which is high quality. Because the funding organizations include the Small Business

Administration as well as your state economic development authorities, the services are free. The SBDC can help you work on the details of your plan. A number of them have great demographic services and are financially astute when you get to that phase.

In a time when unemployment is high (and in some areas, going even higher), new business startups have slowed only a little. People who had already been considering the move to entrepreneurship are not going to be dissuaded, and they will be joined by new participants trying to find a way to develop sufficient work to create income for themselves. There is safety in numbers and most likely new incentives coming every day to encourage you. The government has always made moves in financing and technical assistance directed specifically at the self-employed. It is working to loosen the requirements on new loans by encouraging backers with incentives as well as funding larger projects, which will allow you to bid or become a subcontractor. Private-sector banks are also marketing more aggressively, although it is best to understand that banks don't give away money; they lend it.

History is on your side because the most productive and creative times for new business efforts have always come in downturns.

The Seven Secrets of Highly Successful Entrepreneurs

As a lifelong entrepreneur and business consultant, I have had a firsthand look at what works—and what doesn't. In addition to the basics for getting a business off the ground, I share tips related to my master list of business success principles:

1. **A business plan is a roadmap.** Write one and keep it updated. (See chapter 3 on developing a business plan.)

2. **You can't win the game if you don't keep score.** (See chapter 5 on accounting basics.)

3. **Always hire the best customers.** (See chapter 6 on defining your customer base, going after them, and keeping them.)

4. **Don't create a monster that you're not prepared to feed.** (See chapter 10 for more on tailoring the size of your enterprise to fit your life and personality.)

5. **A successful business is a team sport.** Don't go it alone. (See chapter 10 for more on enlisting the help of bankers, vendors, employees, and the community.)

6. **Even if you didn't invent it, you can improve it.** (See chapter 10 for more on how innovation can put you ahead of the pack.)

7. **Never get so deep into the forest that you can't see the trees.** (See chapter 10 for more on the importance of the big picture.)

CHAPTER 1

THERE'S NO TIME LIKE THE PRESENT TO START YOUR BUSINESS

There has never been a time in our nation's history when new businesses were not being formed, including during the Great Depression. Every economic downturn has produced a group of optimistic entrepreneurs who believed in themselves and what they set out to do. And regardless of the time and the financial circumstances, one person can always take an idea and make it happen in a very big way. Consider the empires of Sam Walton, Bill Gates, Steve Jobs, and others. Many successful entrepreneurs have started more than one venture during their lives, either by necessity (the first one didn't quite work out) or desire.

Some entrepreneurs have always known what they wanted to do, and some even started their first ventures in college. And then there are those who become the reluctant volunteer dragged into the family business by a parent and given few other choices. (I fell into the pool this way and have loved every minute of it.)

And during every time of economic change, many businesses are started by those who lose the job they had for a long time or those who no longer find their work meaningful. The self-employed business effort may begin with part-time independent work or doing odd jobs for a variety of people; however, there is a moment when the worker realizes that he is creating something new and decides to stop looking for a traditional job. He is now in business for himself.

If this has already happened to you, there are some things you need to go back to learn and perhaps reorganize. On the other hand, if this is just a new idea, the time you take to learn in advance and prepare will pay great dividends in the end. I guarantee that if you spend less time worrying about the time it is taking and more time thinking about developing your idea and implementing it, you will increase your own odds of success.

Becoming a Consultant in Your Field

Why would you want to begin a business at the same time companies are cutting back? One of the most interesting opportunities can be found in those cutbacks themselves. Many larger companies lay off entire departments, yet they still have functions within those job duties—simply not enough to justify full-time employees along with the cost of their benefits. Your first effort may be to develop a prior employer into a new prime customer. The total project money you charge could even come close to or exceed your former income, but the company will no longer have to pay the expense of you as a part of the overhead support. This could be a win for you both. The employer gets the accounting changes and you get the cash. And you also get the chance to establish yourself in the community as an expert in your field and the free time to develop other clients.

MARY JANE TURNS A LAYOFF INTO A CONSULTING GIG

Mary Jane was an IT manager at a large money-center bank that merged with an even larger institution. She knew weeks in advance that major layoffs were being planned. Most of her coworkers were thinking about and negotiating their severance packages. Mary Jane was working with the transition integration team, knowing that their work would not be complete before the in-house group became a good deal smaller. She intended to come back as an independent contractor and that took some planning.

Every chance she had, Mary Jane trained on the successor bank's software. By the time she was ready to leave, she was one of the few with working knowledge of both systems. She left information with the internal project manager promoting her interest in assisting with completion of the work. It was a home run that resulted in a year's contract, which was more than enough to turn her into a self-employed consultant.

Having a core volume of work as base revenue from day one makes any startup venture 50 percent easier. Getting to the point where you have a revenue stream is the hard part of getting started.

The Benefits of a Down Economy

A few years ago, when the economy was on a roll and money was flowing, it almost seemed as if anyone could open a store and sales would come. In theory, this might have made success look easier; however, the reality was not all as it appeared. Profits were the challenge (as they still are today). The careful operators were successful and those who were too casual were not.

Rental space was at a premium and landlords were charging top dollar, creating a burdensome overhead. Business owners were getting long-term leases with personal guarantees. This downturn has left store owners with these same high overhead costs; only now they have to be covered by substantially less volume. Margins are tight and entire shopping areas are closing, leaving a lot less foot traffic than the fairly new owners were counting on at opening. High costs at a time when you are building a new customer base can shorten the life of the business.

But now all of that has changed. New business owners have a lot more bargaining power than they did just a few years ago.

New Assets and Costs Are Cheaper Than Ever

The costs to start a new business are lower than they have been in decades. Rental rates in some parts of the country are 50 percent of what they were a year ago. Unfilled space is perishable: the lost revenue will never come back, so building owners have an incentive to be flexible. You may be able to get accommodations from the building owner, such as a period of time of no rent to start and lower rent in the first few months. Motivated landlords will give you incentives if you ask for them. Do your homework. Know what is important to your business in either cash or improvements to the space at a low- or no-cost basis. Then, negotiate for them.

All types of machinery and equipment that you may need to purchase (or lease) are in excess supply or can be purchased on the used market. Is the value of a shiny new truck for delivery or service really worth $10,000 more than a used one? Consider that all the money you save at this point actually translates to cash flow into your pocket. And the new equipment dealers are offering bargains at the same time. The choice is yours and now there are many.

Looking for office furniture? How about some of the expensive but now unneeded desks and credenzas that have been moved out of corporate offices? Some cleaning, refinishing, painting, and accessorizing and you'll look like a pro. Computers are no longer the high-priced items that they once were, and smaller notebooks can be used as your primary communication center. eBay and craigslist are great places to look for deals on used furniture and computers; just make sure you know what you're buying before you make the offer.

Store Fixtures Are Available

You've probably seen this sign even if you weren't interested at the time: "selling down to the bare walls." This signifies that a company is selling inventory as well as all of the shelving and racks. Sometimes these are marked with prices and sometimes there are auctions at this level—it usually depends on the quality of the fixtures. Either way, these are items you need never purchase new. See listings in your newspapers or call larger retail stores to check out what is available. There are also large fixture-liquidation centers you might want to visit. The retail closings will be going on for the next few years.

Caution: As I try to encourage you by letting you know that you don't need nearly as much money these days as you might have only a short time ago, I also want to make the strong point that no business startup should be based solely on low entry costs. You don't succeed without customers; so you must know, as certainly as you are able, whether there will be a market for your product or service once you have opened.

Finding a Winning Business Idea in a Recession

The next question might be this: How you can sell anything when we are in the middle of a recession? At the end of 2008, the U.S. gross national product (GNP) dropped over 6 percent, which is a significant number. But that also means that 94 percent of the purchases (and production) of goods and services continue. Individual needs continue for food, clothing, shelter, and entertainment. Businesses continue to make purchases for their own operations. Government needs may even grow; there are continuing military requirements as well as projects to stimulate the economy. Your challenge is to figure out where you fit in.

You have an advantage in these times because you can learn first about the changes in needs and wants and start up a new company to meet new and growing markets. The aging baby boomer population has created demands in health-care services and housing modifications. There is a demand for information and tools for economizing; for example, people are once again growing some of their own food. Energy efficiency is on everyone's list. Both home and business properties are being modified.

How does this apply to small, independent new businesses? Here are some examples of people who capitalized on trends:

- A company in Oregon selling seeds and plants meant for these new home gardens grew from 2 employees to 18 in less than one year. It produces the seedlings organically, sells them by word-of-mouth referrals and strong Internet presence, and ships all over the country. There is room for more companies catering to the growing home gardening crowd.

- A two-man plumbing crew that specialized in modifying bathrooms and kitchens to make them safer and more accessible to older people remaining in their homes grew its clientele from individual homeowners to larger contracts in cluster housing for senior citizens.

- A perennial hobby gardener started a landscape company specializing in what he called "grandma's gardens," which enable younger people to work side by side with grandparents on easy-to-plant and easy-to-care-for yards.

- Two young women began a resale shop where all of the inventory was on consignment; so they paid for only what they sold. Their trick was to merchandise the goods in the most upscale way.

We are in a time of major change; products, services, and attitudes are evolving in new ways. In the past few days, I heard someone say, "I wish I had a butcher who knew my name." I agree; I try to do business with shopkeepers instead of big-box stores. Spending habits are changing to emphasize quality over quantity. New opportunities are opening up all of the time. Look around at what is happening in your local area and you will probably draw great inspiration.

Your call is to balance what you want to do and what is still a marketable product or service. Or better yet, you can use the opportunity to get in on the ground floor of something innovative that offers opportunity. Web design is now a mature industry; thus, prices have been driven down. But online services such as virtual assisting continue to grow.

The Internet has provided vast opportunities, but with some accompanying cautions. You can market what you do to a large number of clients; however, the first step comes in being able to drive a good number of potential customers to your site. With literally hundreds of millions of Web locations, the competition is fierce. And the real cost of driving demand is kind of obscure. Attracting customers you can't see or call on takes some out-of-the-ordinary expertise. I am skeptical of all the ads about online stores that make millions.

Proactive Marketing Is the Key

The entire business transaction—from marketing to sales to customer service—becomes more intense during soft economic times. You need to see each customer as a valued asset. Your first step is to let customers know you are around and eager to do business. Sound simple? This may be one of the trickiest tasks for many business owners: how to get your name out and create an image that will motivate your potential new customers or clients to want to begin a relationship that ends in a sale.

Marketing is a particularly elusive art. You are creating the opportunity rather than making the sale. You can use mail, the broadcast or print media, the Internet, or even large signs and balloons—or some combination of all of these concepts. You can find yourself spending a lot of money on what seems like a little activity and if you haven't hit the right chord, it might not work. And because there is a delay between the time you start this process and the time of your first transaction, you might have doubts about what exactly is working.

Try to familiarize yourself with who your best customers may be. Determine what they read, listen to, or respond to and be there, as often as you can, with your message. If your budget can stand it, a good marketing pro is a worthwhile investment. There are also some great books on the topic. The classic is *Guerilla Marketing* by Jay Conrad Levinson.

Driving Sales and Extending Credit When Money Is Tight

Selling is the transactional aspect of a business—when the deal is made between buyer and seller. This is when money changes hands. This is also a place where current economic conditions present some challenges. Money is tight and credit may be even tighter. If you are in a business where sales are exchanged for cash, this will not be a concern. But if granting credit is one of your sales tools, used as a way to incentivize the deal or encourage a larger sale, a credit crunch could slow down your growth. However, when payment is in question, you will have to set some reasonable credit limits regardless of how much you want the revenue. Not being paid is not really completing the transaction.

When cash is flowing and credit is easy, business can be more casual. We might never return to that time again. At best, the recovery will take years. So new business owners will need to be more cautious and knowledgeable.

Sit down with a business counselor or a banker and discuss this aspect of your new venture. Find out whether you can partner with a money vendor such as a leasing company that will finance what you sell. Can you get contract financing from your bank and perhaps guaranteed by the SBA so that you can draw cash flow as you complete work? A source of outside capital is an important resource.

Money flows in and out of a business all of the time; however, this flow may be the major challenge as a result of this financial downturn. But it should not be enough to stop a motivated person. Good credit policies are very important to all ventures, but especially those that are new. A single large payment default may wipe out all of the profits.

These are areas I will cover in this book and they are skills you can learn. The courage and the creativity have to be yours.

CHAPTER 2

GETTING INTO THE GAME: RESEARCHING YOUR OPTIONS

If you have read the first chapter and continue to like the idea of being your own boss, now you must think about the preparation needed for starting your particular venture. You cannot become a hairdresser without taking classes and securing a license; and you cannot become a certified mechanic without the same process. You can be the owner of these businesses without a single training program—but it wouldn't be a good idea. Why would you think that you could start a business and put everything on the line without any preparation? Why would you want to? Don't go out on a limb without information.

If you haven't been doing it already, the time to start your research is now. Look around and decide where you will start. What type of business will you get into, and in what industry? How will you find customers? And how does your business fit in with your future plans?

Weighing Your Options

You have several options for getting into business. The next sections take a look at some of them in detail.

Buying an Existing Business

The first strategy to consider is buying an existing business. Businesses are always going up for sale because people's lives change.

The toughest part of starting any new business is trying to estimate when the customers will begin to appear and how long it will take to have enough of them to make a profit. The value of buying an existing business is that you will have a revenue stream (customers and money) coming in from day one. Most new business owners are overly optimistic. They think that during the weeks and months that they've been planning the business in their heads, outsiders also somehow know what is about to happen and can't wait for the big opening day. That doesn't happen. Most new startups show revenue one-third to one-half less than they expect. And often, that is less cash flow than they need.

There is one notable exception to this rule and that is restaurants. New eating places do create a buzz and all sorts of new customers want to find out what is happening and give it a try. The challenge of this business is to sustain the quality and the customer demand over the long term. Early profits may well turn into borderline performance. And then, if customer expectations aren't met, a new restaurant may meet the fate of the average, which is a life span of less than one year. That's a lot of work for a short-term company.

Do Your Due Diligence

Many businesses do not have a formal exit strategy. One day the owner decides that he or she finally wants to retire. Some business owners want out because they just don't like what they are doing anymore.

Some of these companies are doing quite well and some have their best years behind them. Outsiders might not know the difference. More often than not, the selling price is based on the owner's perception (and financial need) rather than reality. If you don't have serious financial savvy when you are looking at these opportunities, find an advisor who does. He or she can give you advice about the actual value as well as help you structure the deal.

Again, the value of buying an operating business is cash flow from day one. But the question for you to research is whether the company is operating at a profit or a loss. Be wary of the person who explains that he or she takes more out of the company than it shows on the books. There is no way of verifying this fact and you may be left with a leaky boat. What shows on the tax returns is the only cash flow you can count on. You have no recourse on a verbal representation.

What Are You Looking For?

Every small business is different. The real truth is that no two operate under the same set of circumstances. They reflect the same differences that exist in families and households. The number of people in charge of any smaller company may be a few or a lot, and the way they decide to spend their money may be conservative or luxurious. You may want to change all of that. The executive offices may be in a back room or wood-paneled and carpeted. Each small business is a reflection of the values, egos, and perceptions of the founders. You decide what means something to you. And if the company you want to purchase makes a profit, that's a good deal. If the company you are interested in purchasing is losing money and you feel confident that you can operate it more effectively, that may be a great opportunity. The selling price could be lower and you might be able to turn it around in quick order.

How Do You Value a Business?

Businesses are valued on a number of different bases:

- Asset value

- Cash-flow value

- Market value

Asset value is what the company is worth if you were to sell off everything that is owned in land, buildings, inventory, and equipment, piece by piece. The other two values are an estimate of the value of the operating company; in short, how much you will earn over a period of time from your benefits as owner of the company (salary, profits, and so on).

This might seem like a complicated formula; however, as you read this book further, you will learn what to evaluate and how to do it. There are entire books on the topic of buying a company and business brokers who can help you with the process.

> **Caution:** Virtually all brokers of anything—including houses and businesses—represent the seller and not the buyer. They are paid on the total selling price, so it might not be in their best interest to sell it to you at the lowest price because they would end up with a lower commission. Ask them about this from day one so that you know whether you need a negotiator on your side.

Reports from the Trenches

I have spent almost 16 years as a business consultant, along with 20 years of running a family manufacturing business. My practice has been throughout the U.S. and it has included involvement in the sales of companies. From my perspective, most owners overprice their companies and far too many new buyers overpay. This presents a challenge for the new owner going forward. Paying back the debt used to purchase the company may be the issue if cash flow is not sufficient. Because many of these deals were based on a payment plan, the seller never sees all of the proceeds, so it is not a great deal for anyone.

I have also seen prospective buyers make very good deals for a company they wanted to purchase. They knew that this was the size of operation they wanted, and in an industry they understood. Often, this results in the assets being sold for far less than they would be if purchased new. The new owners have a competitive edge from day one because they have low debt to retire and excellent value.

The best strategy for achieving this end is to be confident about what you are buying and what it is worth. You learn this skill only by comparison-shopping. See as many businesses as you can; look at as many financials and tax returns as you can get your hands on; and talk to many owners. You will find that most of them love to talk about their work—the good, the bad, and the ugly. You will get a great education and the only cost will be your time. Bring someone along with you who has business experience so that you can get an outside opinion.

Have You Looked at a Franchise?

Where does a franchise begin? One person creates a new concept, takes it into the market, and is well received. The owner decides that the idea would work in a multitude of locations, so an ambitious group forms to create a franchise operation. Meeting state and federal laws to make the franchise offering is a complex task.

What You Get

When you buy into a franchise operation, you get the following:

- An innovation that is proven to draw customers

- A great name

- A recognizable name and product or service that, from day one, has value

- Benefits from national advertising programs

- Organized backroom procedures that make it easier to get started

- Training

Ask in detail about how much training the franchisor will provide. Good training is the sign of a good franchise operation. A set of manuals is not sufficient. You need offsite training or a representative sent to your site to work with you.

A red flag when looking at franchises is how much territory the franchise will protect for you once you have made the purchase. Buying a great fast-food restaurant or a gym doesn't work quite as well when there is another one within a few miles. Franchise operators are often more interested in selling licenses than in creating successful new businesses.

By law, a great deal of information is available about any franchise business, including territory limitations and financial results of various franchises. Do your homework! Read *all* of the documents you are given. If you find one that you do not understand, take it to a professional to interpret.

Ask Someone Who Has Been There

If you think you might be interested in a franchise operation, start by visiting one in the chain that is operating. In fact, taking a road trip to see a few is not a bad idea. Ask the owners what they have experienced and what type of corporate backup they have gotten. Don't go to just the locations suggested by the parent organization; they are usually handpicked to show the best aspects of the business. Check online to find out-of-the-way operations within the chain and talk to the owners, even if you are able to do so only on the phone.

Find out how your prior experience compares with the operating owners' experience. If you think you want to own a single operation of a food chain and you have no prior restaurant experience, make sure that others who have not had years of this training can make it based on the name and the very uniform food recipes. Remember, the owner fills in for anyone who doesn't show up. You may find yourself working as the chef one day, a daunting task for someone who does not know much about cooking.

A Franchise Type for Everyone

There are many low-startup-cost business ventures such as cleaning franchises and senior home care. Some of the value is in the name and some of it is created by tenacity and hard work of the new franchisee.

The recent success of Curves is a good example. The name is great, as is the concept of being a safe and low-impact exercise studio for women. The individual owners, however, must put their personal touch on each one of their operations and make sure that the employees are qualified and concerned about the customer. This franchise has had a nice run and still seems to be growing. Curves franchisees tend to rent in lower-cost areas and can finance equipment purchases with leasing companies connected with the franchisor.

Then there is what might be referred to as a midsize food service buy with a large and established restaurant chain. McDonald's is the most expensive example of this type of franchise. The costs of the land plus the buildouts are fairly high, as are the initial franchise fee and ongoing royalties.

Network Marketing Businesses

A vast number of companies are selling a wide range of products and doing so via a network of distributors. These opportunities range from the excellent to a step or two above a garden-variety scam.

The key element to look for here is whether the drive for recruiting others is far more important to the success than the drive to sell the products to the public. For example, most Mary Kay reps and directors spend as much time with their personal customers as they do with their recruits. The more subs you bring on, the less selling you are doing and the more your income depends on the sales of others. If the product seems secondary, the opportunity may be of less value over the long term.

We all have met people who have generated big revenue at the higher levels of these companies, but you seldom get to see or learn from the many who have spent more money than they made. If you know the product well, are willing to sell it, and are particularly self-motivated, this may work for you. But in reality, few people really enjoy selling, and less often do they like doing so to strangers. Be honest with yourself here. The money will not flow without the sale of products coming first, so don't be enticed by the thought that this is less critical than recruiting others to do the work.

Work at Home and Make Big Money

Ads offering opportunities for home-based workers have existed for years, in part because they appealed to women who were caring for young children. I can remember the promise of a payday for stuffing envelopes (now mostly done by automated equipment) or being a secret shopper. Consider that there is a *big* difference between starting a home-based business and working for someone else's company in your home. Just sending the work to you and getting the completed work back is almost too costly to make this work at all. So there is little hope to make any real profit you can share.

But a lot of tasks can be done at home on a computer. There are a variety of record-keeping jobs, such as medical billing, and virtual assistant operations, as well as accounting, public relations, and marketing. Think of it as the exchange of information rather than goods. These operations are usually independently started and operated rather than a division of a larger entity.

Coordinating home help-care workers is a fairly new field and it is promoted by a number of smaller franchise-type organizations. The clients need help with grocery shopping, light cleaning, and getting to the doctors. You recruit the workers and maintain the schedules and the billings. The work is intense because you must have a group of workers who will show up when expected and billing is critical. But the need is there and finding older workers who need part-time work is not as difficult as you might think, especially since so many people recently lost a chunk of their retirement savings and need to keep working.

Another exception is the party plan companies, which allow you to sell a wide variety of products via an in-home sales event. One of the big original players was Tupperware, and then there was Avon and Mary Kay. They have been joined by Pampered Chef, jewelry such as Silpada and Cookie Lee, and ever newer ones such as Sabika and gold parties where customers bring gold to sell. This category also includes baskets, candles, scrapbooking, lingerie, and even adult toys. The home salesperson recruits a hostess who invites the guests and shares in the profit. Inventory costs are only for what is shown and orders are then placed with the company for a drop-ship delivery. It is possible to make a few hundred dollars or more out of one party and have several parties a week. But the territories are seldom protected at all and it becomes a continuing effort to meet new people and schedule new events.

If you are going to sell a product, be sure it is one you would buy yourself because you are likely to be dealing with customers who have much in common with you. If you wouldn't make the purchase, customers will be hard to find.

The Phenomenon of Online Selling

Online business is something of a personal fascination to me because I started a company called Safety Exchange almost 20 years ago. The concept was to use the available technology (which was still short of an active Internet) to sell excess protective clothing and gear between safety distributors. We used e-mail and faxes. The few customers who were able could even log onto our computer, which was operating as the informational server, to actually see what inventory was there. We had fun and we learned—and we even made some money.

Popular Online Selling Sites

eBay turned this type of selling into an art form. Many people use this tool in more than a few interesting ways. They commit a lot of time to being full-time eBay traders. eBay enables you to run a store without a storefront, which cuts overhead dramatically. Even if you're home based, you may have access to millions of buyers by knowing how to list and price your goods.

Some of the keys to success on eBay include the following:

- Carry unique, collectible, or hard-to-find merchandise so that you will develop a following.

- Make sure that you handle your transactions with accuracy and speed.

You must also correctly represent what you have to offer and deliver it to the buyer quickly and in good condition. eBay refers to itself as a community. True to that designation, there are community values and there is gossip. Only here, it is official. Sellers and buyers evaluate each other. Make too many mistakes and your business is in trouble. Buyer and Seller rankings are listed on the site.

Other shared selling sites include craigslist, which also operates on a negotiated-price basis without the auction (the look is different as well). You can also launch a small store on Yahoo! or Amazon, where you set a fixed price for your goods. You can think of the Internet as a constantly changing village or shopping mall. Open your site where the traffic you want is already surfing by. And play by their rules.

Starting a Standalone Store

Then there is the standalone online store, which you or a developer create yourself and put up on a shared server for customers to use. The question with this type of store is "how will they find you?" That answer may be far more challenging than you first assume.

Many early online sellers believed that the look of their Web site would make it a great success. I remember sites that flashed and sang and generally made me want to go away. I was not the only one who felt that way. It was not easy to complete an order because the software loaded so slowly. Only a few years ago, it was estimated that more than two-thirds of online orders were not completed. That equals someone walking out of a store in the midst of paying for an item. The tools have improved and they are not that expensive to install and maintain. You can pay a monthly fee to use prepackaged storefronts that are marketed by software companies.

But do not count on all your volume being generated by strangers who come across your site. Marketing is critical in this type of venture. Try out a smaller and less expensive site to begin with. If you gain traction, you can enlarge the site and the product line.

The Key to All Business Is Finding Customers

There are several hundred million Internet users in this country alone and each one is a potential customer for an online business. Getting someone to order something online sounds a lot easier than getting someone to drive to your local outlet, doesn't it? For some, that may be true; but for most, it's a tough game. Driving traffic (the customer to be) to your site is really an art and involves many technical aspects, such as optimizing search terms and some heavy lifting such as going out to other sites and letting people know you exist. Like a needle in a haystack or worse, a random potential customer is unlikely to find you unless you do some marketing.

And then there is the other world called "click and mortar," in which you have a physical location that generates traffic to your site. The interesting opportunity here is that a customer may visit your shop or office once only, but will continue to conduct business with you through your site. You can grow a lot faster using multiple touch points to your work. I worked with a candy-supply business that was one of the few in town but was located in an out-of-the-way place. Customers came to the store to look around before big holidays but purchased online or by phone when they needed fill-in material.

Your job is to develop the contacts by getting the e-mail addresses of everyone you do business with. That's a good idea even when you don't have a Web store; it has become as important as a mailing address or a phone number. You need to know where your customers are. And they need to hear from you as a reminder that your business is still eager to serve them. Do not e-mail blast them out of their homes, but do keep in touch and announce when you have something new going on.

Consider Industry Conditions and Your Future Goals

The business you choose should be in a viable industry and fit with your life plans. The following sections go into more detail on these aspects of choosing a business.

Industry Conditions

All industries have cycles. There are the early days of new development, bringing the product or service to market, and then the growth phase. And, finally, there is the age of maturity, when growth slows and some of the early players leave the field. This may be almost impossible to imagine in the beginning days when there is a launch and all the excitement. Each new online service or site looks as if it is offering the ultimate, starting with AOL, Yahoo!, or YouTube. What people perceive as the newest, hottest technology seems to change almost weekly.

The small-business landscape is littered with the remains of good concepts that became fads and services that became unnecessary. You cannot get away from the fact that your industry might not last as long as you need for it to in order earn a living from it. You need to be in an environment of growth in terms of technology, demographics, or some other factor that will propel your development. You can get statistics through your library, marketing consultants you may hire, or the Small Business Development Centers. Consider in advance what the future will look like and decide whether you can reinvent your business as you go along. This ability will give you a longer business life.

What Are Your Future Plans?

If you are a 50-year-old who is trying to reinvent yourself, you may want a business that will go on for only 10 to 12 years and that is a different concept than the one desired by a 30-year-old trying to build a lifetime empire. Getting into a mature industry when the entry costs are low and the cash flow is above average is the ideal scenario for an older entrepreneur. Younger business founders may spend more in the early phase and get a larger payout over the long term.

GETTING A BUSINESS AT A BARGAIN AND TURNING IT AROUND

One of my friends who retired in her mid-50s took over an antiques business from a woman looking to retire. She paid only the wholesale value of the inventory still in the store, in great part because the previous owner did not keep good customer records and the ongoing business opportunities had less value. The new owner immediately began marketing to local buyers and listing items on eBay. Within six weeks, she had made back 50 percent of her investment. And her interesting offers helped her become an eBay success. Her goal is to have a more independent career and positive cash flow for 10 more years; and then she plans to sell what she has built. She is well on her way.

FAILURE IS A RITE OF PASSAGE

I consulted with two young men who partnered to create a new generation of restaurant software to predict sales and control costs by establishing staffing levels and food orders. Both had been through high-tech startups that closed once they ran out of venture capital. Thinking they could use their time while on unemployment benefits, they ran up their credit cards trying to finish the project and had no money left for marketing. New money partners had to be brought in and they exchanged money for 60 percent of the company. This startup cost 10 times more than was anticipated and the product still did not make it to market.

But the two founders received an education worth far more than the cost of time and money and they are busy creating a new venture. Many successful entrepreneurs have failure in their path—this seems to be almost a rite of passage. When you are young and have fewer responsibilities, you can take greater risks.

You need to consider your age, your energy, and your life goals and match your business choice to your personal needs. This is a very important place to begin.

CHAPTER 3

MYSELF, INC.: DEVELOPING YOUR BUSINESS PLAN

The steps reviewed in the preceding chapter may take you only weeks, or can be planned out over months. But now the real meat of the work begins. What are *your* specific plans and how will you put them into action? The document in which you answer these questions is referred to as a business plan. Fortunately for you, the business plan does not have to be nearly as formal and uniform as many new business owners fear. This chapter describes the required information, how to go about finding it, and how to structure it.

I will make one strong recommendation: Your business plan should be written primarily by you. Get help if you need it, but do not pay anyone else to do the work. This is the map to your future and you need to be the one who is involved. Would you let someone else date the person you are going to marry? Starting a business is a big move. If you can't make it through the prestart steps, you will not make it on the field of play. Appendix B includes a sample business plan. For now, let's walk through the steps of putting together your plan.

Caution: I will say this again for more emphasis: Do not ask or pay anyone else to work through the issues of *your* business plan.

First, Determine Which Legal Entity to Use

Companies can be formed as a number of different legal entities, ranging from the very informal to the very complex. Becoming a business means a lot more than choosing a name and designing a logo. You have to make a registration with your state and identify what type of entity you have chosen.

Your choices are the following:

- Sole proprietorship
- Partnership
- Limited Liability Company
- Corporation (S or C)

Caution: If all you do is register the name with your state, you will then have to open your bank accounts under your personal name and you will be considered a sole proprietor by default.

What should be the determining factor in choosing a legal entity is the exposure to liability. Will you generate a good bit of business debt that might put you at risk? If you have unforeseen problems with the work that you do, is it possible that a client might sue you? (Win or lose, you pay the lawyers.) Or will you eventually have employees who will act in the name of the business and leave you personally exposed?

BUSINESS STRUCTURE MISTAKES CAN COST YOU BIG

My own heating contractor had his wife "doing his books" and it turned into a sad story. She sent out bills and recorded them but did not keep copies. They knew customer A owed $500, but not what specific work had been completed. Calls came in, disputes were created, and some bills were paid in part or not at all. He owed his suppliers but never had the money to pay them. He was thousands in debt before the reality began to hit. This money would have to come out of his own pocket because there was no corporate protection.

I also worked through some major trauma with a woman who owned a very successful and quite large restaurant (also not incorporated). During a bad spell, she did not pay her sales tax and the debt grew substantially. In addition, this is a state crime and she ended up being charged and put on probation. Quite often, even a corporate shell will not protect the owner from tax liability.

An additional complication comes when you decide to sell the company. If you are not incorporated, there really is little value beyond actual assets because there is no separate company to transfer. Many of the intangible assets you may have spent time in developing, such as a known name and customer list, cannot be easily packaged with the equipment and property.

Sole Proprietorships

A sole proprietorship consists of a single individual who owns all of the business and its assets. The sole proprietor is responsible for all of the liabilities as well. No matter how many employees you eventually hire, you are still the one on the spot.

This business entity seems as if it would work well, and I have heard many advise this because it simplifies tax reporting. All of your income and expenses are reported on a single tax schedule (Schedule C) and that becomes a part of your personal tax return. Tax forms should never drive this business decision, however; these days, there is user-friendly software to handle virtually all types of corporate reporting. But, the fact is that you will need to hire an accountant as soon in this process as you can afford one.

Would a Partnership Protect You?

Partnerships, which are difficult for a number of reasons of governance (ever meet two people who *really* think alike?), are not a solution for the issue of liability. In fact, with any potentially large liability such as taxes or legal judgments, there can be complications because creditors can come after you both, together and individually, regardless of whether the fault was with only one. At that point, there is little hope that the business entity will be able to continue to operate. The pressure of these events adds strains that are difficult to overcome.

Note: The wealthy partner may be required to handle more than 50 percent of the debt. The first dollars collected from either partner can be used to retire all the debt. The liability is not split 50/50.

Limited Liability Company: A Simple and Legal Solution

The easiest and cheapest way to protect yourself is with a Limited Liability Company (LLC). An LLC is a separate entity unto itself. The owners of the shares of the LLC (there may be one or many) do not own the assets of the business outright and they cannot be held personally liable for the debts as well. Both are carried in the name of the corporate entity and all actions are directed there. The shareholders are referred to as members and will govern under an operating agreement, which you should have if there are multiple members.

Caution: Although boilerplate forms are available at office stores and online, you really should have a lawyer review any documents you decide to create.

The tax responsibility and benefits of the company pass through to the individual. You can elect to be treated in one of three ways:

- A single member (you report on a personal schedule)

- A partnership (which files a return as such)

- A corporation (a separate corporate return is required)

All profits are taxed back to you as an individual. Any losses are deductions for your benefit. Employment and sales-tax responsibilities that the corporation incurs that are not satisfied may revert back to the owner or the responsible party.

Tip: Once you have employees other than yourself, you will have to file for a Tax Identification Number and begin submitting tax reports to the federal, state, and local government.

Becoming a Corporation

This provides the greatest shield to everyone involved, but it does come with costs. There will be choices (a Sub S or C Corporation) and you will need to write agreements and bylaws. This is the time to use the services of both an accountant and a lawyer. If this is within your area of expertise, there are online services that will walk you through the filings. The SBA's SCORE program gives classes on business startups, as do many of the SBDC centers. This book will answer some of your questions; however, those that pertain to your personal needs or expectations should be addressed by a local professional. No two businesses have exactly the same circumstances and there is not a one-size-fits-all solution.

The creation of a corporation does not have to cost you a fortune; however, forming it well may pay great dividends in the future.

LAWYERS AND ACCOUNTANTS LOOK FOR GREAT CLIENTS

Many local professionals aggressively market to develop new clients. Many are very interested in getting in at the early stage of a new business with potential and may well give you a discount so that you can grow together. Ask around and look for these advisors at network meetings and seminars. You may get some solid advice at a discount and also find a long-term business relationship. You need to start here and find a good match.

Writing the Sections of Your Plan

The business plan puts into writing your own concepts and helps you sell them to others—sometimes lenders, sometimes vendors or landlords, and sometimes potential investors. This is the written evidence of how much work you have been doing in advance and how feasible your concept really is.

Your business plan will include some or all of the following headings:

- Executive Summary
- Market Analysis
- Sources of Revenue
- Operating Strategy
- Management
- Pro Forma Financials

Executive Summary

The first section of your business plan is about the details of the company itself, so you must make those decisions before you begin to tackle this document. Here you will state what type of company you have formed and what its primary purpose is.

Begin with a strong statement about what your company was formed to do and why you are planning to be involved in a venture in this field. There are several issues to cover:

- Describe the current status of this new venture. Have you already purchased the assets of another company to use? Will you be involved in a franchise operation, or are you starting from scratch? Answering these questions allows you or any reader to understand how many steps you still have to take in order to get the new venture up to speed.

- Why did you make this choice of business? Is it because you have previous experience in the field? Is there a growing demand for products/services that you feel motivated to meet? Or is the current climate of federal stimulus and support a good opportunity for you to create success in a worthwhile effort?

- Where do you expect to take this company in the future? Here is where you show yourself and anyone else who reads the plan that you have taken time, thought about where you are taking this venture after day one, and done some of your homework. Show that you understand the size (or limitations) of the potential market and your likely place in it. Even if you have thought of a completely unique concept, others will work to catch up—be sure of it. How will you get there first?

This is the section where you can fully describe the business you are going into. What is your product or service and how do you expect to create, manufacture, source, or sell it? Most important, why is it different from other products in its category? No neighborhood needs 10 stores selling the same thing and no industry needs 20 printing companies going after the same jobs. This drives down profits and leaves one or more of the operations vulnerable.

You are asking one important question in this section: What will your sources of revenue be? What are you working on that will turn into cash and how much of that cash will you or your company retain as profit? These are the most important considerations upfront, because revenue should be the driver of all planning decisions.

Perhaps you will start out in one product line and expect to expand both products and services. Will you have enough revenue in the early stages to make a go of it? If not, can you hold out long enough until the second phase comes into play?

Writing this down (and it does not need to be book quality) helps you think over issues for yourself as well as present them to any reader. You may want to share it with friends and advisors and ask for their opinions. You may believe that a new product or service will be a great thing, but you will need to convince a whole lot of new customers that your idea is that good. Test it before you put the money on the line.

Market Analysis

Two elements make up this section:

- Statistics on the size of your target market

- A plan for how you will reach this market

Defining Your Market

The first element, which has been looked at along the way, is how big is the market you are planning to enter? In short, you need to know how many potential clients you may have.

In 2006, I founded an online social network called WomenEtcetera.com. We were determined to create a community for women over 50. At that time, the total number of women between the ages of 50 and 69 (which was our real target audience) was more than 32 million, with an additional 20 million in the 40 to 50 range, giving this demographic bulge a long shelf life. We knew who our audience was. Our question was how to reach them. And then the bigger question was how to make a profit from the effort.

Make sure you have a big enough target, or at a minimum one that is readily identifiable. A very directed marketing pitch that goes to a very specific customer is referred to as niche marketing. An ethnic food store or restaurant that is one of only a few in an area where there is interest and demand for these products is a good example of this strategy. The industrial version of the same strategy is to make replacement parts for equipment still in use where the original supplier has stopped doing this work. This is becoming an issue in the auto industry as the regular suppliers no longer produce parts for cars that are no longer in general production. There is a good bit of manufacturing equipment still in use that demands specially tooled parts. Price is not the issue—availability is.

The bottom line to your bottom line is this: Are there enough potential customers who are likely to choose your business so that you will be able to generate profitable revenue? Changing habits of the buying public is never easy unless you are innovative and tenacious.

Reaching Your Market

The SWOT analysis is a marketing tool that is taught on a high level in most business schools. But it is really not that difficult to do for any company. SWOT is a four-point challenge to your business idea. Including this in a business plan indicates a strong level of potential interest in your new venture and may well impress the reader.

The SWOT acronym stands for the following:

- **Strength:** What will you and your company be doing so well that it will get you noticed and bring in customers? What makes you better than the competition?

- **Weakness:** What elements of the business are you most concerned about? What type of help do you need to overcome this challenge and how have you planned to handle this?

- **Opportunity:** Why is there a chance for your success at this time? What new need will you fill? Is this a limited window or a long-term opportunity?

- **Threat:** Are there some unknowns out there, such as a bigger player trying to take the same customers? Are you undercapitalized and hoping to leverage the money you have once a revenue stream begins? Showing that you understand these potential problems and have considered how to handle them will be of interest to others who read this plan.

Sources of Revenue

The revenue stream is the most critical issue for any new business venture, and, sadly the one that is most often ignored. This was particularly true in the dot-com era that went bust. The main strategy was to create a Web site, get a lot of hits, keep the visitors' attention, and figure out later how to make money from it.

A number of sites were very innovative and popular but never made any money at all. I was an advisor to one called MizBiz.com. When I asked the founders about their stream of revenue, they explained that I did not understand the "new economy." They burned through two million dollars and the adventure was over. There is no new economy, even when the technology is cutting edge. You still need money to change hands from buyer to seller.

The Sources of Revenue section is the place where the rubber meets the road. What are you selling, how many will you sell, and how much will you charge? This is the basic math that equals the number described in a financial plan as income or revenue.

In addition to being specific about your product or service, you need to understand how your pricing compares to that of others who are in a similar business. If you plan to charge more, explain what the added value is to the customers/clients that will motivate them to pay more. You are testing your business model here, so make sure you know what it is.

If yours is a service business and charges by the hour, how many hours can you bill and what is your rate? If you expect to sell a product, how many units will you sell and what is the selling price? Later in the plan, you will identify the profit margin (the revenue less the costs) and determine how much of the money will flow to your bottom line. But you begin with the revenue.

Have you planned for more than one way to bring a stream of revenue into your business? These days, having multiple strategies to generate sales is a great and often necessary concept. If you sell a product, can you also provide service for it? If you sell one category of products, are there others that you can also carry? A hair salon may sell the product line it uses. A restaurant might sell additional food for customers to take home after enjoying a sit-down meal. As the potential value of each customer rises, the bottom line will increase; this is your goal.

You can also generate revenue from an alliance with others in compatible businesses. An IT consultant might work with a software company or a graphic artist could partner with a local printing concern. In many of these cases, commissions are involved and these will add to your company's revenues.

PARTNERING FOR SUCCESS

Being self-employed means that you need to be as creative and expansive as you can be. Find out where there is good synergy. This has been my personal strategy since I was in charge of our family business. We were safety clothing manufacturers and we often partnered with a company in the Midwest to fill orders with both of our products so that we would not lose the business. As a consultant, I partner with other professionals such as lawyers and accountants and we work on projects together. Not everyone is good at this, but it can make your company grow faster and enable you to focus on what you do best.

Operating Strategy

This section on operations allows you to identify all of the resources—in terms of equipment, space, inventory, additional employees, and cash—that you will need. You may be working out of your home and your only needs are a computer and the accessories. Or you might plan to start the business at home and eventually expand to an office once the revenue begins to grow. Retail sales require a storefront or an online store. Whether or not you have made a final decision on the likeliest space to rent, you should include the details in your criteria.

Also review questions such as the overhead cost in addition to the startup costs. You might discover a need for capital you did not think of in the beginning.

UNDERSTAFFING CAUSES PROBLEMS

I stopped in to meet the owner of a dog bakery (yes, making doggie cookies and other treats) and accessory business because I was curious about its range of inventory. Dog lovers are very serious about their pets, and I don't see how one could walk out of this store without making a purchase. This was a great shop in a great location. The main problem was that the high rent prevented the owner from hiring much backup staff. If she or her one employee were not in, the store could not open. Even during busy times, there was only one person working because the owner could not cover the long retail hours except by the owner or the employee working alone. The business lost sales sometimes because a customer could not wait. The store opened late on occasion due to the lack of backup. There was an operating challenge that would have been uncovered in a detailed business plan.

Your operating strategy is how you will actually create or sell your product or service and where and how you will deliver it to the customer. You need to develop enough information for this section so that any reader will be able to understand the business model that you envision. You also need to become confident that you have a strategy that will make it work.

WHAT WILL YOU LEARN?

I would not be surprised if you are beginning to think that this is a difficult process. Starting a new business requires time and effort to think about a number of issues at once. Do people want what you will sell? How will they know that you are providing this product or service? What will you charge and how much can you sell? This is where your operating strategy explains how you will generate your sources of revenue. Have you chosen a location that generates sufficient buyer traffic? Does your staff have the capacity to produce as much as you expect to be able to sell?

All of these sections really come down to answering the question of cash flow: Will you create enough? In the final section of any business plan, you need to put actual numbers to the theory and show what the first year or more will bring in terms of actual revenue, profit, and cash flow. If the theory seems plausible, the numbers will have greater potential. You may well go back and forth redoing sections of your plan as you go along. You will be able to show the credibility of the concept as you begin putting theory into practice.

Management

Particularly if your plan will be used to go to lenders or investors, this section will be of interest to others. You need to describe your own experience and background, emphasizing what makes you prepared to be successful in your own venture. If others are coming in as partners or employees, or even those who will have an alliance with you, their experience and expected contribution are part of this discussion. You are identifying the human resource needs of the business. Talk about the team. They are the ones who will be on the field when the game begins.

Pro Forma Financials

This is the section that most new business owners find to be the greatest challenge. If you can break it down to the most basic components, the confusion should be less. A pro forma is just a prediction in numbers about how a new business will do in the few years after it opens. You are estimating the revenue and expenses and coming up with a profit. That profit becomes part of a cash flow, which tells you how much capital you will need. A growing venture will require funding capital as it moves toward its goals.

Here are the basics of a pro forma and the profit-and-loss statement, which ties into cash flow.

Income (expected revenue from all sources)
— Direct expense (the actual cost of the goods)

Operating or gross profit

Gross profit
— Overhead (fixed costs such as rent)

Net profit (before tax)

Net profit is used to pay off the principal of the debt, to fund growth, and to be returned to investors as a dividend. This positive cash (or negative at times) will add to your monthly cash balance.

Here is how a cash-flow pro forma is structured:

Beginning cash (in the bank, etc.)
+ All revenues (all cash sales or collections)
+ All loan proceeds and investment (all capital)
— Direct and overhead cost
— All debt service

Remaining cash (which starts the next month)

This is similar to a look at your personal cash flow in a family budget. Every month you start out with money; you earn more and you pay bills. Hopefully, there is some left over and that is where you begin the next month. I will cover the finance side in more depth in chapter 5, and you can see an example of a pro forma section in the sample business plan in appendix B.

This Document Is a Roadmap

Just like any mapping service, you start with where you are and you lay out where you want to go. Once you have begun the process of putting it on paper, you will know where the tricky turns are and what roadblocks might be out there. You might be able to find secondary solutions for the detours that will be there if you need them. You are more likely to reach your ultimate goal, or get close to it, if you see what the journey will involve.

CHAPTER 4

SETTING YOUR BUDGET AND GETTING FUNDING IN TOUGH TIMES

This might surprise you, but it has been my experience with many new business ventures that too much money is often a more difficult challenge than too little. Startups with too much capital tend not to make an effort to control themselves. Often they just spend money for anything they think they might need and don't keep to a budget. And when some of the money you are counting on actually exists in loans or a credit line, there is a real risk of getting yourself into serious debt. Try to create a bare-bones budget and then fund as if every dollar were critical—because it is.

One of the primary reasons that you developed your business plan was to determine how much money you would need and where it would be going. By now you have realized that every business costs some money to start, and a few need a lot more than the founder ever realized when he or she began the project. If you spend more on one line item than you budgeted, try to get it back from another.

UNWISE BUSINESS DECISIONS CAN SPELL DISASTER

Many of us have seen a restaurant owner spend tens or even hundreds of thousands of dollars in design before an opening. I worked with owners who spent $1.2 million in buildouts and decorations before opening day. They thought they were lucky to be in a hip new area prior to anyone else. But it took

(continued)

(continued)

> a year for others to be a part of the new development. By then, the high loan costs and missed payments as well as back rent had this investment in jeopardy. In another example, Southside Works in Pittsburgh was not one-third full when the first tenant got into trouble. And the only reason that tenant lasted as long as it did was that the developer cut the owners some slack because he didn't want new prospects to see someone close. This was not outside investor capital at risk; this project was funded with the owners' money.

In this chapter you will learn how to figure how much money you will need, get that money, and spend it wisely.

Question #1: How Much Money Do You Need?

The pro forma of any business plan seldom includes a startup budget, even though this is a critical element of any new venture. Knowing how much you will spend upfront will tell you about how much it will cost you on a monthly basis. A portion of your monthly payments will be any borrowed funds you have required for startup. So before you decide where the cash will come from, calculate all of the costs. Then you will know whether you already have enough money or how much of a loan or investment you will need.

If you have looked at the pros and cons of the different business structures and decided to stay a sole proprietor, the legal and filing costs will be minimal. Any form of incorporation will require professional fees as well as registrations. Accountants are also critical advisors on filing your documents; so depending on where your business is located, your fees here will range from $1,500 to $5,000, and perhaps more. In addition, if you plan to have investors, you will need more complicated agreements, which will increase these costs.

Other startup costs include the following:

- **Preparing the business location:** Will you be using machinery or equipment that requires heavy wiring or Internet lines? Will you want to add or subtract any walls? How will you need the space to be finished?

- **Deposits, fees, and licenses:** Budget for deposits and other fees for the property and for any insurance you require. Plan on paying up to three months' worth of fees in advance because you have no existing business credit.

- **Marketing material:** At a minimum, you need business cards and a brochure. It might be sensible to limit yourself until you know more about what works. Before long, you are likely to need more, so allow for that increase. Still, spend your marketing dollars slowly.

- **Lease or purchase of vehicles and equipment:** A lease costs less, but you may discover it is not easy to qualify for one. Consider purchasing used equipment to start out with and perhaps purchase some of your items on credit terms from the seller.

- **Inventory or raw material:** You will need to stock a shop and a factory floor with products to begin. The replacements should come from cash flow from sales.

- **Working capital:** The money to pay for what you will need to sustain you until the cash begins flowing. You will be paying overhead for a while before you begin to operate at a profit.

The last of these—working capital—is the most difficult to predict. The first try you had was when you created a pro forma for your business plan. You were estimating money in and money out for a time in the future. All the cash you need to sustain your business over the early months and then to grow is considered working capital. If you underestimate the amount, you may be right in the middle of getting launched and be so strapped for cash that you can't get the company where it needs to be. The only answer is to leave a little extra in the budget to cover the unforeseen—and perhaps leave a little bit of credit untapped, as well.

Getting Money Without a Loan

In the early years of this century, a lot of new business owners were finding most of their cash needs funded by loans based on the equity of their homes and available cash reserves on their personal credit cards. This is no longer possible because plummeting home values are soaking up everyone's equity; meanwhile, credit card companies are slashing credit limits even for longtime cardholders. That is not all bad because such practices were a questionable idea, even though a lot of small-business owners were doing it. Your business must be able to make it on the cash flow it is generating now or in the future and not just a flow of borrowed money.

But that does not mean that all loans are bad. Business startup loans have always been a challenge to get, and this is one of the reasons for the existence of the Small Business Administration (SBA). The SBA uses a federal guarantee program to encourage the banks to loan money. Then, if the borrower defaults, the banks will be at risk for only between 10 and 30 percent of the loan. The SBA can pre-approve smaller loans of up to $35,000 for its guarantee program. Another benefit of working with this SBA approval program is that you will know what you have available as you are finishing your plans, even if you have not yet chosen your bank.

But before we go through all the elements and ways to apply for a loan, let's discuss some of the more creative ways to finance a business. Everything does not have to be on a strictly cash basis.

Have You Thought About Bartering?

The concept is to think of ways to exchange services you provide for services you need, thereby lowering your need for capital. Every dollar you save will be less you have to borrow and pay back. And there are times when this type of exchange even helps to market a new venture. You will create a user already in place who can serve as a reference for your work.

Here's an example of a mutually beneficial bartering arrangement. Assume you design a Web site for someone who does work for you, such as a carpenter who is helping with your business buildout. The carpenter gets an essential business marketing tool and you get a discount on your carpentry as well as a sample to show future customers.

Can You Co-venture with an Existing Entity?

Another source of cash or cash equivalents (items of value that will be converted to cash) is a company contribution of material (inventory) to your startup. Perhaps it is a company for whom you will resell or the creator of a raw material you will utilize. This entity is gaining market exposure and you are saving the cash. This may take the form of some free samples or easy credit—for example, inventorying goods on consignment (not having to pay until they are sold) or with extended credit terms of over 90 days. This will allow you to grow into a revenue stream without drawing all your capital. Many companies are cautious with startups, but quite a few are learning to be aggressive in order to grow their own businesses.

Negotiating Back-End Payments

The most important need for capital in many new ventures is to pay the rent and perhaps the leaseholder improvements on the space you require. Many landlords that have empty space are happy to have a tenant signed up and their own cash stream beginning again. They may well give you a few early months of free or reduced rent as an incentive. They may also allow for lower rent for the first year and the difference will be added to the last year when there should be more cash available from your more established business. As you look at spaces, find out what the offer might be and use this benefit as part of your thought process. You want to be in a great location, but there are some slightly less appealing ones with motivated landlords.

RESTAURANT OWNER GETS SWEET DEAL

A number of years ago, an old auto dealership that operated in a huge historic building in Pittsburgh closed. The space was empty for some time. Finally, the development group in the neighborhood got together the funding for reconstruction. It was turned into a mini-mall. The one business the group wanted to attract was a restaurant. There was a successful

(continued)

(continued)

> upscale rib joint not that far away and the team putting this
> property together went on a recruiting trip. The restaurant
> owner was offered a lease that started at two percent of his
> gross and went up one percent per year for the next few years.
> It was an offer he could not refuse.

Using Credit Wisely

Most potential business owners can understand that a traditional loan
is one way to fund a business startup. But few see that a cash loan
is only one instrument that provides credit. Exchanging anything
of value for a promise to pay is a loan of some form. Equipment and
vehicle leases may actually be financing agreements that are a form of
a loan to purchase. The key element is whether you are paying the full
value of the agreement over the life of the lease, in which case your
final payment for title will be $1 or less. Most auto leases are regular
leases.

The other type of credit you may be eligible for is vendor credit.
Anything that is shipped to you with terms of net 30 days or more
allows you to add and collect your markup (gross profit) before you
have to pay the vendor. This is not as good as a longer-term loan,
which allows time for you to establish yourself. But if you purchase
carefully, you may be able to turn inventory quickly and pay for it
after you have sold it to your customer. Having a business that only
takes special orders to be shipped directly will allow you to collect
your sale and send the purchase portion off to your vendor.

Getting Loans

What most aspiring entrepreneurs think about is the cash and where
they are going to get it. The easiest place is from savings that are
not essential to your present and near-future well-being. Regardless
of the source (yours or someone else's), capital invested in a business
venture is at risk. Banks charge interest and fees based on that risk.
Investors will seek a return on a higher basis when the venture is new
or unproven. Unless you're using your own money, be prepared for
this cost of money.

One Size Does Not Fit All: The Business Loan

You have a great idea and a well-thought-out plan. But you have very little money to spare. So now you are wondering whether you can qualify for a loan. For the most part, it depends on how much you need, how long you will need it, and how much security (collateral in the form of property or other assets) you can pledge to the lender.

Finding the Right Bank

Your first step is to find the right bank and the right banker. Large money-center banks (you know, the ones that are always in the news) might seem like the place to go because they have many branches and lots of services. But the best place for most new and smaller companies is a community bank—not a one- or two-branch institution, but one with a presence over a regional area that might cover two or three states. The employees are more active members of the local community and could be people you have known for a long time. More importantly, they know you. Banks are as good as the people who manage them. Find out from friends and business associates who they would recommend.

Banks have different areas of interest. Some are more consumer oriented and focus more on home, car, and personal loans. They will make a business loan and they may even assure you that this is something their bank is seeking; but if it is not an area of expertise, your local banker at the branch may not be equipped to give you the advice and support you need. A good place to find a business banker is at your local Rotary Club or at a Chamber of Commerce or other business group.

Talk to more than one banker and find out whether he or she has expertise doing SBA-guarantee loans; if so, it is one of the signs of a small-business-friendly lender.

Approaching the Lender

You want to approach the branch manager to begin with and ask whether you can discuss your new venture and what you think you might need in the way of a loan. This is where you total up your startup requirements and your working capital needs and have a target number of what you will need.

Your Loan Proposal

Most traditional banks are interested in what I classify as the 4 *P*s of a loan proposal:

- **Purpose:** What will the money be used for?

- **Payments:** How will the loan be paid back?

- **Protection:** Is there any collateral to secure all or part of the loan?

- **People:** What is the experience and reputation of the company's owners?

Purpose is the specific use of funds. At this time, you might include quotes or invoices for the equipment or inventory that you intend to purchase. You might even include competing quotes to show that you are working on how to be economical. You should have already estimated your working capital requirements in the pro forma section of your business plan. The more you show that you know about how you will productively use the money, the more convincing your loan request will be.

Payments represent the specific amount you are able to repay monthly on the loan you are seeking. The amount of this payment will be determined by the original amount borrowed, the interest rate you negotiate, and the term of the loan. Not all banks charge the same interest; you might want to ask at this point what might be available to your company. A short-term loan is less than two years in length of payback and a long-term loan is over four years. Make sure that the cost of using the loan funds will be returned by increased revenue and profits within the time you have to pay them back.

For example, inventory should turn in less than 90 days, so very short-term money is all you need to finance this. But a major purchase such as property or manufacturing equipment may take anywhere from as few as 5 years to well over 10 years to provide extra funds for the payments. Loans are structured to take this into account. That is why commercial mortgages are often for 15 years. The payments must be low enough that the owner can make them in the early years. Any equipment provides tools to generate revenue but does not earn direct dollars. The funding comes from the profit of your work.

Protection signifies the secondary source of funds to pay off the loan. Theoretically, in the past, mortgages were easier to find because if you didn't pay, the house or building could be sold to pay the amount. Lenders are far more conservative about property values these days. Equipment may also be the collateral on the loan account, as well as any other deposits the bank is also holding, such as a CD or savings. You will still own the CD, but it will be pledged to secure your loan and released back to you when the loan is paid (there are times when a partial release of collateral is permitted). And this is where the SBA can be helpful because when they step in with a guarantee, the lender knows that less of their funds are exposed to loss. This guarantee becomes a form of secondary payment. The SBA or other entities, such as state and local development authorities, will underwrite 50 to 90 percent of a loan in most cases.

People is the term for the underlying background and credibility of the borrower. This is where your credit score comes into play for most banks. You should already know your credit-score number for personal reasons. Many lenders will not look at a business loan with a principal who has a score under 680 to 700. If yours has become a problem and you know it, address the issue first and explain the circumstances. You can find out your own credit score by logging on to www.MyFico.com or other credit score sites and checking it out. You are entitled to one free credit score per year so that you can protect yourself from identity theft.

PERSONAL CREDIT PROBLEMS CAN SINK YOUR BUSINESS

One of my clients needed to borrow a small amount of money to fund operations and there was a development authority which had a program that was a great match. I put together the loan plan and was sure that the business could well support the payments. The owner neglected to tell me about his personal credit problems, however, and his application was denied as a result. On top of that, he was questioned at length by the loan committee, which was very uncomfortable. We might have been successful by addressing the issue before the loan committee asked. Instead, it ended up being a waste of time and money. If we had started the process with an explanation of what had caused his personal credit problem and how that was being handled, we might have had a different outcome.

Non-traditional Sources of Loans

Most people typically think of banks when they think about a business loan. But there are other options:

- **Credit unions:** Have you ever been a member of a credit union? Credit unions operate with a different set of regulations and will work hand in hand with each member to meet their individual needs. Many of these credit groups originated within a single company's employees, but they have opened membership to the general public. The attention is more one-to-one and the underwriting often is more liberal. You must open an account to become a member of the credit union and be eligible for a loan.

- **Veterans Administration:** If you are a veteran, try going to the VA and asking what special assistance you can get. One particular program is the Patriot Loan overseen by the SBA, which is intended to meet the needs of returning Iraq/ Afghanistan war veterans to restart their working lives by going into a new business venture.

- **State economic development departments:** Check with your state economic development department and request a list of all programs it is supporting. Some loan guarantees are available, as well as low-interest loans. Remember, these guarantees serve to secure a loan and make it easier to get. Go to the Small Business Development Center at a university near you and talk to one of the consultants. They are familiar with local funding sources.

- **Micro-loan funds:** Community-based micro-loan funds will lend anywhere from $500 to $35,000 from a revolving loan fund. This pool of money comes mostly from grants or public program funds and is meant to support businesses that meet the needs of the community. If you are able to create (or save) a job or move into an area that is a target for development, you are a candidate for these programs. Micro-loans are available in both small and large communities throughout the U.S. Call your city/county department of community affairs to locate one near you. There are special funds for women and members of minority groups, as well as the disabled. In recent years, there has been a directed effort to make at least some funding available to anyone committed to starting his or her own business.

Should You Borrow from Friends or Family?

More misunderstandings between people who may otherwise care for each other come from money than virtually any other issue. So understand that this is a high-risk way to find funding. One of the few exceptions is when you have your own money in another investment and you might lose by taking it out now, but it will soon be accessible. In this circumstance, if you have some problems with your business, you will be able to make the lending family member whole again. This will create less risk of family tension, which would happen at the time you really don't need the added stress. Having business worries is enough strain without adding a sense of personal guilt.

BORROWING FROM FAMILY ADDS STRESS

In the midst of some very difficult conditions, I have a former client who has a loan due to his father for over $100,000 and there is no way he can even pay the interest and keep the doors open. Added to this is the fact that his dad has lost money in the market, and what seemed like a non-issue to his financial well-being is now very much of one. This wears on them both and is almost guaranteed to hasten the end of the business, which will further hurt them both. At the time the loan was made, no one could even imagine what problems were right around the bend.

Make sure you offer competitive rates (you can find a chart on www.bankrate.com) and make sure you have the agreement in writing. You can go to an office-supply store and buy a book of blank forms or make up one yourself. If things change and you must modify your agreement, do that in writing as well. It might even be a good idea to ask a lawyer to draft a simple agreement.

THE DIFFERENCE BETWEEN AN INVESTMENT AND A LOAN

You might hear, "That sounds like a great idea; I'll give you money for that business!" but the unsophisticated speaker may mean something other than what he or she is saying. An investment is an "at-risk" contribution to capital in a business, which is usually exchanged in return for equity in the company. The investor becomes a partial owner. And being a minority owner in a closely held company is not much of a benefit. This small interest is one that seldom entitles the holder to any ongoing return unless there is an official dividend declared. What it usually means is that if the company is sold for more money than was put in, the investors get a return over their original amount. When the company is successful, everybody wins. If the company struggles, everyone holds on hoping for the turn.

What About Other Outsiders?

There are people with excess money who enjoy investing in new business concepts, and they like to participate in management as well. These are not the formal venture capital groups that you might be thinking about. These funders are referred to as angel investors because they will work with early-stage companies with a reasonable chance of success. Members of angel networks must be high-worth individuals (over $1 million) and they often pool their money so that the investment risk is spread around.

Money is not their only feature. High-level advice is also available and usually required. An angel will sit on your board and may well be looking over your shoulder, perhaps like an angel but perhaps not. This depends on your own level of expertise. But if you have a need for a lot of capital and it is not available through a loan, this may well be the way to go.

There are also individuals who act informally as angels and they will give you capital in exchange for equity. In all of these situations, however, there is an interest in an exit strategy so that the investor can cash out his or her interest. You may be able to buy back the investment at a premium. But if you are looking for a long-term venture, this may not be the way to go. Most investors have an expectation of getting out within three years.

Be as sure as you can that you are likely to work well with your investor. Some of them become overly intrusive on the business and its management. You do not need to agree on every move that you make, but you must have a way to govern the differences without trying to force people to take sides. I recently overheard one of these investors try to convince a friend to take over a business he had invested in and I am sure that current management had no idea they were even at risk.

Caution: I have mentioned throughout this book that your initial source of funds should not be from a home-equity loan (if you could get one) or credit cards. They put you too much at risk personally and often the interest rate is too high, particularly on the cards. And it can be too easy to fall into the trap of paying only the minimum and

keeping the cards close to max. In a credit crunch, your availability
may be dropped and you will find yourself short of cash. And you
should not cash in retirement programs such as 401(k)s to fund your
new venture. You will incur a tax burden if you do and you will put
your future at a higher level of risk.

Do Not Let Money Stop You

The most important document you create before the grand opening
may well be your business plan and the section on the pro forma. Even
if your accountant works on the numbers with you, it is still your job
to understand them and be prepared to secure the capital you will
require.

You may have to lower your expectations or use more creative and
lower-cost strategies; but if you have a viable concept and you are
committed to making it happen, the capital will come. You may be
able to start your business on a part-time basis and use the results
to enlarge it to a full-time venture. Find a partner and work as a
subcontractor. If you have the will, you will find the way.

CHAPTER 5

KEEPING SCORE: A BRIEF INTRODUCTION TO ACCOUNTING BASICS

This is a chapter all about finance and accounting, and I am asking you now not to flip the pages without reading because this is a topic that bores or intimidates you. Accounting and finance are the meat and potatoes of any business and provide an understanding of how you make money. You wouldn't send any sports team onto the field without teaching them first how to score. Your financial results are the scores of your business. First, at least, learn the rules. I will go over some of the finer points. You can come back and refer to them as you become more comfortable with the terms and experienced at looking at the reports. In other words, this book should stay with you for a while.

In this chapter, you will learn about the two options you have when it comes to recordkeeping methods: cash or accrual.

This chapter also tells you what you need to know about the two primary reports that you will generate as a result of your operations:

- **The income (profit and loss) statement:** Records all of the revenue that you take in from operations and deducts all of the expense you incur. Then it tells you how much money you made or lost. Think of it as the game card that details the actions and reports the final score.

- **The balance sheet:** Think of it as the season card. It will tell you how much you have in assets and how much in liabilities. It lets you know whether you have created a growing value in your company. At the end of each month, the profit (or loss) adds (or subtracts) from that value.

In short, you'll learn how to keep track of everything and analyze the results of your business efforts.

Cash or Accrual?

Recordkeeping can be on a cash basis or on an accrual basis. This is a timing question and it describes how you handle transactions within a certain period. You need to decide whether to record only the cash transactions during that period (cash method) or to record all of them (accrual method).

Cash means that only the cash that is received is counted as income (or revenue). The only sales you will report will be cash sales. If a customer buys something or accepts a service on credit, that deal is booked when the cash is received. For instance, if I sell something in April but it is sold on credit and not paid until May, I will record that transaction in May when the cash is received.

On the other hand, in a cash-basis system, only those bills that are actually paid are recorded as expenses. If you run up unpaid debt, it will show up when (and if) it is paid. The cash-basis system works best in an all-cash business such as a restaurant because every diner pays in full after the meal, and even a credit-card company will send payment to the owner within a few days. Most food bills are paid when the product is delivered or very close to the purchase date. Employees are paid weekly or biweekly, and that is also by cash or check, and the taxes are due shortly thereafter. The money in and the money out for each month provide a fairly accurate indication as to how the business is doing. On the other hand, although most retail stores sell for cash, they might not pay for inventory for a few months. Keeping the books on a cash basis would provide results that were not representative of the real results.

For a company that bills its clients and pays suppliers on terms, the only way to accurately keep the books is on an accrual basis. When work is completed and billed, the income goes on the books. When debt is incurred, whether or not it is paid, it is treated as an expense. For example, in manufacturing, you may have a number of different materials and you may pay for them over a period of months. So you must expense them when they are first purchased. This permits you to see a snapshot of how you have done over a 30-day period. You will manage your cash as it becomes available and is needed.

Virtually all accrual systems are kept in computer programs and they will show variances that may make a single month irrelevant, such as an extra week of payroll or a last inventory purchase made at the end of the month. Looking at these results on a quarterly basis may be more productive, giving a more accurate picture of how you are doing.

Profit-and-Loss (P&L) Statements

There is a great deal of information to be found on a P&L statement, although it is relative to how you are recording the information. The more detail you put into a system, the more usable information will be available.

To begin with, you can determine the exact sources of your revenue by keeping track of them by category or type. You can do this yourself or have an employee do it by using a very simple-to-operate software system such as QuickBooks or Peachtree Accounting. Or you can retain the bills that you issue to customers and the ones you receive from suppliers and get an outside bookkeeper to post each one to an income account or an expense account. If you are working on a cash basis, all you need to turn over to your outside bookkeeper are the deposits and the checkbook.

Fixed and Variable Expenses

The P&L statement is set up to give you a look like this:

> Sales
> − Returns
> Net sales

> Net sales
> − Cost of goods sold (variable)
> Gross profit

Gross profit

− General and administrative costs

Net (before-tax) profits

Figure 5.1 is a sample P&L statement.

	AZ Commercial Printing
	May 28 - Jun 24, 09
Ordinary Income/Expense	
Income	
Sales	
Sales - Keystone Agencies	1,700.50
Sales - Keystone Corporate	365.00
Sales - Retail	8,373.65
Sales - Sign Department Retail	
Sales - Sign Department Port	1,038.85
Sales - Sign Department Retail - Other	2,718.74
Total Sales - Sign Department Retail	3,757.59
Sales - Wholesale	63,138.69
Sales -Sign Department Wholesale	526.85
Total Sales	77,862.28
Sales Discounts	-207.03
Shipping and Delivery Income	4,909.49
Total Income	82,564.74
Cost of Goods Sold	
COGS- Direct Labor	20,056.55
COGS - Finishing Operations	
Boxes and Cartons	217.30
Miscellaneous (FO)	28.76
Total COGS - Finishing Operations	246.06
COGS - General	
Chemicals & Solvents	121.50
COGS - General - Other	656.44
Total COGS - General	777.94
COGS - Printing Presses	
Ink	545.16
Paper	10,254.06
Plates	
COGS - DI Plates	5,370.00
COGS - Heidelberg Plates	891.10
Total Plates	6,261.10
Total COGS - Printing Presses	17,060.32
COGS - Sign Department	
Banner Inks	700.00
COGS - Sign Department - Other	551.94
Total COGS - Sign Department	1,251.94
Freight Costs	2,809.98
Purchases - Subcontractors	
Sublet Finishing Operations	1,178.24
Total Purchases - Subcontractors	1,178.24
Total COGS	43,381.03

Figure 5.1: Sample P&L statement.

Gross Profit	39,183.71
Expense	
Administrative Payroll	
Office Salaries	7,617.54
Total Administrative Payroll	7,617.54
Commissions	3,250.00
Computer and Internet Expenses	
E-mail Blasts	91.95
Total Computer and Internet Expenses	91.95
Employers Tax	4,131.28
Equipment Rental	794.36
Garbage Disposal	140.00
Gas, Oil & Fluids	55.00
Insurance Expense	1,444.01
Mailing Services	398.00
Merchant Fees-credit card sales	794.02
MFG - Maintenance & Repair	
MR - Copiers	61.07
MR - Heidelberg 52PM	1,875.00
MR - Kodak DI	432.00
MR - Polar 78x Cutter	128.40
Total MFG - Maintenance & Repair	2,496.47
Miscellaneous Expense	750.00
Office Supplies	144.77
Operating Supplies	65.55
Payroll Expenses	50.49
Postage and Delivery	966.41
Professional Fees	2,850.00
Telephone Expense	309.31
Utilities	1,282.98
Total Expense	27,632.14
Net Ordinary Income	11,551.57
Net Income	11,551.57

The first cost you are looking at (cost of goods sold) is described as direct, or variable, because these are directly connected to each sale and vary according to your volume of sales. For example, if you own a restaurant, the direct costs are food and labor. The higher the sales, the more food you will consume and the more cooks and wait staff you will have to employ. In a retail store, the more you sell, the more inventory you will have to buy. This formula is true in any business: The more sales you make, the more you will consume materials and time. The more clients you serve, the more direct costs you will have. Just remember that the costs which go up (and down) with your level of sales are the ones that are described as variable.

What is left over after you pay for the actual cost of your products/ service is described as your gross profit. Assuming that you sold the goods from the trunk of your car, that might be the profit that you get to keep. But because no company operates without some overhead, this is the category called fixed costs: the costs you have every month just to open the doors, whether or not you make a sale. Think about yours:

- Rent
- Insurance
- Support staff
- Marketing and advertising
- Phones and utilities
- Professional fees
- Internet and computer
- Dues and subscriptions
- Travel and entertainment
- Your own salary or draw

Although not all of these costs are the same each month, you will incur some in each category and they will average out over a year. The monthly average is the overhead budget, even when some months you actually spend less or more. The interesting element about this is that you can grow sales and keep your overhead budget the same, and that extra profit is yours to retain. The other side of this is that you also can lose sales and if you do not lower your overhead, your total losses will increase over time. The challenge for any business owner is to watch the sales trend and manage overhead closely when they need to adjust during slower periods. That is why annual budgeting is a good idea.

Why It's Important to Understand a P&L

Most new companies have limited access to capital and you will need to begin to operate at a profit as quickly as you can. Many costs will be slightly more or less than you anticipated and these will show up once operations are actually in place. After a few months in business, take a good look at your P&L and see how you are actually doing compared to what you anticipated. You will see where sales are softer than you planned for or costs are higher than you projected. You'll know what actions you have to take to correct the situation.

LOWERING OVERHEAD FOR A SMALL PRINTING COMPANY

I worked with a small printing company that had a sophisticated estimating system but a poor accounting side. At the end of the year, the tax return showed that the company had lost more than $300,000, but the owners did not know why this was happening. The people at this company had been working very hard and still were putting themselves out of business. We went in and made major corrections in the finance side, while making sure that all costs were where they should be and each statement showed exactly what the problem was. The direct labor was far too high and the owners cut one job and lowered production overtime (which can really throw off your labor expense). And then we went line by line on the overheard and cut it by 15 percent, most of it by getting competitive bids on insurance, phone service, and freight. It took almost six months to turn a profit, but it did happen.

You need to track trends over time by comparing one quarter to another and one year to the ones before. At the end of your first year, you want to see how you have done by comparing the results on a quarterly basis. Have sales continued to rise in the same quarter from one year to the next, or have they leveled off? Are you maintaining the same cost structure, or have your material costs started to rise? Are your overhead costs starting to go up because no one is watching them? If your labor is also growing as a percentage of sales, is this because you are hiring and training newer and less skilled workers who may be less productive? Or have your existing employees become comfortable and less productive? Knowing this information is the job of the business owner. If the company needs change, you are the one who will have to initiate it.

All businesses, over the years, need to compare quarters and analyze trends. The decisions about next year are based on past performance. You need to use the experience of past outcome as a basis for projections. I use the example of quarters because a month-by-month analysis may have too many irregularities. A late-month big sale or a bill that comes in late may throw off results; however, these elements seem to balance out over a quarter.

Use the P&L to Set Pricing Standards

What percentage are you marking up your products and why have you chosen that number? How much do you charge for your time and what is the actual cost? Analyzing your own profit-and-loss statement will make all of this more understandable because you can see that a product you sell takes time to order, ship in, store, market, deliver, and bill. And for every hour of your time that you bill, you probably spent one more working on preparation and recordkeeping. You might also have marketing costs associated with every sale that you make. Once you can read in actual numbers how much it costs to operate, you will have a better idea of what you should charge. As a startup, you need to budget for overhead and estimate your sales. Your gross profit margins need to cover those costs.

Throughout this book and throughout your business life, you will be working on pricing strategies. Sometimes you will lower them to drive volume. In other times, you may raise them to cover increases in your own costs.

Analyzing Sales

You can also break down your P&L statement into more descriptive categories to show where your sales are in a number of areas. Assume that you sell a type of product such as clothing. You may want to know how much of your revenue comes from the clothing lines and how much comes from the accessories. You can code each sale by type and then total all sales of each type to make up the entire revenue.

I just finished running a meeting for a Web site I founded and we had various categories of participation as revenue for the seminar. In our P&L, I broke them down as follows:

- **Sales—Sponsorships:** Money paid by companies to have their names included as underwriters

- **Sales—Advertising:** Revenue from companies that paid for an ad in our program book

- **Sales—Exhibitors:** Fees from companies that had booths at the event

- **Sales—Registrations:** Registration fees from those who attended

This allowed us to look at where we needed to focus our time going forward so that we could increase the total amount of revenue. We had as many exhibitors as we could handle, but we needed more sponsors and registrations. We will create a pro forma model for the next event based on this information.

Balance Sheets

The other primary financial report that is easily generated by any accounting software, or may be provided by your accountant, is your balance sheet. This is an organized listing of your assets (cash, accounts receivable, equipment, property, vehicles, and so on), as well as your liabilities (all accounts payable, loans, payroll due, and so on). Once your assets and liabilities are balanced against one another, you will find out how much your business is worth, an amount referred to as the owner's equity.

A balance sheet will show these items as current (due now or within a year) or long-term (due in more than a year) so that you can see what current resources you have to meet current obligations.

The balance sheet formula is this:

>   Current assets (cash and cash items, accounts receivable, notes payable [short-term], inventory)
>
> \+ Fixed assets (land and buildings, machinery and equipment, autos and trucks)
>
> − Accumulated depreciation
>
> \+ Long-term notes
> _____
>
>   Total assets

Current liabilities (accounts payable, payroll due, taxes due, current portions of loans)

+ Long-term liabilities (mortgage, long-term debt)

= Total liabilities

All assets

− All liabilities

Owner's equity

Figure 5.2 is a sample balance sheet.

Many of the transactions that go through your profit-and-loss statement will also flow onto the balance sheet. When a sale is made, the value of that sale becomes part of your cash balance (if paid in cash) or will flow to your accounts receivable (if purchased on credit terms). When the accounts receivable item is paid, that money flows back to your cash account. If you make a purchase with cash, the available cash balance will be reduced or you will add to the liabilities in the form of your accounts payable. This is how you build value in the worth of the business.

Making a loan payment is a bit more complicated. The interest goes only to the expense line on your P&L statement; but any principal reduction will lower your total debt on the balance sheet and raise your net worth. The name of the balance sheet report implies its purpose: to make sure everything remains in balance.

A Z Commercial Printing

	May 28, 09
ASSETS	
Current Assets	
Checking/Savings	
National City Checking DIP	57,849.27
Payroll	11,496.46
Petty Cash	1,020.13
Total Checking/Savings	70,365.86
Accounts Receivable	
Accounts Receivable	64,052.83
Total Accounts Receivable	64,052.83
Other Current Assets	
Inventory	20,000.00
Prepaid Insurance	4,240.39
Undeposited Funds	-391.44
Total Other Current Assets	23,848.95
Total Current Assets	158,267.64
Fixed Assets	
Accumulated Depreciation	-105,523.00
Equipment	350,320.42
Total Fixed Assets	244,797.42
TOTAL ASSETS	**403,065.06**
LIABILITIES & EQUITY	
Liabilities	
Current Liabilities	
Accounts Payable	
Accounts Payable	16,814.87
Total Accounts Payable	16,814.87
Other Current Liabilities	
Accounts Payable Control	48,125.00
Customer Deposit	10,498.59
Payroll Deduction Payable	983.61
Sales Tax Payable	106.01
Union Dues	-1,872.99
Total Other Current Liabilities	57,840.22
Total Current Liabilities	74,655.09
Long-Term Liabilities	
Notes Payable Control	
NP - GMAC 2007 Delivery Truck	-318.27
Notes Payable Control - Other	365,555.39
Total Notes Payable Control	365,237.12
Total Long-Term Liabilities	365,237.12
Total Liabilities	439,892.21
Equity	
Capital Stock	7,912.80
Opening Bal Equity	-0.13
Retained Earnings	-47,770.81
Net Income	3,030.99
Total Equity	-36,827.15
TOTAL LIABILITIES & EQUITY	**403,065.06**

Figure 5.2: Sample balance sheet.

Other Insights from Your Balance Sheet

Fixed assets are items that are tangible and have long-term value, such as vehicles and equipment. Unlike your inventory, which may build and then be sold off, these remain on your books at their purchase price using another entry to signify their change in value. That entry is referred to as depreciation.

In short, a car you paid $20,000 for a year ago may lose 20 percent of its value in depreciation. For business purposes, however, there is a schedule you must use for this number. In some cases, the new value overstates the loss; in others, it understates it. You may write off a piece of equipment over 10 years, but it may still have a value. The purpose of this is to provide a tax write-off that will free up cash to replace the equipment with new assets.

You will need to reserve extra cash for maintenance, repair, and replacement of assets; so consider that aspect of the tax advantage. In some companies, the depreciation allowance is where the profits come from. Where the ownership is able to take advantage of this, the tax benefits become personal. This is not additional salary for the owners; it should be seen as reserves to be put aside should the business need them for investment.

Business Liquidity (Solvency)

There are a number of important uses of your balance sheet. Perhaps the most important is that it will show you how well your company is able to retire current debt from current assets. This is why you list these two categories as current and long term. If you have bills coming due and no money in the bank to pay them, you will be worried. But if you have cash in your accounts receivable where checks will be coming in soon, you are in a better place.

In order to determine your position, you will need to total your cash, your accounts receivable, and your inventory and compare that total with your accounts payable, any payroll or taxes due, and the current portions of your outstanding loans. Remember that a certain portion of all inventory will end up unsold, so you want to write down this number at the end of each year. You need to watch the trend in this area because as solvency (the ability of the business to retire current debt from current assets) goes up, you are building a healthy business.

When it goes down, your options become more limited. You may have to take action such as moving out some unused inventory or equipment and selling it to improve your cash position. This is the kind of action large corporations take when times get tough.

Why a Balance Sheet Matters

Both the P&L statement and the balance sheet are important as snapshots of different measures of how a company is operating. How much profit have you made over a quarter or a year? What is the book value of your business at this time? If you make profits, the value of the company increases and you will see this on your balance sheet. If you lose money, how it affects your worth will show up on this report as well.

One of the ways that a company finances losses is through building debts. This leads to increasing liabilities, including accounts payable/ taxes due. Over the short term, a business can absorb losses. But if your debts are trending up, you will have some growing risks. And if your assets in the form of your accounts receivable start to grow, you may have a collection problem.

Vendors may be patient for a while because they like you and they want to make the next sale. But when they are owed too much for too long, some may begin to take action and even file lawsuits. These black marks on the company's credit history will impair future credit and loans going forward. I discuss credit in other chapters of this book; however, the takeaway is that your reputation, in the form of your credit history, is a valuable asset and one to be protected.

Account Agings: Another Trend to Watch

You can watch the numbers inside your balance sheet by creating a report that will show you not only how much is owed to your company or by your company, but also how long these funds are outstanding. If you are buying or selling on credit, the money due you and the cash that you owe will be recorded on your books. At the end of each month, you can look at a report called an aging. This will tell you what is current, what is over 30 days old, and what is aged out to over 90 days, which is the danger point on both sides. The report for a business with $50,000 due to it from a variety of customers looks like this:

A/R Aging				
	1–30	31–60	61–90	Over 90	Total
ABC Company	$3,000	$3,000	-0-	-0-	$6,000
EFG Company	$2,500	-0-	$5,500	$1,000	$9,000
JKL Company	-0-	$15,000	$10,000	-0-	$25,000
Total	$5,500	$18,000	$20,500	$6,000	$50,000

The total of all accounts by customer and by time is the same, but now you are seeing that some amounts are past due and may be in jeopardy of collection. Having a company owe you money for more than 90 days is not good business practice and you want to be careful about making more sales to that customer without payment.

Tip: You can set credit limits by several methods, considering how much you are willing to put at risk and how long you are willing to carry the customer. Depending on what you are paying for any loans you have, this is not free money.

You should do this same type of aging on your accounts payable—what you owe to vendors. The total amount shows as a liability on your balance sheet; however, the details of when the debts are due are found on an aging. As I have said before, vendor credit is a source of capital but it is not one to play with. Over the years, you will find out that you need good vendors and keeping that relationship requires payment in terms that are agreed to by both parties. If you see an invoice cannot be paid in full, pay part of it as an act of good faith.

Break-Even Analyses

There is an old line about business challenges that originated from as far back as the days when there were medicine men driving horses and buggies to travel around and sell their wares. Their first goal was to "make their nut," which meant, at that time, that bills that represented their overhead on the road had to be paid before they could move on. This practice was enforced by the local sheriff, who took the wooden nut holding the wheel onto the wagon and held onto it until all the locals were paid for what they had provided. The wagon and its owner were stuck until then. Modern business is really not that different; a company and its owner are often on the hook for the costs that represent overhead.

For a business, this is about producing or selling enough to cover your overhead. These are the obligations that continue day to day and month to month, no matter how high or low your sales are. Remember that your variables are a part of each sale or project and what is left over pays the operating costs. How do you find your number?

Finding Your Break-Even Number

Think of it as a reverse-engineering problem. You begin with the costs you need to cover. Then you must know your profit margin. The margin is what percentage of each sale is gross profit. If you sell an item for $100 and it cost you $65 in direct costs, your margin is 35 percent. If your overhead is $3,500 per month, you must sell at least $10,000 of goods to be at break-even.

Don't expect to start a business and break even in the first few months. You will more likely grow into that number in the early stage of operation (the first three months to a year). By creating a low-cost structure in order to create a faster start, you may find yourself without enough resources to become the size venture you have wanted and even planned for.

DECIDE HOW BIG YOU WANT TO GET

Years ago, I did some work with a woman who was a doll designer and was doing quite well creating dolls for a major manufacturer. Loving her work, she began to create a small line, which she actually produced at home, for limited distribution to only a few local stores. These were very expensive and often referred to as "grandma dolls" because they were most likely purchased as gifts for beloved granddaughters. Totally handcrafted does make a difference, but when volume grew beyond the small operation, she

(continued)

(continued)

decided to take a leap of faith and open a small factory. Sales grew, and in six months the company finally grew into a break-even, even with the new and higher costs. But now it had debt for equipment and excess inventory. But the demand continued to grow and the company attracted the attention of investors. Now, it was off to the races.

The company rented an even bigger location, and now it was making some of the parts for the dolls that it used to buy in a finished state. It was then that demand leveled off because the company did not have much of a sales effort in place when it was growing by word of mouth. Not able to grow beyond the break-even and mostly losing money (some months a lot), the whole operation shut down, leaving the investors as well as the original owner heavily in debt.

The lesson is to choose a break-even level that accounts for your goal of what size of a business you want to be when you have met all of the early challenges. Starting too small because you do not want to take the risk may leave you without the room to complete the necessary early growth. Yet, taking on too much, too early, may also mean that you are never able to make "the nut." Use a well-worked pro forma to make this choice (see chapter 3).

There Are Ways to Lower Your Break-Even

Pricing has a lot to do with where your break-even point is set. If you are in the position to pass along to customers a meaningful increase in prices (few smaller businesses are), you can solve a lot of problems. The other solutions are to increase sales or cut back on your overhead. And the fact is that you can do a little of all three. You can make a big difference in your bottom line by raising sales by 2 percent, raising prices by the same, and lowering costs by the same. A 10 percent increase in any of these categories is quite a goal to achieve, but a 2 percent change is within the margin of effort. Most customers will not notice this pricing; a few more customer calls can bring a slight increase; and overhead cuts are found with an increase in efficiency. When you do the numbers, you will be surprised.

The Value of Understanding Finance Is Critical

Every job you ever have will have some aspects that are more interesting and satisfying than others. All jobs have chores that you love to do and those you do because you have to. The finance and accounting side may start out on the necessary side, but you must keep at it until it is at least understandable. You cannot run a successful business without this knowledge.

I hope you will find, as I did, that when you begin to master some of the information, these numbers become tools for you to use and are infinitely more interesting because of that. I learned this from a banker who was my mentor when I was a manufacturer. I really look forward to looking at the numbers side of every new business I try to help. Ask questions of your accountant as you need to, but work on having your own benchmarks for the company to reach.

CHAPTER 6

KNOWING THE MARKET AND HIRING THE BEST CUSTOMERS

If you are a shopper who enjoys and feels that you require the service provided by a Nordstrom-type department store, you are unlikely to be very happy shopping at Walmart. Although you may go there for some reasons, it will never be your primary place to shop. If you live in a house in a moderately priced residential area, you are not likely to seek out and engage a high-priced designer to create a dream kitchen because most people realize that it is not a wise investment in the property. (Well, perhaps a few would do that, but not enough for a kitchen company to build a business around.) The companies that market upgrades to this type of homeowner will be in the middle price range, as well.

Defining Your Customer Base

You want to learn as much as you can, in advance, about the clients and customers you expect to serve so that you can communicate with them easily and serve their needs well. You are building a clientele to be with you over the long haul—not just trying to make a single, isolated sale. So, before going out and trying to be everything to everyone, stop and consider some good advice.

The 25 Percent Concept

A college professor I studied with many years ago suggested the following explanation of human behavior: No matter what you do, 25 percent of the people will like you for the right reasons; 25 percent will like you for the wrong reasons; 25 percent of the people will dislike you for the right reasons; and 25 percent will dislike you for the wrong reasons. Although I did not realize it at the time, this is a very good business rule of thumb. The best idea is to focus on the one in four who likes you for the right reasons.

Analyzing this thought as a business theory will help you proceed in developing your business. Imagine if you opened just the right type of restaurant but it was in the wrong location for some customers? Or you could be located only minutes away from some potential customers but not serve the type of food these people are looking for at that time or most of the time. How do you turn any of these situations into a potential sale? You don't. Customers will always have their reasons why they patronize a specific business as well as why they do not. Their reasons may be wrong, but you will find that working too hard to connect with them is not a worthwhile effort when there are potentially right matches that you can focus on instead.

If you are opening the only 24-hour gas station, shop, or deli in a neighborhood, you are likely to see everyone around at one time or another. This is an issue of convenience and falls into the 25 percent who like you for the wrong reasons. These customers are not worth great attention, either, because they will come only when they really need you. It is almost impossible to be price-competitive due to your costs, and you are likely to stock limited items. But at 4 a.m., the choice between one flavor of overpriced soda and another seems not to matter.

A competent and responsive heating company will develop a great following of customers who feel safer knowing that this is the person to call. The company may be able to limit its emergency hours to existing customers. These clients like you for the right reason and they need the best attention you have. The ones who do have emergencies are likely to look for bids if more work needs to be done later.

And finally, consider the customer who really isn't convinced that your bakery has the best cakes in town, but all of her friends can't stop raving about your shop. Here is an example of the customer who likes you for the wrong reason. Give these people the best that you can, but don't ignore your top 25 percent in order to do it. Keep your eyes on the prize.

Just think of it: If one out of four potential customers for your products or services could be converted into a regular, you could build a great business. So let's find out who these prime candidates might be and how you will attract them to your business.

Start with a Competitive Analysis

You know what kind of a company you are going to start, so now you need to know as much as you can about others in the same business. Ask yourself these basic questions about similar businesses:

- Does location matter?
- Must you have great parking?
- Is the physical look of the business important?
- Do you require a deep selection of merchandise?
- How wide is variety within a product line?
- Are hours extra-convenient?
- Is pricing competitive?
- Is the business well staffed?
- How is the follow-up attention?

Determine what elements will differentiate you from others in the field and focus on those. They are your best hooks.

For example, my favorite restaurant has two things that keep me coming back frequently: great parking and very fresh food. I am one who runs in on my way home, and I don't want to drive around looking for a place to park. The freshness of the food is also high on my list, although my choice of spots has very little in the way of decor and the prices are just a bit high. Having said that, enough people have the same requirements as I do, so the place is always busy. It also helps that the place has great pizza.

A CAUTIONARY EXAMPLE

Look at what has happened to the big traditional retail chains as well as box stores in the last few years. Many of them went from having a loyal customer base to trying to bring in everyone, including the rock-bottom-price shopper. Perhaps they saw this as another way to compete, but the regular customers are turned off. They took out some of the amenities in the stores, such as restaurants and small boutique departments, and added incessant sales programs to their strategy. There's always some sort of deal going on and no way to know whether the price will come down even further next week. So customers started looking and not buying, and the big chains have taken big hits. A few are trying to reinvent themselves, but many of them will become extinct. A few have already filed for bankruptcy.

What exact needs do you intend to fill? Where do you fit among all the other businesses doing something similar to what you expect to do? You need to know this as specifically as possible so that you can advertise your message clearly and hire the best customers—the ones who do business with you for the right reasons.

How Do You Define Customers for a Service Company?

There are also questions to ask if you are beginning a service company:

- What type of individual or business is the perfect client for you?

- What size company has an internal gap that you can fill?

- Why are your skills a good match for the company's needs?

- Are you priced in a range that gives value to your service?

- Are you big enough to provide sufficient service?

- Do you understand the values of the companies you want to develop as customers?

The business-to-business transaction is different from those directed at consumers. Companies are far more sensitive to the return they receive for their purchase. If you can provide a service that adds to another company's sales—or better yet, to its bottom line—you will increase your value. Whereas consumer behavior is based on want; business investment, for the most part, is based on need.

Think about your thought process when you're choosing professional service providers. Do you head for the largest law firm in town, the one with the biggest and plushest office? Or are you fairly sure that you cannot afford the fees and are not likely to require the top guns in the area to handle your day-to-day issues? Now translate this to what your potential customers are thinking. What can you provide as a value proposition to your customers? Do you need to rely on ambiance as a calling card, or does your service affect their bottom line?

Differentiating Your Company

Most new business owners will tell you that they plan to compete on quality and price, but this is a simplistic view of how a business positions itself. If you expect to provide high, personalized quality, there is a good chance your internal costs will be higher; therefore, your prices will not be the lowest around.

So these days, more than any time in decades, you need to understand exactly where you stand in the value proposition. And if you do expect to compete on cost, you need to have a strategy in place that will drive high volume (with fairly low service) because that is the model that works. Think of Walmart. It runs an extensive number of product categories as well as brand names through its stores and it has a definite purchasing edge, being one of the biggest buyers in the world in most of its lines.

This is actually the reverse of hiring an employee. In that case, you list a set of skills and find someone to meet your qualifications. Here *you* are trying to meet as many of the requirements and preferences of your customers as you can so that they will choose you repeatedly to use as a preferential vendor.

Some of the ways to differentiate your company:

- Be open longer hours.
- Be easy to contact via phone/fax/Internet.
- Offer delivery.
- Offer special orders.
- Run frequent-user programs.
- Provide parking/child care.
- Provide in-home or in-office consultation.
- Follow up to make sure customers are satisfied.

MOBILE SUIT CONSULTANT STRIKES JUST THE RIGHT NOTE

I know a man in western Pennsylvania who has a very niched but successful business selling high-priced suits to customers by calling on them at their places of business. His clients are primarily attorneys and funeral directors, both of whom have busy and complicated schedules along with the need for high-quality clothing. He has a few good suppliers and works with a few tailors in the area.

Once every few months, Joel stops in to see his clients, bringing along fabric swatches and a few new style samples. He takes an order, makes sure that all of the sleeves and cuffs are perfectly tailored, and delivers a ready-to-go suit in a month. Clients pay only slightly more than retail, and they love the convenience. And because he buys directly and maintains no inventory and little overhead, Joel enjoys a good profit margin. It's a great deal for both vendor and client.

Do not be surprised; there are many opportunities to serve a niche market at a good price. What Joel knows about his best customers is what you want to know about yours: everything.

If you are selling to consumers, you want to know the following:

- How old are they?

- What other products do they tend to need?

- Do you appeal to one gender more than the other?

- What is their family status and income level?

- What other interests do they have?

- What is their education level and job category?

All of these items are important because you want to match your communication with the target. A company gives off many messages in the way it does business. These messages either welcome the customer it wants or make it daunting for them to do business.

The auto industry is a great example of making purchasing daunting. Ask most women what their experience has been around choosing a car for themselves or with their family. They will likely tell you it is at best intimidating and at worst something they hate. Car companies have always said that they understand this, but they don't seem to be able to change it. And the reality is that this is mostly up to the individual dealers. However, going forward, more than half of all new buyers will be women (and they participate in 80 percent of all car-buying decisions). So you would think that they would have to make the process easier for women, who make up a large part of their top 25 percent of customers. What are the disconnects?

- Showrooms are crowded and not merchandised well. I am never sure what I want to do when I walk in the door.

- Salesmen are primarily male and they often ignore women. And women tend to visit more dealers before making the decision to purchase than do men, meaning that they are not closing the deal as quickly as the male buyers. Perhaps part of the issue is that they are ignored.

- Women do not know much about the mechanics of a car and that tends to hurt them in the selling process. Information is not made easy to learn, either.

- Price negotiation is very uncomfortable for many women. They tend to end up paying more than men (and most know it).

- To make matters even worse, women have a difficult time with the service department. I believe that the service department is where most customers develop a dealer relationship that predicts where they will purchase their next car.

What can the average business owner learn from this? Once you have attracted a good potential customer and he or she is the one who is most likely to value you (that right 25 percent), make sure that everything about your business is geared to service this customer in a welcoming and comfortable way. You are building a long-term relationship that will have great value in future sales, and referrals and recommendations to others. The cost of attracting a new customer is high. Don't make it a one-time deal. Doing business with a company or individual who is not a good fit may distract you from your primary goal: providing more than what is expected from you to your loyal customers.

Taking on "Emergency" Clients Has Consequences

One of my clients is a small printer whose strength is both the quality of its work as well as the fact that it can turn around short-term print work very quickly. Regular customers understand that when they need a job completed in a few days, they get it in a few days. This service has built strong relationships.

However, every so often, a new client will call with a job that has become an emergency, something typically caused by someone else's misstep or the fact that the client is not sure of what they want or what they are ordering. Most entrepreneurs are driven by making new sales and my client is no different. It takes the challenge. But three out of four times, these new customers will create havoc in the shop and an incumbent customer will have his or her feathers ruffled. Is it worth it?

Not over the long haul. You must consider each opportunity on a cost/benefit basis. That is, in fact, also how you hire a new employee. It is important that the salesmen as well as the management balance the demands of new customers against those of their loyal customers.

Sending Messages to Customers

You'll communicate with your customers in many different ways. It's important to send messages that are consistent with what you do and what your customers want.

Name and Logo

Your initial contact with each new customer is likely to be with your name and your logo. Have you made a call to action from this first touch? Or are you sending out an unclear message? Have you ever driven past a storefront, thought it looked interesting, but could not figure what the business was? Many new entrepreneurs do not consider this. Their drive is to be different from others, or sometimes just to promote their own name. You will make greater impact if you are clear about what type of business you are in or what service or product you provide.

One of my favorite business names is for a chain of bakeries and gift shops for dogs. The look is that of a traditional bakery but the name is Just Dogs, and that says a lot. Another franchise is Maid with Care, which is a cleaning service that makes me feel as if its employees will treat my home and my possessions with some extra effort. The name is clear but reassuring.

Decor and Merchandising

Your decor also invites customers to come in and linger—or provides less in the way of a welcoming message. You may want to encourage one behavior or the other depending on what you do. Going back to my auto dealer example, you'll find few showrooms with comfortable places to sit and get information or negotiate comfortably. Most salesmen have either small offices or will seat you at a desk in front of the windows so that people can watch you as the dance of the deal goes on. My own response is that everything is structured to get the deal made quickly. I am someone who likes to find out more before I make the second largest purchase that I would typically make, and I know that most women agree with me. I wonder what it's going to take to make them change.

Merchandising your store gives yet another message about what type of customer you are trying to serve. You want your most desirable clients to see something that attracts them as soon as they walk in the door. Pulling out the glitziest or most expensive products may seem like an interesting idea, but if you know where the "sweet spot" is, you want to play it. Put your best sellers out where people can see them, even when you sell a range of products. Feature those that might not sell as well in other places in the store.

Note: What is a "sweet spot"? This is a term often used to describe the best place on a tennis racquet that, when hit, gives your shot the longest and most controlled impact. Every business has one of these: those customers who are satisfied with virtually every transaction— your own 25 percent who love you for the right reasons. If you've had them in mind from day one, good job!

Is Your Communication Directed at the Right Person?

There are so many ways to market to new and existing customers and you need to choose the most effective ones. And, in fact, your existing list of regular customers (if you have one) will give you a lot of information on what works best. If you are new, you can purchase a mailing list, but you also want to track your most active clients to add as soon as possible. First, let's consider the options:

- Telemarketing

- Direct mail—promotional and catalogs

- Advertising in newspapers, on radio, or on cable TV channels

- Publicity from news outlets and special events

- Internet, including e-mail blasts

You are likely to use all of these at one time or another and you need to track the results. When your existing customers respond to a particular campaign, you are onto something. If you are sending regular e-mail blasts and getting very little response, you may want to try another technique. There is no doubt that most people are deluged with all sorts of material and some of it is just plain ignored.

Joy Gendusa, owner of a successful printing operation in Clearwater, Florida, called Postcardmania, uses her product to attract her customers. Each month she sends out tens of thousands of postcards to potential businesses to promote how they may be able to do this to drive up their own business. Direct mail tends to be a game of numbers, so the more you can get into circulation, the bigger the response. In the past, a response figure of 2 to 5 percent was considered excellent. This may be the most broad-based campaign you can run; you are trolling for numbers here, not specific leads.

Clients of higher-end companies tend not to respond to mass-appeal marketing. Advertising in high-end publications and sponsoring special events are often far more effective in reaching the decision makers you want to hire as customers. Know who they are and meet them where they pay attention.

Networking for Business

Word of mouth can also be a very effective marketing tool. There are as many business network groups as there are stars in the sky. They organize by location, gender, industry, and intensity of tip generation. In some groups, each member gives a promo on his or her business and then gives some effort to providing and receiving leads from other members. In the more formal groups, you are expected to generate leads for others as a part of your own participation. In many, only one member per business category is allowed in each chapter. The numbers of leads are predetermined and you can be fined for not participating.

There is no doubt that a personal referral is the best way to develop new clients for a lot of companies. But know your best customer well enough to decide whether he or she looks for vendors such as you this way. You will get the name of your company out, but you may have a difficult time closing a deal from a casual lead where the recommender knows little about your goals or those of the potential customer he or she is offering.

Caution: Do not spend your time and energy or serious money working on customers or projects that are not a good fit. You may be able to get some new business, but you won't keep it for long.

When to "Fire" a Customer

One of the toughest things I ever did while I was managing my family business was to fire a long-time customer. There comes a time in the life of some businesses when they realize that one customer is demanding an excessive amount of resources and lowering the company's overall profits as a result. You already have an investment of time in your customers, and I can tell you that my concern was that the revenue would not be easy to replace. I wrestled with the decision for weeks before I finally took action.

One of my oldest customers was a multi-location distributor that sold our products along with its own. By value, ours was very secondary. So, even though the company's orders were small, its demands were high. The owners did not want to inventory our products, expecting us to produce on demand when clothing or gloves were ordered from them. This made scheduling our production quite difficult because we had to jump on smaller orders that were almost always a "hot rush." The reps from all of the locations would call and speak harshly to anyone who answered our phone if they did not like the answer. I knew that there was growing resentment, but I was responsible for the whole operation and this distributor did pay its bills.

So I made a last-ditch effort to resolve this issue and save a business relationship of over 50 years and several generations. I spoke with the powers that be. At the conclusion of my pitch, I invited them to tour the factory so that they could see that production took time and worked only when we produced larger quantities at a time. We could produce their products best along with other similar items. True to form, they made insulting comments in the factory, offending more people than ever before. At that point I had no choice. As they were leaving, I was strong when I informed them that after the current shipments, we were no longer willing to be their vendor. They were shocked and I was shaky. I revisited this conversation in my head for a few days and realized that I had made a good decision.

We cannot expect to have a personal relationship with everyone we do business with. We all have personality quirks that make us different. And we don't always have a good business experience with people we might really like. But what is non-negotiable is mutual respect and trust.

Can You Change Your Direction Midstream?

These days, there is much talk about corporations reinventing themselves to meet the new demands of the marketplace. The unanswered question is can this really be done? Can a major auto company which has been making cars that are no longer relevant suddenly produce new models that generate new demand? And as a sub-question, can you do the same thing to your company to change it? I would make the argument for two elements that are critical to this working:

- Can you make a change within a short amount of time so that inventory that is not moving, costing money, and taking up space does not turn off your customers?

- Do you still have customers, and are they loyal enough to your company for some other reason that they will stay onboard until your conversion process is done?

The department stores will be in an interesting transition for some time. The vulnerable chains that dotted this country virtually all now belong to what was the Federated Group and is now called Macy's. Some parts of the country are very comfortable with that name and the style. Others—such as my own in Pittsburgh, which lost our Kauffmann's; and Chicago, which lost Marshall Field's—are not equally happy. I have been hearing about a new Macy's regional strategy that will customize the stores more to the desires of the areas where they exist. The resentment lingers and the window to change may be short.

Two Restaurant Reinventions

The most dramatic change I ever saw in a smaller business was in a restaurant that was not doing well and continued to slide. The owners, in a desperate attempt to save their business, closed it for renovations and renamed it before the new opening. It worked. The location was good, customers liked the staff (most of whom had stayed on), and the food was better.

I saw another restaurant do this twice, although it was little more than the name and some minor decor. It got worse each time. Last called Friday's Harbor, the company finally was forced to close and the owner was completely bankrupt and lost the building. The food and service had deteriorated so badly that regulars no longer wanted to patronize the establishment. The owner hardly came in and no one took any responsibility about how things were going.

This was clearly an operational problem because new owners bought and restored the building and the place is now called the Willow. The last time I was there, it was a 30-minute wait for a table.

A manufacturing plant cannot change its product on a dime, although in our situation, we began on a very short cycle to manufacture firefighter gear as heavy industry was getting very soft. I am seeing contractors turning to more green work such as solar panels or other "green" products such as insulation and energy-efficient HVAC. The change part takes vision, financial resources, and loyalty on many fronts, including your skilled employees. But with times always in change, it may be a skill you want to acquire.

Take Time to Find Good Customers

The startup phase of business has so many things to consider, including deciding what you are going to do and then learning all the ways you need to put together the business structure itself. I know that few think finding customers will be easy, but I am almost sure that few new entrepreneurs think of customers in terms of good ones and not-so-good ones. I hope this chapter has made you more aware.

CHAPTER 7

SMART MARKETING: DON'T SPEND THOUSANDS TO MAKE HUNDREDS

The first sale is always the toughest; finding the initial vote of confidence in your concept means a lot. And in the startup phase, you might have spent a good bit of effort and cash developing the best way to attract clients. You might have spent capital on outside marketing advice and materials, but you will learn that this becomes part of the intangible assets of your business. This is an investment and it will be earned back over the years as awareness of your business helps to draw in customers.

What I want you to consider in this chapter is how much you will spend on ongoing direct marketing as well as sales efforts, making sure that your return justifies your expense. The place to start is by determining the value of each client over a period of time.

What Is the Value of Each Customer?

The first question is this:

Are your sales repetitive to the same customer, or are they a collection of major one-time purchases?

For a restaurant that develops a loyal returning customer and can see thousands of dollars of revenue come in year after year, spending money in the early months is a good idea. In fact, this is one of the few business types that has a big bump when it opens. The challenge is to keep it up. Everyone wants to check out the new spot. After a new customer has come in a few times, sending over a free drink or a special dessert makes good sense. When the customers or clients are regular, retention becomes the major issue.

An appliance dealer, on the other hand, may make one sale to a customer every few years. But remember, there isn't just the revenue to consider, but also the profit value of each customer. A sale of $500 for a stove may bring 50 percent in gross profit, which is $250. You may want to allocate 10 percent of that to marketing and advertising.

The next question is this:

> How many customers come through your doors and what percentage of them actually make a purchase?

All of these questions generate insights, and this is the kind of information you need in order to spend your marketing money wisely.

KFC GIVEAWAY WAS WORTH IT

In April 2009, one of the major fast-food chicken chains had a coupon on its site for a free meal, no strings attached, with the exception that you had to buy your own drink if you wanted one. Did this make sense? When you consider that KFC was introducing a new version of its product to the market and that this particular promotion (with a major celebrity attached) brought millions of dollars of attention, this was a good deal. KFC sells a lot of food on a daily basis, and picking up another category of customer is a win. The typical KFC customer is a repeat customer.

Your new startup would not be likely to get this level of media hype or the continued loyal customer sales from a promotion like this (unless, of course, you can come up with something so clever that it stops traffic—and does not get you cited). Although many new owners want to see bodies in the door to assure themselves that the concept is a winner, you need to carefully reconsider driving these crowds at any cost long before grand opening day.

The value of each customer is a math question with a developed process:

What is the value of your average sale?

How often will a customer buy from you or hire you?

What percentage of that sale is profit?

Value = sale × frequency, expressed in profit margin

Here's an example. You are a consultant and each project has an average value of $10,000 and your profit is 75 percent. Each client engagement brings you $7,500 and you develop repeat work. Multiply $7,500 by the engagements over a few years. One customer may be worth $15,000 or $30,000 to your venture. A small retail store may generate average sales amounts only in the hundreds, and its profit per customer will be only a percentage of those dollars times the volume of transactions. The first company can afford a comprehensive marketing effort for attracting each client. The latter cannot.

Where Do You Begin with Marketing?

The first thing to understand is that marketing is a process to help you create opportunities to make a sale. This works by bringing positive attention to you and your company that motivates potential customers to explore what products and services you have that may meet their needs. People are reluctant to change from existing providers, so you have some work and investment of time ahead of you.

First you look at organizational branding—creating an image, with a logo and Web site, that reinforces your message. Then you begin to do target marketing that speaks directly to the customer you want to reach. You will expense these efforts in the overhead category, which should tell you that they are

- Necessary to build a successful company

- Not always directly related to your revenue

Unfortunately, you may begin a large and expensive marketing campaign that brings few results. Your safest bet is to budget for each step and not spend in excess of what the return may be in the short term or over the life of the business.

These days, consumers as well as businesses get their information in a variety of ways. What used to be advertised in newspapers is coming out in other formats as the local daily papers are losing readership (and in some cities folding). I still remember the very large editions of my local paper before the holidays that were full of sections on department stores, grocery stores, auto dealers, and small specialty operations. They have not been around for years, and there are some stores I have forgotten about because of this. This is going to be a challenge for many types of consumer businesses going forward.

Direct mail has increased in that same time, so what used to be printed and distributed to everyone in the form of newspapers or supplements in those papers is now sent to a more targeted market. You can purchase a very targeted mailing list at a reasonable price. Information is king in the current world we live in.

The Internet has opened a way for a business to get in the door of a home or another business by getting onto a potential customer's computer in the form of e-mail. The cost is far lower; but the results have been going down, as well, as the clutter of e-mails has inspired defensive action known as spam filters. Some of these are set to be so sensitive that they block out wanted mail.

The social media format is now coming into play with blogs, Facebook, LinkedIn, YouTube, and Twitter. And then there is the formerly expensive television ad that has come down substantially with the evolution of cable; however, the fact is that there are far fewer watchers at any time. But the stations know more about their individual viewers for any one show than ever because the programming is so targeted.

Your question is what is the best way to get your message across? Is it visual, or will just a still image work? Or do you need more time to be able to describe who you are? Multiple points of contact are often the most effective, but you don't need to use them all.

Where Should a New Company Invest Its Early Marketing Dollars?

Branding and image are the first costs to cover. Find a name and a look that welcomes new customers and at least create a letterhead package and a basic Web site presentation. Having a site has become similar to having a phone book listing: Everyone expects to be able to find you somewhere on the Web. You can leave the deeper development of pages to a later time when money is more readily available, but do put up your name on the Web. Even before you get your site up, you must register your domain name to keep your right to the name and allow it to be opened on a hosting server. There are a number of places to register your name, but Network Solutions and Register.com have been around the longest and they both give you tools to create your own site. If your first choice is gone, they will also suggest alternatives such as .biz or .net domains.

How Much Should You Spend on the First Day?

How much should you spend to open the doors of your business? The opening budget is a tough call because you are trying to get the venture from zero to break-even without running out of money. The value you will get by purchasing an existing business is that some revenue stream will already be in place. Even if you need to grow the company to get it back into the black, the existing customers will help. If you spend your money wisely at this point for a new business, you will be creating that same intangible value in your company that will build its value for the next owner (if eventually selling out is your end-game strategy). Your spending at this time should be based less on the return on investment of customer spending and more on establishing a brand identity in the marketplace.

The Importance of Choosing the Right Business Name

This is another reason to choose a company name that represents what you do and not who you are. A Jones and Company store that no longer has a Jones involved as an owner has very little long-term value. Even the venerable older law firms have learned that adding the names of some living partners is a good idea. Use a name and customers will want to speak to that person. I learned that because years after my father passed away, people were still calling to speak to him. On the other hand, I had a client operating under the name of Creative Kitchens and More. With its generic name and a visible and attractive storefront, a new owner could ease in and take over the business.

Remember that your corporate name could be the family name and you can operate using a more descriptive one. But it is important to register the trademark with your state. If you will use it nationally (or internationally) on a Web site or in a product you will ship, you also need to look at having it federally trademarked. And remember that the real strength is created by strong marketing across a wide area that makes the name a household word.

Do not spend all of your budget driving customers before you have some early success under your belt. You could learn from watching the hotel industry, where there is a lot at stake when a new property opens. Prior to that time, the property has what is called a soft opening where guests are in the mix, although they may be friends and family and may rent fewer rooms. Each department has a shakeout opening to identify any problems that might be lurking ready to pop up after the real opening. Guests are continually communicating with staff (because the staff is asking for feedback) and everyone is ready for day one. Restaurants and retail stores also often have soft openings a few days before the real opening. You never know what you will uncover and you don't want that to happen with a crowd around.

When you were creating your pro forma financials in chapter 3, you made an allocation to the budget for marketing and advertising expenses. You should spend approximately one-third of this for the early days of business. This is needed to create some buzz over the venture but still leave you some reserve for a second marketing wave, which you will likely need.

Be Judicious with Grand-Opening Specials

Some store owners use balloons or loud music, whereas others use the appearance of a special guest from the community, to let everyone know they are ready for prime time. Ideas vary and all may have some sort of success. The idea is to bring on some attraction, and bright lights and excitement will do that.

The really tough question is what level of discounting you should use to get people to try your product or services. Let's get back to the KFC free chicken coupon. KFC tried to limit the use by limiting the distribution, but even I knew quite a few people who found a way around that by converting the electronic file. It may well be possible to give away thousands of dollars of anything that you offer. But will you attract people who are interested in coming back to purchase the product or service, or are you drawing only those who would go anywhere for something free? You are the best judge of this.

Many new professionals offer free consultations to potential new clients in the hope that this is what it will take to convert them. This method works only when you screen your prospect to make sure that you seem to be a good match for each other and that he or she could afford to pay for the service from you or from anyone. There are some individuals who, although they might be in need of some high-level assistance, are not in a financial position to hire anyone. And then the meetings must be structured so that there is a way to close the deal if the criteria are met. You must handle the balance of giving out some good advice yet holding back enough that you seem like the go-to person. If you talk only in generalities, you might not sound as if you would be up for the job.

The point of this discussion is to help you analyze what you are offering as incentives along with what they might bring you in value, both in the beginning and over a longer-term period. Marketing is an investment in growing your business and you need to be a bit of a prognosticator as well as a business expert.

Instead of a wide-reaching grand-opening sale, consider a draw that has a longer-term effect on your customers' or clients' behavior. Their first visit might bring a discount of 5 percent, but that value goes up with every new visit up to a maximum. You are encouraging them to return. The other most frequently used technique is a user's card, which will earn some free product or service after it has been validated a certain number of times. This is all based on the value and profit on your product or service. If you are marketing to a more upscale clientele, perhaps you would rather conduct an occasional private sale for just your best customers.

Client-Retention Programs

A number of years ago, most major airlines created their own frequent-flyer programs designed to maintain loyalty with their highest-level users. Before long, credit-card companies and other stores jumped into the game, adding points for other usage. Once the entire system was up and running, it became quite the game—and one that appeared to work better than anyone anticipated. I know because I was one of the ones who would fly in strange patterns just to stay on my airline of choice. It wasn't a matter of time or a matter of convenience; it became the drive for miles and then the one to maintain the status you had achieved on that airline. Hotels joined in and then the rental-car companies. Travel could be a real adventure.

The programs started to get old and mileage piled up. After 9/11, the world of business travel slowed down considerably. Upgrades were no longer available on smaller planes and free tickets were hard to come by. Then routes and entire cities were abandoned by some carriers, most of whom had gone into bankruptcy. Now, instead of being an incentive to fly a certain carrier, these programs became a source of anger among most of the loyal cadre of road warriors who could not get the benefit of them. And the low-price, low-cost airlines have reaped the rewards of these conditions.

Although you should never ignore existing clients in the rush to find another new one, you need to be thoughtful about what you are offering. Good attention and a reasonable extra benefit should do it. But mostly, make sure you are communicating with them and continue to live up to their expectations.

PR: Getting Someone Else to Talk About You

When you buy space or time on media to tell the public about your company, that is advertising. When you are able to have someone else interview you and write about what you are doing without paying money, that is public relations. This is a very important tool in the marketing basket.

I don't want to give the impression that public relations is not usually a very expensive proposition, because you can ask any author or other prominent person who has sought publicity and he or she will give you numbers that will turn your hair grey. A great PR agent is someone who works constantly to get his or her clients into the news and in the front of the public's attention. The name of the company (or book, or movie) comes along with that exposure. But you can get some of this attention at a far lower cost if you have the time to focus on this or you have someone within your organization who is a good writer and interested in this task.

Sending out press releases is one way to get publicity. You can find online information about the format of a standard release (try, for example, these tips on PRWeb: www.prweb.com/pr/press-release-tip/best-practices.html), and there is no shortage of places to send them. Then every time you have an opportunity to announce a new hire, a new account success, the achievements of some of your staff, or even how your business can solve a problem that is in the news, you should be releasing that information to the local newspapers, radio and television stations, and other media outlets. Some will follow up on your information and may even get you a few minutes of fame.

Is there something in the newspaper that directly relates to your industry and you have an opinion or important new information? Write a letter to the editor. Start a blog about the issue or put up some footage on YouTube. The idea is to get your name and that of your company out into the public domain. Needless to say, you want to keep it in a positive light. The old-style press release that announced an event or a change in a company will no longer get much space. You have to make your information relevant to the time and current events.

Can you write an article and submit it to a magazine for publication? Once it is out, you can get reprints to send to your customers. Can you write a small book and have it self-published and then send a copy to good prospects? Can you offer to teach about your expertise at the local university, community college, or even a meeting of an organization? All of this leads to making you a familiar name in the community and serves to improve the awareness of your business. Talk to many insurance agents and they will tell you that has always been one of the descriptions of the job.

Guerilla Marketing — What Does That Mean?

Popularized in a book by Jay Conrad Levinson 25 years ago, the term "guerilla marketing" is a description of a grassroots system of promoting anything, relying more on energy and ideas than money. There are many versions of this strategy. Some are very unconventional, such as having people outside your business passing out flyers or samples or imploring people to come in. This isn't just about catching customers off guard to get their attention. It may also include the owner catching the media in a place where he or she will get attention. Being found in the stands of a championship game wearing a costume with your company's name on it is an example. There are a number of books on the market by this author and others and I strongly recommend that you read or browse them.

And now there is the electronic version of this type of marketing. You can blog on a variety of sites and say controversial things to get noticed while linking your blog back to your site. You can make and put interesting audio and video clips on YouTube, which may be picked up on by your customers or the mainstream media. And now you can use Twitter and Facebook to create a following that will follow you back to where you want them to be. And by the time this book has gone to print, I'm sure there will be several newer ways to do this all.

The Goal Is a Return That Meets the Expense

The entire point here is to learn that although marketing is a critical issue to the success of any venture, it is unwise to spend more than you will ever see come back in profits. The experts who sell marketing programs are great at promoting themselves, so it is not surprising that more often than not, you see a big price tag on the projects they promote. Your primary goal is to design programs that will create awareness and desire for your products and services while not breaking the bank to do so. Your customer pays the freight at the end of the day with the prices, so if you get too ambitious, you will become too expensive to do business with.

CHAPTER 8

MAKING A PROFIT

The most frequent interest and vocational strength that motivates people into the world of entrepreneurship is a talent for salesmanship. Give them an idea for a new product or services and they are off and running, convinced that they can create an empire. The second driving force is from those who truly love what they do and want to be able to accomplish their work without the interference of someone else (the boss). But whatever the reason for the venture, everyone knows that they need to make the sale. The challenge is to be the one who will make the sale at a profit. But not everyone knows what profit really means.

In an age when we have had much discussion about greed, you need to separate the issue of fair profit from the perception of too much. Businesses exist because they are able to make a sufficient profit that will provide the positive cash flow to continue their operations. There is a line some may cross that may be too much; but few, if any, small businesses get to the edge of this question. The more creative and innovative you can be, the more profit you should be able to make. And that is a fair reward.

There are some items that we see and consume on a regular basis that carry pricing structures that make us shake our heads—the range is so wide. Although airfare pricing has become a bit more logical in recent years, there was a time when an airline flew a plane from point A to point B carrying passengers paying fares that could be as low as $49 and as high as $800. As confusing as this was to the traveler, the airlines were relying on a computer program or capacity-control system to sell fares at different levels at different times. The walkups or last-minute flyers picked the short straw. The strategy has not shown much history of success as airlines have lost more money in the history of aviation than they have made. The major reason for the recent fare hikes has been oil prices; but the underlying industry failure was the fact that pricing inadequately drove demand and capacity was higher than use.

The other pricing that seems to defy reality is that of pharmaceuticals. The pricing in the U.S. is the highest in the world, and for the individual payer, it depends solely on the type of medical coverage that you have. The wildcard here is that much of the cost is based not on the price of the product itself but on the cost of marketing and the allocation of the recovery of development costs before the drug is actually released. You are unlikely to be in the world of these types of decisions, but you still need to know how the pricing question is answered and what elements are used.

How Do You Set Your Prices?

This may be the most challenging business decision for all new entrepreneurs, with the exception of those who are franchised and have their pricing ranges set by the franchisor. In most cases, you must know what your costs are to start with. Then you must decide whether you should base your end-user pricing on a cost-plus basis or one that is more closely based on market value. Is your product or service innovative and unique enough to set its own pricing? If not, you must price it competitively.

Influences on Pricing Decisions

The three most frequent influences on pricing decisions are the following:

- The actual direct cost of product or service (See chapter 5 for more on direct cost.)

- The amount of costs that is sufficient to cover overhead and anticipated or targeted profit margin (This number is based on your total revenue.)

- The competitive forces that allow you or prevent you from adding a higher margin—the prevailing prices in the market that will influence your profit

Your price must be more than your actual direct and overhead cost, regardless of what competitive forces there are. Operating at a loss—even to get more market share—is a high-risk strategy that has ended the careers of more than one entrepreneur. Sometimes it will seem that competitors are pricing below their cost, and you cannot be drawn into that game. Even if it is only over the short term, this strategy erodes cash and makes any business vulnerable. And you never know whether your competitors are delivering what they say they are or whether they made a particularly good buy and are luring you into a dangerous price war.

Selling at cost is occasionally a workable strategy when you are trying to reduce inventory (by liquidating older models or hard-to-sell goods) or to make a big push to drive volume to its next level. Again, this is tricky enough that you should do it only on a short-term basis.

What Is a Reasonable Profit Margin?

The next decision you will make in the pricing game is what profit margin (the percentage you add to overhead) is reasonable and will easily be absorbed by customers? If you sell or make a variety of items, the markup may well differ from category to category. Many companies work on a product mix basis, meaning that some of what they sell is at tight margins and some is high, giving an overall level of profits that is acceptable. And sometimes you win customers with the lower prices and your relationship allows you to sell them higher-profit products as well.

For example, a restaurant may sell some food very competitively but make its margins on alcoholic drinks. Or a grocery might have sales on generic products but merchandise its deli products, which are far more profitable.

How Are You Viewed in Relation to the Competition?

And finally, you need to be aware of what competition you have and how your customer views you in comparison. Are you just another pizza parlor in the neighborhood and your large pizza must be the same price as it is in the shop next door? Or is your product superior and worth a higher price based on great taste?

With certain value-added items that give you extra meaning to customers, you can produce higher markups on some or all of your services. Not all pizza restaurants deliver; can you increase prices in exchange for that convenience? Not all clothing stores include free alterations. Could you mark up your prices to cover the cost of this added service? You do not want to set your prices in a vacuum, unaware of what the market is supporting around you. However, you also must give yourself credit for what you are able to do that others are not and roll that into the pricing equation.

SOME CUSTOMERS ARE NOT SENSITIVE TO HIGHER PRICES

My plumbing contractor client in New York City was a union shop. That added considerably to its direct labor costs—and even overhead, as that is where some of the benefits were accounted for. On the other hand, it added no additional costs to the markup of the material included in the job, which could be up to 50 percent of the job. For some clients, using a union shop was desirable or an absolute necessity. The contractor added a markup on everything because it had a customer base that wanted to use its services and that was not price sensitive.

As you are developing your business and setting price points, you may actually decide to modify your strategy a bit. Selling a wide variety of items or providing a large number of services may seem like a good idea when it comes to revenue. However, the different products and services may carry vastly different profit margins. And the lower markups will undermine the most profitable ones unless you are using them as a draw for customers. Experienced business owners understand that it isn't the total revenue that matters; it is the bottom line—how much you are making in profit. It is not really that hard to create a big venture giving away value rather than charging for it. But that model isn't sustainable.

How Supply and Demand Affect Prices

Even if you weren't aware of the concept of how prices work, over the past few years the oil companies have made a public discussion out of it. Their claims have been that disruption in supply or a shortage of refinery capacity drives up prices. This is a bit hard to understand as demand has been dropping as well, and the price fluctuations have been major. But the general theory is that demand that exceeds supply will increase prices and supply that exceeds demand will drive them down. You are more likely to experience this in your purchases than in your sales.

For the small-business owner, the theory of supply and demand has a limited impact unless you are dealing in commodity-type products such as metals or produce. When supply is high due to good crops, for example, prices will start to fall. When demand is down, prices will be lower, and more companies will be willing to make deals in order to be the one to get the sale. You will have to make a call on your own strategy. You want to keep your customers even when times are tough, but you need some profits in order to continue.

When there is an actual disruption in supply or distribution, prices will go up. And when demand returns (as happens in an economic recovery), prices will move upward as well. Capacity and demand are seldom in balance. You are likely to see these cycles more than once in your business career.

The theory of supply and demand also suggests that when prices get too high, the cost will make demand go down. The $4-plus-per-gallon of gas in 2008 served as an example of that theory: When prices got too high, people found ways to use less gas. This is called the inelasticity of pricing, meaning that prices cannot continue to go up forever without a change in demand and some downward movement. And prices also will go to different set points. For example, in mid-2009, it is being suggested that the real top for gasoline is closer to $3 per gallon. The last run-up caught consumers by shock and did not allow them a chance to cut back immediately. Driving patterns have certainly changed in these volatile markets.

Few new business owners should attempt to open businesses where the pricing is erratic on an ongoing basis. You need stability in the material and services you purchase so that you can pinpoint your costs. Life becomes far more complicated when you are constantly changing your selling price. Check out what has been going on in your field and try to make some of your decisions based on the need and desire for stability.

You will not get away from the changes in demands because they are always in the market. Sometimes they are based on seasons; sometimes they're based on fickle taste; and sometimes general economic activity is the cause. But it might be a better strategy to arrange for a short-term discount sale than to lower prices across the board. In some economic turndowns, there is no discount deep enough to drive demand.

Find a Niche and Fill It

Rather than go toe to toe with other companies, why not be different enough so that your pricing can be cost driven and firm and your profits will stay in place? The markets for niche products are small by definition, and few empires are born from this strategy. You might continue manufacturing something in smaller demand, sell items with limited usage, or provide a specific type of consulting. There are a number of benefits to this that surely outweigh the downside of having fewer potential customers. You know exactly who you are marketing to and can target everything that you do. Your customers are often out looking for you and seldom want to haggle over price. They will stay with you because their options are limited and you can make a fair dollar. Consider this as an alternative. Costs may well be less and margins better.

I had a client that purchased a small division of a larger company that made flexible hinges for larger drilling equipment, particularly the type of equipment used to drill for water. The total market had gotten too small for the original company to have much interest left in this specific type of part. My client bought some of the old company's equipment, added some newly tooled elements for productivity, and moved the entire operation to a small site outside Erie, Pennsylvania, the original home. Volume was not high, but it was steady and the profit margins had been healthy from day one. Markets have not grown by much and they are not likely to, although there are big projects that come up. But the demand is steady and should go on for many years as developing countries work on their water supply and that provides a steady flow to the bottom line. And now, the company is known for hard-to-get parts and may yet have a chance to expand.

There are retail stores that specialize in a distinct product, such as Just Dogs, which (as I mentioned earlier in this book) is a bakery and gift store for dogs. There are construction companies that work with converting properties to make them accessible to the disabled or to the elderly. The aging population is driving this need even if it isn't the most glamorous aspect of building. There are consultants like myself who work with companies in need of a turnaround or those going through other types of transitions, perhaps between generations. Our work is very specific to a problem and not just business consulting in general. Now that some are working under the term "coaching," finding a specific area of improvement to promote is always important. The more definable your specialty, the easier and cheaper it is to market what you do and you take away the clients' desire and ability to find hundreds doing the same work and then make a comparison purely on price.

Cutting Prices to Drive Volume: A Good Idea?

No matter how many times you try to explain to a newer business owner that the total revenue number is not nearly as important as the profitability, there is that little voice inside some of us that wants to run an empire. The magic million mark sticks in many people's minds. Surely anyone with revenue in excess of $1 million could make money with that kind of volume, you might think. The truth is that revenue and profitability are not directly connected. Making 10 percent margins on $1 million is less than making 35 percent of $500,000.

If you are making a fair markup on all of your products or on your services, you will, in fact, make more as you grow volume. But if getting to that number requires you to start out under-pricing your goods or to lower prices to drive sales, you will not enjoy the outcome. And you might be surprised how a price increase and lower volume can achieve the same bottom line. Let's do the math.

A Sample Exercise

For the purposes of this exercise, we will assume that the product you sell goes for $10 per unit and that the direct cost is $6, so the gross profit margin is 40 percent.

1,000 units @ $10

Sales income	$10,000
– Direct Cost	$6,000
Gross Profit	$4,000

This allows you $4,000 to cover the cost of overhead as well as make a profit. What happens if you lower the price to $9?

1,000 units @ $9

Sales Income	$9,000
– Direct Cost	$6,000
Gross Profit	$3,000

This lowers the available cash to cover costs and profits by $1,000. But the intention of lowering the price was to grow sales, so what happens if you do?

Selling 1,300 units at $9 (a 30 percent increase in sales—almost impossible) would provide the following:

1,300 units @ $9.00

Sales Income	$11,700
− Direct Cost	$7,800
Gross Profit	$3,900

Your profit to fund overhead would be slightly less than selling 1,000 units at the higher price, even with this substantial increase in volume.

Try Adding Value and Raising Prices

The concept that I have just described is even more complicated than my simple chart would lead you to believe. The fact is that a sales jump of 20 percent takes time and a whole lot more marketing and advertising to get customers in the doors to increase those sales. You may need more employees and you may incur costs of higher inventory, and so on. So, although the gross profit dollars could be at the same dollar level, you could actually lose money with this strategy. On the other hand, if you could add something to make this mythical $10 product more desirable or add some value that your customer was willing to pay 10 percent extra for, your sales could go down by 20 percent and you would still earn as much gross profit!

Here are the actual numbers:

800 units sold at $11

Sales Income	$8,800
− Direct Cost	$4,800
Gross Profit	$4,000

There are a number of scenarios you could project that I will not spell out for you here, such as an additional price increase and a slight sales increase. This will actually increase your gross profit. Remember that the overhead, although not directly related to each sale, is still impacted by the level of business. Fewer units may mean fewer customers and fewer transactions. That will inevitably lower your overall costs and raise your bottom line.

Moving a Company from a Loss to a Profit

You can grow out of a loss by increasing sales. You can cut costs across the board to keep afloat. But the really savvy business owner understands that corrections of minor and achievable amounts will have the same dramatic effect on your bottom line. Try raising prices by 2 percent, increasing sales by 2 percent, and lowering overhead by 2 percent and you will see what drops directly to the bottom line. Price increases that are limited and perhaps not on all items may pass unnoticed. Growing sales by a small amount may require a few more calls each week or a little extra effort by salespeople. And the overhead always has some excess in it that you can trim. Don't think that you can hit a homerun in every area; but a few well-placed singles can give you the score that you need.

SUBTLE PRICE INCREASES CAN WORK WONDERS

One of the restaurants that I consulted with was always teetering on the edge. In the winter when things were slow (with the exception of Valentine's Day), it became grim at times. There was barely enough money to pay for food deliveries. We used this small change, big result strategy and it worked very well.

We designed a new menu. Then we used a trick I learned from the owner: Do not raise the price of the highest-priced item. At the time, it was $22.95 and that is where it stayed. But a $4.75 appetizer went to $4.95 and a $17.50 entree went to $17.95. A few people asked, but there were new items and some were dropped and not a customer was lost. In fact, the new menu brought in customers and people came to try the new items. Overhead savings came out of the linen service company and a new produce supplier. In fact, the profit increase was more than expected. Profits were once again very healthy and no one was laid off or run off by the revised prices.

Pricing Strategy for Consultants or Other Independents

All independent operations have overhead expenses. We have to run at least an office space; we need equipment; and often we hire subcontractors. There is depreciation on our cars (and the cost of running them) as well as on our office or other equipment. And there is the time we spend working on a client's project when we are not billing them. Some consultants (very few, but some) use a law-firm-type billing system and account for each minute they spend. I think the majority do what I do: Reading on a topic I need to get up to speed on, checking out a site or vendor to see what it could do to participate, or even making a quick return call is not billable. I also do not charge for time when I travel, but I do charge mileage. I charge by the project and seldom by the hour. The rule is that you are likely to be able to bill 25 hours each week and the rest of the time you will spend marketing for new clients or managing your own administrative needs.

So, to project your hourly rate, decide what your weekly goal is and divide it by 25. If you need $2,500 per week to run your business, your fee is $100 an hour. That does not mean it cannot be more, but that needs to be your goal. If you are in demand at your current pricing level, the market is telling you that you are under-pricing and it is time to increase your rates.

Most independents undervalue their service because it is not easy to set a high price on your own somewhat intangible work. A number of years ago, at a writer's conference, I heard a commercial photographer give the best description of the process I have ever heard. His main focus was pictures of Hawaii and most people considered him to be among the best. He was approached by United Airlines, which asked to buy some of his pictures for its ads. He had no idea what to charge. So he called a friend who was more experienced in the field.

The answer was short but complicated: "Whatever you can say, you can charge." The rest of the conversation went like this:

> *"I don't think I could get $8,000 for each, do you?"*
>
> *"Apparently not, because you can't say it."*

"Well, they should be worth $5,000."

"You seem comfortable at this point, so I think you should go for it."

The end of the story was that he did indeed get that amount for the first five pictures he sold. Just a few years later, he was getting $85,000 for each one. If only I could learn to be so bold with my publishers.

The lesson here is that you are worth what you think you are worth and what you can convince someone else to pay you. The real estate market has been based on just such a theory for years.

The Psychology of Pricing

Is one seat on an airliner headed from point A to point B really worth that much more than another? These days, first class has far less added value than the pricing would suggest. Yet, there are those who are willing to pay a premium to get some real or perceived value. This can be as a result of branding, which adds to status, or something a company adds to the product that really has meaning to the customer. And it does not matter what business you decide to go into, there is a range of low- to high-priced options in every sector of the economy. In recent years, this may have blurred and the trend may be moving toward being more frugal, but the premium buyer will always be there.

The strategy of pricing for profits is worth repeating in a number of different ways so that you can work through the best and the most likely way for your company to achieve a healthy bottom line. Profits are not only the way to sustain the operation in the present, but they form at least part of the capital to take the business to the next level (and there will be several levels in your business life, I can assure you). You can set out to sell low-priced items in high volume with low overhead and you will inevitably drop something to the bottom line. Grocery stores are good examples of this: They do high volume on fairly low margins. You can sell higher-end goods or services and have an office or shop worthy of such a pricing structure and you are likely to drop something to the bottom line. And both of these customers will stay loyal as long as you continue to deliver what they expect.

But the majority of new companies will aim for the middle, which means to provide the products or services that a large percentage of the population of consumers or businesses might be interested in and to do it with a manageable overhead. We soon learn that although it might be the name or logo and the look of the surroundings that draw people in, it is the quality of what we provide that completes the deal and causes them to come back. For example, most auto dealerships look the same from the inside (it has been only recently that many cities have seen the huge new mega dealerships—and for thousands of dealers in 2009, it may have come too late). Often the pricing of cars is very close from place to place and the financing and leasing deals are almost exact. What makes us buy and then what brings any loyalty is the quality of the treatment we get from the salesman, the staff, and particularly the service department. A happy car buyer will tell 10 people about it, and the greatest source of leads in virtually all types of businesses is from happy referrals.

So when considering how you will make the profits that you seek, consider first how you are doing at pleasing your customers. If they walk away the first time feeling as if they were paid attention and their needs were meet, the price (and your profit) will be a non-issue. And an unhappy customer can be turned around into a loyal one if you show that this matters to you.

The Secret About Profits

Your first goal is to understand all of your costs so that you know what money you have put into the project or product. Your second goal is to know how the market values the work you are involved in and what the common range of pricing is, and then to stake out a place in that range, hopefully on the higher side. Then work as hard as you can to create happy customers and clients and keep up the relationship so that you get their repeat business and that of their friends. Profits are not rocket science; they are the result of good business practice.

CHAPTER 9

WHOSE MONEY IS IT, ANYWAY? KEEPING BUSINESS AND PERSONAL FINANCES SEPARATE

The ongoing theme of this book has been about budgets, pricing, and profit. Being in business is about a lot of things, but the main thread is money: cash, loans, or investments. It is all money. And with the exception of what you still have in your hands, once it goes into the company, the money is no longer yours. Try to think of your business as a separate entity and then treat it accordingly. Capital cannot flow in and out without causing a great deal of confusion and liability.

This chapter also addresses issues of business credit and how to keep it separate from your own personal credit.

Keeping Business and Personal Assets Separate

You must begin your business with an understanding of separation of business money and family relationships. Businesses have a life of their own, driven by the idea and energy of the owner and the needs and demands of the local and general economies. Conditions that are in play when you start the company may change down the road, in months or years. In fact, the actual roads may change, closing off access to your place of business. Or you may become viable and fabulously successful, and every dollar you borrowed will be considered investment and the non-bank lenders will expect a jackpot return. Or every unemployed cousin will expect a job. The sooner you see the lines between you and your business, the better.

BUSINESS DEBACLE CREATES A FINANCIAL MESS

Rosemary had been a legal secretary for almost 20 years when she decided that if she ever wanted to open the store she always dreamed of, it was now or never. Shoes had long been her passion. She had haunted shoe stores for years, knew virtually every stylish brand, and could anticipate the new styles and the likely colors coming in. The second major motivating factor was the availability of an interesting shop in a small but well-regarded community. It was only a few doors away from a stylish clothing store that had been around for years. Because the location was along one of Pittsburgh's well-traveled river roads, an excess of potential customers went past, many of whom stopped to window-shop or eat in one of the interesting bistro-type restaurants. The space was unfinished but the rent was initially very reasonable. This looked like a no-brainer.

And so a store was born. The idea was great, and Rosemary was able to convince a friend to lend her $80,000 (they did not make it clear whether it was a loan or an investment) along with an SBA loan of $50,000. Had her investment been recorded as such, her investor would have been required to sign for the SBA loan, as do all owners of more than 20 percent of the company. Her investor might have felt too exposed in the debt. Although the company was still just in the early planning stages, the amount seemed more than generous. But as she started working on her plans, a friend suggested she hire a team of retail consultants. They came with a top-of-the-line concept that was clearly excessive for the business area. In 60 days, they had used up two-thirds of the money with their fees and the one-of-a-kind fixtures they found. Much of the balance of funds seemed to dissolve paying deposits and buying a small amount of initial inventory. All budget plans went away.

Rosemary forgot along the way that all of the money had to be paid back. She used it doing all of the things she had thought about over the years when the business was only a dream. She attended to details that no one would ever notice, such as placing the chairs for fittings into alcoves to enhance customers' privacy. She ordered the most current styles, although it was almost too late in the current season. The most popular sizes sold out and in reordering she had to accept unneeded inventory to make minimums. Details are complicated, but this store was in full meltdown in less than six months.

Now there was the investment, the SBA loan, an additional family loan, and some personal credit-card debt. All of the mistakes of mixing money and business that you could make were in place here. There was not a happy ending.

How Much Should You Pay Yourself?

This has been the topic of much debate in recent times, but the majority of it has surrounded publicly owned companies, investment firms, and banks. There is an answer that includes privately held companies as well. Your salary should be based on the value of your work and a percentage of the profits you help create.

What does that mean, exactly? If you were to hire someone to do your job, how much would you have to pay that person for his or her skills and devotion? Is your company making money? If so, you should increase your compensation with some of those profits. On the other hand, is your company losing money? Think about how you need to control your own draw to conserve cash. There won't be any outsider to say no, but you will be putting your career and your assets at risk if you take out too much money for yourself.

It is an interesting sensation for most business owners to set their own salary for the first time. There is no one to negotiate with or disagree, and that can make the CEO a bit bold.

I was hired to do a turnaround at a company in New York City that had been doing well for years and everyone was making money. When I was called in, the company had been experiencing devastating losses for well over 18 months. My first move was a 20 percent temporary reduction in wages for management because cash was dwindling to dangerous levels. It wasn't permanent, but we did furlough the buyer, who no longer was serious about watching costs, and replaced him by adding his duties to another employee who was more motivated. The owner did not like having his pay cut one bit and he made his opinion known. I would have liked more leadership from him, but I admit that I understand the disappointment. He was the highest-paid man in the building, however, and it would have angered everyone if he had been exempted.

Don't Put in More Money to Cover a Loss

The owner tried to negotiate that he would put in some of his own money to cover the short-term needs if we would not cut his pay. I resisted that solution because you are never quite sure exactly when the loan can be paid back and the transaction must be very well documented. And why pay income tax on the pay you are drawing when it is being covered by money you are putting in? There was a strong ego issue here, but it was not worth the aggravation. If the company did get into serious trouble, the owner might well need all of his personal money to maintain his lifestyle until a solution was found.

There are times when putting in personal funds might be the way to go: to up the investment in the company and take advantage of opportunities such as an acquisition or major purchase of equipment that will pay a return. In these circumstances, you can project the additional profits and set up a schedule to redeem your money. When you are shoring up a loss, that is not possible.

The Business Is Not Your Piggy Bank

We all have times when unexpected expenses create a deficit in our personal budgets. Some of these challenges last longer than others and some go beyond our individual resources. If the company has the extra cash, this might be a tempting place to go to get the funds. And you might take a loan on rare occasions. However, make sure that you put it formally on the books as a company asset (under loans payable from stockholder) and that you pay it back on time with a reasonable interest rate. Interest-free money could cause a tax problem or an even thornier one from an audit perspective: This could be considered as compensation and taxable as income. Borrowing from the company should be an infrequent tactic. Try to get it paid back as soon as you are able. The more you commingle the money, the greater the possibility that any corporate protection you assumed that you had will not hold up if you are sued.

Using the company credit cards as if they were your own falls into this category as well. This distorts your actual profit report, perhaps keeping you from being able to get the credit that you do need. It can also become a recordkeeping problem down the road.

Don't Pay Company Bills with Your Own Money, Either

The flip side is a caution not to pay company bills personally. This scenario is a frequent occurrence in the small-business world: The available cash in the business is short and a creditor is hammering you to be paid or it won't ship the material you need on open account. You pull out a personal credit card and give the creditor the number. This satisfies an immediate problem but creates a few new ones. The first is paperwork and the second is accounting.

You cannot just pay the ongoing monthly charge as if it were a company bill and think that solves the problem. The credit balance sits on your account and becomes a part of your credit score—not the company's. If you miss a payment, it shows on your credit record and that hurts both you and the company in the long run. Your credit score will be taken into consideration when you apply for a company loan, so down the line, credit may be denied to both.

Also, you really need to have the total debt sitting on the company's balance sheet so that you have an honest picture of how you are doing. If the credit-card balance is really owed by the company, the entire amount should be on the company's books.

Even though you are the one who gets a call when someone is looking for money, you need to discuss the circumstance of the company and realize that it is not about your personal ability to pay. This chapter discusses credit in depth. The more objective you can be about it, the better off your company will be. These issues are based on how much either side wants to make a sale and how they believe the business will succeed and be able to pay the debts eventually.

Giving Credit Where Credit Is Due

The giving and taking of credit is one of the trickiest issues in business. The following sections detail some of the things to watch out for.

Giving Personal Guarantees

In chapter 3, I made recommendations about deciding on a legal entity based in part on the issue of liability that would flow through to you personally. This is not just about debt. No new business owner thinks that he or she is going to go into business and then default on his or her obligations. Most work very hard to meet them. You really need to be concerned about any legal actions that are brought against the business also including you personally. Situations come up in a business environment such as damage or injury during a job or a disgruntled employee deciding to sue. Your company will have to defend and it will be at risk. But you don't want a second target attached to the trouble—namely you.

On the other hand, an increasing number of businesses use a credit application that asks you to sign as a personal guarantor of the vendor debt. This follows the procedure of most banks and leasing companies, which have this policy as well. They are not likely to do a deal when you do not sign. And I have a banker friend who always argues that if you are not willing to guarantee the risk, then why should the bank? So this issue is very complex.

My advice is that you should not sign these instruments personally unless there is no way around it. If you sign as an officer of the company, you are obligating only the company, so use your title. And if there is a second line for your name again, send it back unsigned. You may or may not get away with it. If the document goes back to the office and gets filed, no one will notice; but if the other company owner is looking, you may be asked. The best answer is to say that your personal attorney advises against this and you feel you must take his advice. The only reason to relent is if this is an important vendor and there are no other options. Make sure that you are using credit that can be repaid and watch it so that the vendor never comes looking for you. And in fact, vendors seldom will. What they are looking for is some leverage to make sure that they will get paid. But in 30 years I have seen only a few lawsuits filed against the owner. In all cases, it was really personal, not business.

And for the most part, these requests are not personal. Your supplier is likely listening to the advice of its counsel, who suggested that the guarantee be added to any credit application. That is why you may be able to negotiate. Meanwhile, you'll want to add that same provision to your own application to show your customers that you are serious about being paid in full and timely. And just like you, they may decide not to sign on that line and you will have to ignore it or insist on it. It depends on the risk you think you are getting into. I just went through this issue with a client because we could not get anyone to corroborate his creditworthiness. And this potential customer had a big order in the house that it would not pay for on a COD basis. So we asked for a signature and that was denied. The problem was the company had only been in business for 12 days and did not understand that no one else wanted to go out on a limb with them.

Don't Take Business Credit Personally

Credit is a touchy subject, particularly in recent years when so many people have gotten in over their heads. Too many large credit grantors became arbitrary about the issue and cancelled personal and business credit—not because the customer was not doing what it was supposed to, but because the lender was having difficulty. Creditors cancelled cards without notice and raised interest rates before the customers even knew it. As the credit noose started to tighten and choke many fine small businesses, other creditors started acting aggressively to protect their own interests. Phone companies and other utilities sent shutoff notices before bills were even due. This situation is unlikely to change for some time.

Your startup may find it hard to get credit and your vendors may be doling it out very little at a time. Don't see this as a value judgment on you and your own honesty. It reflects business conditions that have swung away from easy credit and moved to the exact opposite. Talk to those you need to work with you and see whether you can work something out in the middle. Perhaps you can have a small limit to start. As you build trust, you'll also build credit. This is why a new company needs working capital: to fund the operation until the cash flow kicks in.

As a vendor, don't be embarrassed to let a new or infrequent customer know that it may not have as much credit available to it as it might want or need. And when this is going to be the case, make sure you let the customer know in a timely way. All business owners are motivated by the desire to get the sale, but don't wait until you are ready to deliver to ask for the money. You put both you and your customer at risk at that point; the customer may need the goods and be unable to pay for them in advance, and you may already have an investment that you cannot get back. This will cloud the decision process. However you work it out, you will both feel somewhat dissatisfied by the transaction and possibly not willing to continue to build your business relationship.

Money can be a difficult conversation topic with your business peers. If you make sure that you keep it focused on the companies and not personal, you will do a lot better. Don't be forced into making a bad decision because someone acts offended. If the collection activity turns bad at a later date, the entire business relationship could be destroyed over temporary strains.

A Sale Isn't Complete Until It Is Paid

Your company works hard to complete its work and make sure that the customer is satisfied with everything it receives. Then weeks go on and no check is in the mail. The money is important to the operation of your company. But even if it is only a little, there is great frustration when a customer will not honor your effort with its payment. This is a lesson I learned really early and well.

The companies that are easy about granting credit terms get hurt quite a bit, and that was true even before the credit crunch of 2009. Some of your clients will be diligent about making sure that invoices are posted and tracked and make it to account in time to be paid. Some may have completely disorganized systems and it becomes a paperwork nightmare. And others are always running on a shoestring and pay when and how they can.

You want to take steps as early in the process as you can to make sure that you do not get caught up in these issues. This begins with sending a credit application to any new client requesting terms in order to meet its obligations. Once you receive that document, you or someone in your organization must do the backup, which is to call or fax the references and make sure that you can verify that this company pays others in a timely way. You can also order credit reports on people and businesses that will give you information as well.

Open credit must have its limits, and that is your call. How much are you willing to extend and for how long? Do not allow any more than you are willing to risk. You are likely to provide a 30-day period to pay. If you grant a limit of $3,000 for that time and a second order comes in that makes the balance exceed that amount, do something about it. You would be surprised how much can become at risk and how quickly. If the account is about to go over the limit, make a call and get some payment before new orders are shipped.

Be Clear About the Project from the Beginning

I have been in a number of businesses in my work life, the first being a manufacturer and the balance being various versions of consulting companies ranging from investment to business management to software. I learned in my early life that there could be misunderstandings about products, quantities, or delivery dates. More often than not, that resulted in some issues over money because when it came time to pay the bill, customers wanted some discount for the discrepancies, even if they had already been resolved. Sometimes we did and sometimes we did not, but eventually we learned how to send purchase confirmations to keep us all on the same page.

Now that my work is with intangible projects, I can assure you that we are more careful about defining expectations and documenting any changes. I am diligent about this with all of my clients as well. It is an issue that can come up at payment time; but from a customer-service standpoint, which is even more important, putting agreements in writing allows both sides to review and notice when there is any misunderstanding. You want happy customers and no client is looking for aggravation, so most are cooperative with this technique.

Getting the Money

Once you've delivered your product or service, you want to get paid for it. This section discusses the finer points of asking for and getting your money.

Invoice Timely and Accurately

My landscaper did not bill for the entire year of 2007. Two years later we still do not have an agreement as to what is owed. He has continued to do some work and I have been sending money, but we both are using different balances. It is not likely to end pretty. The way to avoid this problem is to send bills to your clients as soon as the work is complete; make sure the bill is detailed and understandable. Include any and all documentation that you have. You may want to print a line on the bottom asking for any discrepancies to be noticed as soon as possible.

The bills that are received without any questions can be posted for payment as soon as they come in. The ones that need further investigation are put to the side until they can be resolved, and that takes time. You want to send monthly statements that include all of the open invoices so that if one has been misplaced, the customer is on notice.

Once an invoice ages for 30 days, you should send another reminder in the form of a statement or a copy. You should begin making calls at about 45 days. The accountant should give you this aging of your receivables at least every 15 days. You need to look into anything that has gone over 30 days without payment. This is the cash that runs the company. If you let it drip out into the hands of customers, you will begin to have cash-flow problems. The deal you made when you first took the order is not completed until payment is made in full.

Enforcing Collections

Making collection calls is a tricky task. If it can be done between your staff member who handles the accounting and the same peer at your customer's company, this may well be the simplest solution. The first call is just to get payment information, asking whether the check has been processed and when it will be released. If that brings no satisfaction, you must do more.

Once an invoice has gone unpaid for 60 days, the chances of getting payment without stronger action are far more questionable. There could be any number of problems: Your client may not be getting paid, or your client may have already spent the money that should have been earmarked for you. As credit tightens, companies that had access to outside credit may lose it without any notice. As volume slows during a downturn, companies have lower gross profits and begin to lose money. They fund those losses with increasing debt, and some of it may be to you. Your job (the reason you are the top earner) is to determine which case it is and be the one to initiate action.

The first step is usually a direct call from you to the principal on the other side. This must always be polite, but you need to insist on knowing what is going on. If you are asked for patience and are in a position to be so, try to accommodate, perhaps by getting a partial payment. If your client is in a temporary problem and resolves it, the client will always remember your assistance. You may have a customer for life.

But if your calls are not answered and not returned, you have a problem on your hands. You have options at this point, and some or none of them could work. It is almost impossible to get someone to pay you when he or she is determined not to. You can go to small claims court, you can turn it over to a collections agency, or you can go directly to a lawyer. You may have to file a lawsuit. Even if you win it and get a judgment, however, this will not carry enforcement action with it. You will have to find assets and then take further action, sometimes hiring a sheriff to serve it. You may get paid in equipment and inventory and not in cash. However, if you have saved a check from the defendant and have the name of his or her bank, that would be the first place to serve. None of these choices is very pleasant and you want to take every step you can to settle with your client before it gets to this point. Perhaps accepting an amount that is less than the full balance owed is a good idea.

When Your Family Is Involved

I grew up in a family business and I understand the seamless way that members of the family start to become involved in the company. In my case it was as a teenager, the first summer I did not go to camp. I was informed that I'd better find something to do; and then my dad offered me a job. I was not overpaid, I can assure you. But then, I did not overwork, either. I joined literally millions of people who are involved in their family's company.

That does represent a number of challenges to the founder. One is that often the other employees resent the son, daughter, brother, or whoever it is and they scrutinize what they do and compare it to their own workload. Where it gets really touchy is when the member of the family is paid more than others and more than he or she is worth. This acts as a disincentive to fellow employees who are being asked to produce so that the company can succeed. And no matter how your payroll is handled, in house or not, do not think that this information will stay private because it won't. The worst case I ever worked with was a wife who was on the payroll for a no-show job. It was the topic of much conversation. And if conditions get tough, the resentment gets stronger.

And then what happens if you can no longer afford to have the family member in the job? Firing a family member can make holiday dinners very touchy for years. I know because my own father fired my brother-in-law.

And then there are the perks for family, those who work and those who don't. Perhaps it seems like a good idea to buy all of the cars in the company name, insure them that way, and buy the gas and repairs. This is certainly a strategy that saves the family money personally and seems to be buried in the books of the company. In an audit, it is not and this may be a difficult thing to disengage should economics dictate it. If you lease the cars, the company will have to complete the lease. If you own them, they will be on your books and have to be sold, with the cash going back into the company or the loss being covered by the company.

Many people start businesses for just this reason: to be able to live the high life and avoid taxation. And some succeed without problems. But they are fewer than you think. My advice is to act conservatively and take your rewards when you sell out, a topic we will cover in depth in chapter 11.

Build Your Assets and You Will Reap Rewards

From the day you start the company, thinking of it as a separate entity is a very good strategy. Make decisions based not on your needs, but on what is in the best interest of the business. This makes the business more likely to succeed and to provide for you as long as you want to be in charge. And when the day comes to exit, you will have a track record of that success that will attract buyers and add to the price. This is the best long-term strategy.

CHAPTER 10

SECRETS FOR CONTINUING BUSINESS SUCCESS

I have been speaking to audiences of business owners for decades, and one of my favorite topics is the Seven Secrets of Successful Entrepreneurs. I have expanded some of these "secrets" into entire chapters in this book, such as hiring the best customers and learning how to keep the score. These topics are worthy of entire books and my hope is that you will read some additional books to enlarge your knowledge base. This chapter covers the rest of the list, in no particular order. Being in business requires you to be a multi-tasker, so you need to consider many of the elements that contribute to your success.

Don't Create a Monster That You're Not Prepared to Feed

Working for someone else means that your employer must generate the business to keep you busy, the resources to make you productive, and the money to pay for your services. Once you take charge, all of these jobs will be rolled into your daily tasks. If yours is a small shop, you will be actively involved in every aspect of this work. Once you have built a bigger company, you will still have responsibility for oversight and leadership.

Who brings the business in the door? The simple answer might be the salespeople, but their work is driven by the decisions on product, pricing, and policy made at the top. These aspects really make the difference in the market, and that is the owner's prime responsibility. Sam Walton built a billion-dollar corporation based on a vision he tested in small stores early in his career. It took millions of people to help build his vision into the enterprise it is today. Even though Sam was no longer in charge at the end, as he was dying of leukemia, he was still making calls to store managers to ask about how they were doing. If you have been creative about what you are doing and how it will be done, you can bring in others to handle the transactions. But you are still the one in charge. As long as the buck stops at your desk, you need to make the calls.

The owner of a local printing company had turned the company over to family a decade ago. But he still called the plant from the hospital on his very last weekend alive to check what was going on press on Monday. He and his family both knew that it is the sales that drive the engines. The growing business becomes the biggest focus in the life of the owner and the family, often requiring effort in excess of what is possible in a day. This may become a monster in their lives. And they live with their monster as their pet, which is possible for some.

Are You Really Comfortable with People?

There are many roles in a company that require the founder to interact with a variety of disparate personalities and create a positive outcome. This is not nearly as easy as you might anticipate. Having a large number of employees, some quite competent and some underachievers, can drive anyone to great frustration, particularly when you need their work product to meet your customers' requirements. And your customers are not going to understand who dropped the ball; they will just know that it was dropped. You need to be the one who drives the team to win or decide which player is cut. Firing is a whole other topic that I will not cover in this book, but I can tell you from personal experience that it is painful.

Not all customers are pleasant to deal with, either; there are some who are unreasonably demanding. Your role is to be patient and pleasant and solve their problems, even for those who appear to have no solution. Particularly in tough times, customers are always trying to cut deals to save money. Are you good at keeping your cool? The bigger the operation you create, the more complicated human interaction you will get involved in. You need to be the one who does the right thing all the time, not just react as most people would when faced with challenging behaviors.

Are You Strong at Meeting the Needs of Many?

Your job as chief salesperson won't end, even with a system full of purchase orders. Fulfilling expectations must be in your DNA. This concern starts the entrepreneurial juggling act. You need to manage relationships with vendors and lenders, as well. And don't forget that you are the ultimate HR department; you may lead, mediate, or discipline. It's all part of the job.

The bigger the company you grow, the more complicated your role. Day-to-day tasks will be replaced by delegating and oversight, which at some times may prove to be more of a challenge than rolling up your sleeves and doing the work. Patience is not one of the entrepreneurial virtues; often, while waiting for others to do what should be done, we go ahead and do it ourselves.

I was the CEO of a family manufacturing company for 20 years and I can count on my fingers the number of days that I did not show up or call the office. Vacations were always punctuated by a certain number of business calls, and that number could get quite high. I remember days sitting in a hotel room in a resort area returning phone calls. I was used to it. I grew up in a family business environment watching my father do the same thing. In the days before cell phones, he had a car phone and tried not to get out of range. Once I sold the company, after all those years, I employed only independent contractors in my later ventures. I was amazed how much freedom that provided.

So, if you value your freedom over almost anything else, make your own enterprise a simple one, which is not as easy as it seems. Every company needs a certain amount of growth to survive. But if you are very ambitious and willing to trade time for great success, the total commitment will seem fair. This is your call; make it wisely.

A Successful Business Is a Team Sport

You'll spend your early days of developing your venture alone while you plan, research products and space, and find resources. Depending on what kind of a company you are beginning, you might be going it alone as the sole employee for a while. Even when that is the case, you will still be forming a team of trusted advisors, vendors you need to rely on, customers who will trust you with their dollars and their work, and lenders who are getting to know you and preparing to make capital available if you need it. This becomes your team. Many of them will stay with you for your entire business life. Some may well become good friends. The more collaborative you become in your business environment, the more successful you can be.

When I was first in business, I met one of the bankers from my bank while we were working as volunteers in a community organization and we became friends. He was the one who ultimately taught me the most about business financial operations and he became my mentor. Throughout the time I owned the company, when he moved to another bank, so did my business bank account. Even after I went on to another career as a writer/consultant, he remained a major resource. We even co-authored a book on small business banking. Not all relationships work out with such long-term value, but it is worth it to try to make that the case.

Maintain Good Relationships with Vendors

It can be easy at times to become impatient with your vendors if they miss a deadline or ship incorrectly. You are the customer and you are always right, except when you are being unreasonable. What you need to find out first is whether this is an occasional problem or an indication that they do not care about their work. You will make mistakes in your business as well and ask your customers for tolerance, so you should provide the same for others. One of my clients spent the last week working hard to get a job right when it should have taken only a few days. Part of it was the client's fault and part was the fault of the customer's poor design. Regardless of whose fault it was, the job still had to be corrected and the customer appreciated the effort. Give your own vendors the benefit of the doubt.

Good vendors can really give you a business edge. They can offer you special terms when you need it or special deals when they are available, or they might expedite something just to help you out. You want to be considered a special customer and that works best if you can earn that status. It's not often granted to the one who can prove only that it is the most demanding.

The Care and Feeding of Your Local Banker

Having a good banker means far more than having a source of funds when they are required, although that is important. Bankers, more than most local professionals, are active members of the business community because it is a necessary aspect of their job. So if you want local referrals, insight into the trends in business, or even strategies about how to build financial independence, a good banker is a great resource. Make sure you get to know one when you start out.

Here as well, you need to be a good customer; understand that handling your checking-account problems is not how your banker shows his employers how much value he can create. Bankers, like every other business representative, have goals. Sometimes it's new deposits; other times, it's new loan applications. Help your banker meet his or her goals and he or she will help you meet yours. Show enough interest to inquire what business goals your banker is trying to reach within the organization and perhaps make referrals. If it is appropriate, try to invite yours to your place of business so that he or she can see what you are trying to accomplish.

Employees Build Your Company

"You work for me!": four of the dumbest words any business owner has ever used to try to motivate an employee. It really seldom works. You both work for the customer, and when your personal interests get in the middle, everyone loses. Satisfying the needs of the modern market requires the joint effort of management, workers, and sales, all putting their oars in the water in the same direction. A stronger and more profitable company should pay dividends to those who contribute to its success. The employees need to understand that they share and benefit from this customer-driven goal, and it is one of the most important roles of the owner to communicate this in practice. It may be in the form of an occasional lunch meant to say thank you, or an actual cash bonus for serving a particularly big project.

THE DIFFERENCE WORKING TOGETHER CAN MAKE

I remember the end of TWA, one of the largest airlines in the country. It had devolved into an open war between management and labor. Flying on its planes was like being in a war zone. All you heard were complaints and no one cared about the customer, an attitude that showed anytime you asked about anything. The other side of this in the travel industry is the Marriott Corporation, which preaches, teaches, and believes in customer service in every department of its hotels. Unfortunate things have happened to me at these hotels, but everyone in the property works to solve the problems. This company understands the life value of a customer. Marriott has earned my loyalty for 30 years with its service.

Be a Good Community Citizen

If you operate anywhere within a definable business community, you are a neighbor and need to act like a good one. Keep your business premises clean and be responsible for what happens outside your place as well as inside. Get to know the other community members who are also in business. Join the Chamber of Commerce or other business organizations and support whatever local drives the members of the community, the local Rotary, or other groups are spearheading.

This might not seem to be a good source of direct referral of work for you, but it does show others how you operate your company and that sends messages beyond where you can see. Not all referrals are direct; some come by way of people mentioning your name and giving you or your company compliments. In fact, there are times when all it takes is to mention the name of the business and a new customer will check it out.

Sometimes the local organizations are more effective than the business-networking groups. I have talked about these groups before and my only additional comment is that if your company needs many leads that do not have to be vetted, and if you have the time and interest, going to a breakfast with a leaders' group once a week might work very well for you.

Even if You Didn't Invent It, You Can Improve It

Innovation is an interesting phenomenon: It's part brilliance and part timing. Just look at the Internet and how the technology has made millions and lost almost as much. In the dot-com era, the enabling technology was developed for anyone to launch a Web-based business. And clearly, now that we reflect on it, far too many did just that. E-commerce sites went up with absolutely no idea how they would find even a small amount of the millions of potential clients. After the loss of billions in investment, the new social media has risen, although far too few know how they intend to monetize their efforts. Blogs are great, but how do you earn money from starting one or writing one? Might you be the one who can create a cash stream from this attention?

Remember that the mighty have fallen in this effort. When Time Warner took over AOL, it was projected to be the major player in media by combining books, newspapers, movies, and the Internet. When AOL failed to keep up with trends and users got more savvy, its value slipped. First the AOL name was dropped from corporate, and then AOL was dropped entirely.

The online media will become the dominant media eventually, likely in just a few years. But it is not clear yet who will be the big players when that happens. Will the shopping sites merge with the news sites and become an interactive replacement for newspapers? Surprisingly, it is often the second and the third generation of technology that cashes in and not the first. Some of the smaller software players who wrote programs compatible with larger operating systems made a fortune selling to their customers or selling out to the giants.

You certainly do not need to start a business in that high-tech world. You will be able to use what was developed by others to turn a simple business into a new business model. I know a small uniform company that existed for years selling customized clothing to health-care and food-service companies through catalogs and telemarketing. This was time-consuming and expensive. A well-designed Web store and e-mail marketing campaign turned this small business into a vibrant national concern. And it was not just the ordering that became automated. Inventory control and delivery information was light-years ahead of the competition. These days, workers come into the office and check the orders, which have already been downloaded into the order-entry system and are waiting for embroidery or shipping. Now they've got more business and more profit.

Amazon is a marriage between one of the most mature retailing industries and state-of-the-art technology. Although it started as a bookstore, the real story behind Amazon was the software that managed the store: interacting with customers, tracking inventory and shipments, and providing a great online shopping system to customers. Now Amazon carries almost everything. Can you think of some improvement in your own field or one you may be able to get into? Build on the work of others to create your own empire.

Traditional marketing methods involved using existing media and mail to get the information out to potential clients. You were counting on what people saw and what they heard. The online media drive information so quickly that it is possible to create a new phenomenon in a matter of days and weeks. Does this have application in your business?

Don't Get So Deep into the Forest That You Can't See the Trees

This may be a very controversial point to make (and this is a self-admitted anecdotal observation), but my experience with new business owners is that having a degree in business or even an MBA is not a predictor of success in an entrepreneurial venture. Many MBA programs are in a single area of specialty, such as finance or marketing. But business needs to be driven by a balance of all interests. One of the unrecognized talents of successful entrepreneurs is the ability to see what you are trying to do in terms of the big picture. And that is not as easy as it sounds. The day-to-day demands of any company may well be such that it is tough to find the time and the energy to get out and see what is going on that will affect your company in the immediate future or shortly down the road. And it could be as simple as a street that might be facing a shutdown, thereby choking off your customer traffic. Have you been watching the street rehab plans around you, or are you surprised when the cones and barrels go up?

Although it might seem logical that the person with the greatest financial savvy can run the ship and find others to handle sales, marketing, and operations, this is not always the case. Entrepreneurial growth is about risk, which is not always comfortable for a person with linear accounting skills.

Here are some big-picture questions to consider:

- Are there upcoming events that might bring traffic to your area, such as a fair or special summer sidewalk sale, and you want to prepare to take advantage of that additional business? You do not need to be one of the special-event vendors in order to have a marketing presence where there is a lot of traffic.

- Do you belong to the Chamber? Even if you don't go to meetings, do you read their reports? Do you pay attention to some of the macroeconomics that might influence your company a year from now?

- Do you belong to a trade association and try to get to at least some of the meetings to see what is going on in the industry?

- Are you a regular consumer of news, both business and general? Do you follow trends in the global economy? Are you watching for opportunities that might arise because government money is being spent or new regulations are being passed into law?

There is much that happens to affect your company that does not happen within your own four walls. I know what it feels like to come in to a desk full of work with phones blasting, text messages going off, and all of those other distractions. I also know that I was surprised once by an event that I did not expect, which was the closing of many of the steel mills that we served. It came at me like a freight train. The papers and the news had been making predictions; but because I did not want to believe it was true, I paid no attention. I could have been better prepared, so now I spend at least a part of my day thinking about my business and not just working in it.

Tip: Get out at least a half a day a week and do something that adds to your learning: Take a course, visit a vendor or customer, or have lunch with other business owners.

Always Keep Two Sets of Books

This is one of my favorite tips because when I say it, people look around as if I am about to tell them how to cheat on their taxes. (That is something I do not recommend because it can cost you far more than you save and it is *not* the right thing to do. I always recommend that you work to minimize your taxes, but pay the ones that are due.) This is about strategic books: keeping the set that shows you how you have done and comparing them to the ones that show you how you expected to do. I am talking about *budgets.*

When you created your business plan in chapter 3, I described these reports as pro forma statements—documents created around your optimism and research, which usually turn out to be a best-case scenario. Once you have had close to a year to see how the sales grow and the costs vary from what you expected, you will have an actual set of books. This is also known as the income statement or the P&L, and it's the monthly record of your sales, expenses, and bottom line (good, bad, or in the middle). You will also have a balance sheet that shows assets and liabilities and owner's equity. The income statement closes at the end of each year and no longer accrues numbers. The balance sheet continues to roll values.

The second set of books is a mirror of the first, with the exception that the numbers are for periods in the future and they are your goals (hopefully achievable expectations). Before the beginning of each year, estimate each month on all of the micro numbers such as total sales, cost of goods sold, overhead costs (perhaps in some detail), and the net expected (before-tax) profits. The basis of these numbers is how much better you think you can do at selling as well as controlling costs now that you have some time to gain skills at your new venture. This should be a month-by-month document that you lay side by side with the actual numbers as they are achieved. Then, at the end of each period, you can see how you made your goals or where you were off and by what amount. It is probably easier to do this quarterly because that allows for some small changes in one month that may not happen again. If your real books are close to your second set, you can start to set even more ambitious goals. If you have missed the numbers, you will know where you need to make improvements.

Keep Up Your Business Plan

Most business owners are not engaged by the creation of a business plan. They would rather work at it than write about it. Yet, this document remains a very important part of your job. You might need parts of it to turn into a loan proposal when the bank is looking for background information. You might also incorporate some of it into your marketing material.

Once the initial plan is complete, I am not suggesting that you continue to rewrite it as you go along—I don't think I could convince anyone to do that. But you do want to create at least an ongoing strategic plan in writing so that, as you are doing it, you can take the time to think through all of the elements of what you are working on now and what you expect to be doing a few years from now. Business cycles are very short these days, and the nature of many industries changes in less than a decade. At the end of each year, sit down and look at what you wrote the year before about what expectations you had for this time just passed. Were you right, and do the facts seem to be the same? Use this in conjunction with the two sets of books I discussed in the preceding section.

I have heard insanity described as doing the same thing over and over again and expecting different results. I can assure you that if your company has had lackluster results from last year and you do nothing to change it, it is likely to have about the same results or worse this year. Although there is no doubt that business gets slow for periods and then has some level of rebound, the interesting fact is that it never comes back exactly as it was. The forces that soften activity will ultimately change it. You need to find out where you are positioned for the future, not just the past. And the truth is that even when you are doing okay, you need to be thinking and planning for what you will be doing next.

I had a 20-year run in my first business and went through a number of cycles. At the end of each, there was something inside my company that was quite different. We changed our distribution philosophy over that time, moving from distributor sales to direct. We changed our product line to include safety clothing for firefighters, and we included the resale of other companies' products. I decided to sell when I did not want to go through the reinvention once again. Depending on how long you expect to stay in business, you need to be prepared to reinvent the business as demands dictate.

CHAPTER 11

EXIT...STAGE LEFT: PLANNING YOUR BUSINESS EXIT STRATEGY

The day will come when you decide that the business is not as much fun as it used to be or that it requires greater resources to take it to the next level than you are able to invest. Perhaps the market has changed and there are no longer the same opportunities as when you began. You may even have started this as a short-term investment and it's getting to the point where you have done what you set out to do. The day to leave will come, and you should be thinking about it along the way so that you can max out your return. Building equity in your company is the long-term profit of running a company.

The time to begin the process of getting a business ready to sell is three years in advance of the time you will be actively marketing it. Like a home that you want to sell, your company will need to be cleaned up both from the external aspect of how it looks (particularly if you own the property) and the internal aspect of how your profits have been and what is being carried on your balance sheet. You can build additional value in a company by taking steps in the operation over the short term that will pay you back at the time of sale. This chapter discusses these in detail.

Exit Strategies

Businesses are started for a variety of reasons:

- Some are started by people who just love their work.

- Some are started by people who need to create work to provide personal cash flow.

- Some are started as short-term strategies to create greater value and sell it off.

Whatever the reason you started it, you have a variety of business exit strategies to consider, including selling the business, grooming a successor, and merging with another company.

Selling the Company

The last reason is the equivalent of house flipping in the real estate market. Investors look for low-entry-cost properties and work to make the value increase while taking out little cash for the effort. The payoff comes when the property (in this case, the business) is sold. The business version differs from a real-estate flip because it might take longer to create a saleable entity and you will need income to support your effort and show buyers that there is value for them as well.

The exit strategy in an investment company starts the day that the first business plans are being put on paper. The books must be set up strictly from day one, and each transaction must have backup documentation. Having a CPA do all statements and taxes from the first year is important because any buyers will want to be able to audit your records. They are buying on the basis of performance, and you will be required to have an audit trail to prove that performance.

For many, selling the business is the most complicated aspect of ownership. The owner seldom knows what the price should be, how to find buyers, or how to complete the transaction. You hope to have the option to make this decision at a time of your own choosing, as well as the luxury to make the best choices along the way. As a rule, it seldom happens exactly like this. There are times when illness or family demands require an early and immediate sale, or you might have hung on too long beyond the optimum selling point or time and no longer have the patience or time to learn what you need to know before you sell it. You need to be thinking about this along the way so that you can make good decisions about this final sale.

UNPREPARED TO SELL

My own situation is a good cautionary example. After 20 years of the responsibility and the ups and downs (which I had gotten used to), I made the decision that I needed to move on. I had no idea how to value the company, although I was aware of a likely buyer. My first call to him had an immediate and positive reception. After very little negotiation, we struck a deal, and I was mentally on my way out.

Knowing then what I know now, I would have done much of it in a very different way. I made that call totally unknowledgeable of the different types of business sales and I did not even have a price in mind. I called the person most likely to buy my company and asked if he wanted it. His yes was followed by my silence. Then he made an offer that I was in no position to counter, so I accepted. I ended up with a few side deals that made it all worthwhile, however.

What should happen at the point you decide to sell? Here's a general outline:

1. First, look at the last few years of statements with your financial advisor and decide on a fair price (more on how to do this later in the chapter).

2. Then you'll begin to market the company, most of the time anonymously so that you do not disturb the ongoing business.

3. Once you have found an interested buyer, get a letter of intent, as well as a confidentiality agreement, before you release insider information.

4. Negotiate until you come to a mutual agreement on price and terms. The more cash you receive on closing, the more secure

your payout will be (you'll read more on this aspect later in this chapter).

5. Sign a sales agreement, which may be very complex and include a number of adjustments to the agreed-upon price.

6. The last step before closing is what is known as due diligence, where accounts are reviewed and inventory is checked. This is where some secondary negotiations may well go on.

7. And finally, the closing! Very similar to real estate, this part includes lots of lawyers and lots of documentation.

As you think more about this method of exit, I will discuss some of the others. Then I will review the sale of a business in greater depth.

Grooming a Successor

Do you have another family member who loves what you do almost as much as you do? Is there a son or a daughter who always wants to go to work with you? If this is the case, I am sure you are at least considering grooming a successor. I want you to remember that making this work takes thought and planning over a long period of time.

The first thing is to be careful about how you characterize your work while the younger one is still impressionable. Don't think that you can come home and complain about work every night and still have a son or daughter who can't wait to get into the nightmare you describe. Instead, let him or her have some good experiences and share the range of challenge and satisfaction. Let him or her work over summers and do more than just being an errand runner.

Most of us need time to be ourselves, so starting out a potential successor with his or her own career can be a good idea. Certainly, you need to encourage him or her to take time out to go to school and study what interests him or her. Perhaps your potential successor needs to consider a job with another company as a good strategy for the start of his or her career. It will give him or her better perspective and help him or her earn the respect of other company employees. Many offspring in family businesses spend time thinking that if only they had a chance to go elsewhere, life would be easier—even when they also harbor a hope to be a part of the business. It is not easy to be the child in the workplace as well as at home.

Once you have actually hired your son, daughter, nephew, or whomever, you need to make sure that you give this person a very specific job description. He or she needs to have some tasks that are measurable in terms of success so that he or she can feel as if he or she is an integral part of the company. Perhaps groom your successor to head a department or handle specific accounts. If your successor is to spend a lot of time with the founder in the picture, he or she needs to develop enough autonomy to be motivated to buy out your interests.

MICROMANAGEMENT CAN SCARE OFF YOUR SUCCESSOR

I had a client whose son worked with him for 15 years and was always under his father's thumb. Just about the time in his life when dad was hoping to take more time off and start the process of making the transition, Max gave notice and left. His dad, Larry, was dumbfounded; but no one else in the building was. Max was now growing into his job someplace else because his father would not let him do so. All Max saw in front of him in the family business was interference for years to come.

The successor does not simply take over the business without any exchange of money or legal authority. The company passes hands by an official sale between the two of them that may take place all at once or be gradual over a period of time. The founder will have obligations and guarantees that the new owner must assume. The founder will have his or her name on documents that show ownership of vehicles and equipment that must be given over to the new owner.

Last, but by no means least, the founder has equity invested in the company that must be redeemed by the new owner. The founder has financial needs that cannot be met if he or she just leaves and continues to draw a check from the company. Also, if the founder still has money invested, it's difficult to get him or her to let go and let the successor run the business. The successor needs to go to a lender and borrow much (if not all) of the money that it will take to purchase the company from its previous owner. And whatever balance may be owed should be paid promptly.

And while this is a financial deal, it is also a symbolic deal because as long as the founder (the parent or older relative) still has his or her money at risk, the tendency will be to manage from the back seat. Even when his or her money is no longer at risk, this can be an issue. The successor might be able to carve out a special project or let him or her handle special accounts, which eases them out of the day-to-day decisions.

When the Founder Just Won't Quit

One of my vendors was a tannery in Milwaukee. The former owner came in every day until he was in his late eighties and was always telling employees what they should be doing regardless of the fact that his two sons were in charge. They moved him out of his office, but that didn't slow him down. They even gave him a retirement party and a gift certificate for a trip, and he was still back early the next morning. Given that this often happens, taking the money out of the equation is a sensible move that can encourage the founder to back off.

Merging with Another Company

Before you formally put your company into play as a seller, consider the possibility of a merger with another player in the industry, either locally or in another city. Is there a competitor that you respect and believe that if the two of you joined forces, a larger and far more profitable company would emerge?

How does that happen? "Economies of scale" is the term used when two companies combine to save money. It means that all of the functions that each of you do on your own could be done only once and the savings would increase profits. There are a vast number of opportunities to make this work:

- A single advertising and marketing campaign to attract customers while spending less money

- A single accounting system to do all of the billing and paying

- Keeping fewer people busier and more productive in product development and production

- The opportunity to purchase inventory in larger quantities and at lower prices

- One surviving company and only a single CEO to draw a salary

The value of those projected new profits would form the resources that would allow the other company to pay for yours. In these types of cases, only some of the money for the sale is paid at the closing. The rest is paid out as the profits increase. Sometimes it is paid as a salary or a consulting fee for you to stay on as a part-time employee. This is why I recommend that you pursue this strategy only with someone you know fairly well and have a lot of respect for. You are going to have some money at risk and very little ability to determine how the successor company will be run. I have seen this work very effectively; one of my clients was paid much of the money at the closing and has remained a part-time consultant for more than five years because he enjoys the work and likes not having the responsibility.

If this is a joining of two small companies, I would suggest that much of the negotiation go on between the principals without outsiders so that they can make the common understandings before the lawyers make it too complicated. I have seen more small deals fall through because they were done by professionals. If the two of you can determine a mutually beneficial deal, that is one that will likely work.

Creating Greater Value in the Business

Throughout the time you are operating your company, you should be building value for the day you will look at selling. Of course, you are also providing for your ongoing financial needs and those of others, but you are creating or purchasing valuable assets at the same time. Take a look at how this all works. A few years before you intend to market your company, you will want to focus more on this aspect of what you are doing.

You must maximize profits by really scrutinizing the expense side, and that includes your own draw and any benefits. Scaling them back to improve the bottom line could pay great returns. Always keep equipment in good repair and consider replacement when the need arises or the technology improves—except during this sensitive time. The only reason for capital investment when you're planning to sell is a genuine increase in productivity. Although you will put the purchase on your balance sheet as an asset, there is a cost to implement any change and that may well cause a short-term hiccup in profits.

Look at your balance sheet as well and make sure that you can document all of the line items. If you have been carrying receivables that are uncollectible or inventory that is out of date, write it off sooner rather than later. You will take a hit on your bottom line, but not doing this will be a contentious issue in any due-diligence activity prior to a closing. Cleaning up the financials by real action will make your company more attractive to an outsider.

What Are the Different Ways to Value Your Company?

The value of a company is often described as the *present value of future benefits.* The condition that I described in a merger is a good example of this. If the two companies will make an additional million dollars over the next five years as a result of the deal, that is the future benefit. The present value of that is some percentage of that outcome. So, as I review the other bases of value, keep this in mind.

- **Fair market value:** A tax-purpose value that is described as the price which a willing buyer would pay and a willing seller would accept. This is often set for estate purposes, but it should also be considered in a sale to an insider. If the deal is ever scrutinized as a result of any tax dispute, the sale should be able to stand up to this standard. This is not easy for most small companies that have many contingencies, such as inventory that has lost value, receivables that you will never collect, or the potential for lawsuits down the road.

- **EBITDA:** Earnings Before Interest, Tax, Depreciation, and Amortization. This is the value of positive cash flow, which is restated by taking out the listed items. Typically, a company may be valued at three to five times this cash flow.

- **Asset value:** The net value of all of the company's assets such as accounts receivable, inventory, equipment, and so on. This type of pricing is for a company that is selling only assets and retiring its own liabilities. This may be of benefit to a company which owns property that is depreciated on the books but has greater value individually. The book value would be a lower number.

- **Dream value:** The opportunity you are conveying to another who may be able to grow the business into a larger and more profitable one than it is currently. You may not have the interest, energy, or financial resources, but a new buyer might be able to leverage an existing operation.

- **House-in-the-middle-of-the-road value:** When your company may hold the missing piece for another business that will allow it to expand and become more profitable. Without your product line or market share, this growth would not be possible. The price here is solely based on serious negotiation.

The last two valuations are my interpretation of what I have seen over the years—they are not produced by authorities or valuations firms. But I have clearly seen them at work. In one case, a nonunion company purchased a union competitor, which allowed it to bid on all types of contracts and increase profit immediately. The value to a buyer has as much to do with its vision and ambition as it does with the technical aspects of the company being sold. Your job at this point is to identify your own strengths and make the pitch.

Putting Your Company into Play

The day comes when you really are ready to sell and you wonder how to begin the process. Let's go through the details and some of the warnings you should listen to. Do not go out immediately and let everyone know that the company is for sale. Once this is widely known, you may well lose customers to aggressive competitors and your valued employees may decide that they need to explore their own alternatives. Considering that these might be two of your biggest assets, you can lose value in a hurry.

The first thing to do is to sit down with your accountant and go over the company financials. You will be setting the selling price (and strategy) at this time and you want to know if there would be some benefit to taking extra time to improve the profits or the balance sheet. If your industry and market are still healthy and you aren't being forced by some imminent event, this should be the first step. Have as many conversations as you need to learn what type of sale you will make and how much of the sale price will eventually come to you. There are some major tax implications that may make one option far better than the other.

When you are ready to begin marketing the company, you will need to see an attorney and have him or her draw up two agreements for you to have ready for any potential buyer:

- One is a **confidentiality agreement** that the prospect needs to sign before you release any specific information such as tax returns and customer lists. This keeps the prospect from sharing with a third party any information found out as a result of your release. You always have a risk when others learn too much about your business, but you must try to avoid any further knowledge drain.

- The second, which may be specific if the sale is a big one or just generic, is a **letter of intent.** This identifies your buyer and the terms, as well as the fact that he or she is entering into these negotiations with the intent of purchasing the company. You may or may not include the price as well.

There is little chance that you will be able to actually enforce these agreements because the court fight will be costly, but you still need to act in a businesslike manner.

You may want to deal with a business broker who will list your business and market it to those who are out looking for a company to purchase. Be careful when choosing one because not all brokers are the same. They may make you promises about how much you can ask for the company, but that does not mean you are going to get it. Brokers are paid a percentage of the deal, although some get paid to help you market the company and then get a lower percentage when it is sold. If you can find a referral, that is the best way to go. You may also be able to find an accountant or a consultant who makes a business out of selling companies and will represent you exclusively to buyers. Brokers really work for the buyers and will try very hard to make a deal because that is their payday.

Price is not the only thing to consider in a deal. The terms may be even more important. Will you be paid everything at the closing, or are you accepting a payout over time? You need to see the personal financials of your buyer before even agreeing to a deal, and if it is a payout, ask for a personal guarantee. If the company does not do well, you will still be entitled to be paid.

The Moment of Truth: Closing the Deal

I have seen business sales agreements that are more pages than anyone could read carefully or understand well. What is included in this document is a detail of what is being sold, what representations have been made, and what indemnifications are included. This means that if the business is sued or held liable for some action after the sale has closed, the previous owner may be held liable for it unless the possibility was disclosed. This agreement will also include a due-diligence list, which is a recap of all documents that may be reviewed by the buyer before the closing and whether any price adjustments will be available if some of the balances are different on the closing date. There is likely to be a physical inventory taken, which will be an addition or subtraction off the price.

The closing will take place at a bank, if the buyer is taking out a loan to be given to the seller, or in an attorney's office. They can be long and arduous affairs full of all kinds of signings. I have been through 12 of them in my time and there has not been one owner who was not a bit sad at the thought of giving over to an outsider the reins of something he or she had built. I had one who made an excuse to walk away from a meeting and cease negotiating for six months to show his resolve in getting the right deal. And I had one who cancelled the deal the night before (for good reasons; see the sidebar on the next page).

Not Giving in to Last-Minute Pressure Tactics

The deal that failed was a purchase of the assets of a company and the forming of a new joint venture between the buyer and seller to use these assets in a larger project. The buyer hired a negotiator from Washington, D.C., to come to this small town in Pennsylvania to complete the deal.

At the very end, most sellers are anxious for the close and good negotiators (for the buyer) know that you can force some concessions at that point. I have worked only with sellers so I have seen this but not done it, and I try to get my clients not to give in. In this case, the buyer said he had discovered a miscalculation in the joint-venture plans and, therefore, needed to pay less for his share of the company—$200,000 less!

My client said no and ended the deal at that point, no counter-offer and no more conversation. I was amazed at his resolve. He explained that if they were to be partners going forward, the deal could not start out like this. I suspect all they wanted was a $50,000 discount and it was a calculated risk that backfired. The deal was gone and the buyer tried for weeks to get it going again with no result. I still admire the seller's resolve.

After the close, the new owner takes possession of all of the business assets that he or she has bought. The new operation begins, at times with the name of the old owner still on the door. Even when the new owner does a bad job, the seller has to stay out. And I can tell you that old customers may call to complain to the former owner.

Life Goes On

How long should you stay in business before thinking about selling the company? This is a question without a single answer. Some founders want to build a company and then sell within a few years. Some expect to be in business for the duration of their working lives, but get disillusioned and decide to get out. There are times when the original owner does not have the resources to take it to the next level and has to either merge or sell to gain access to what he or she needs. These circumstances can appear after a decade or a number of decades. The challenge is when the sale happens to someone who is not quite ready to retire and the problem is deciding what will be next. Well, I can tell you that really interesting opportunities may be in front of you.

After I sold my business, I continued my writing and this is book number 13. I have been teaching other entrepreneurs and I have spoken throughout the U.S. on topics that concern us all. And I have started a few new businesses, which is what many of us do. We start smaller ones and sometimes take on partners. But when you have the DNA of an entrepreneur, it never quite goes away. What new idea can you think of that fits with your current lifestyle?

EPILOGUE

The business startup environment has changed drastically over the past five years, and even more rapidly in the past two. The news is mixed, but by no means all bad. Technology has allowed us to sell to customers who are farther away and for longer hours, collect money faster, manage inventory better, and improve business processes of all types. On the other hand, credit is so much tighter now than it was only a few years ago, when money seemed to be flowing without limits. New business may be a bit tougher to start, but the ones that will make it to opening day are far better prepared now than the ones that were born of easy credit. And as the economy grows, well-planned and well-executed companies will show even stronger performance.

Keep an Eye on the Hot Trends

Many of the older industries, such as steel production and domestic auto manufacturing, have almost completely disappeared and the supply chain that served them is far smaller than it was before the downsizing began. There were many small businesses among the group that served these product lines. But the global opportunities that have replaced them have created new chances to create services for international manufacturing and distribution operations. Change is a constant in the world of business. The businesses that will be thriving in five years are likely still on the drawing boards and yours can be there with them. You need to link your business aspirations with growing trends to ensure that the business model isn't over before you start.

The entry costs to begin are quite a bit lower now than they were a few years ago. You can find used assets and unused space that is being marketed by motivated owners. Creating a new brand and getting a message into the marketplace is often more a matter of work than cash. If you are knowledgeable and committed to building an Internet presence, you can market on effort rather than cash. Bootstrapping on your own road to success was an engaging story years ago and it remains so today.

There are real opportunities in the health-care field in general, and elder care in particular, with an increasingly aging population. Digitizing medical records is work that will take years to complete and remains in high demand. Medical transcription services will be needed to convert years of files into accessible databases.

Home health and home help care are both growing fields as we try to keep people in their homes with on-demand support staff for as long as possible. Being a liaison between adult children and faraway parents is a new concept and one that makes great sense. I can think of other services to offer to this market as well; can you?

New energy concepts are being developed, offering new manufacturing and installation openings. Grants are available for the development of designs and government money is in the pipeline to retrofit public buildings and housing to be more energy efficient. Have you considered becoming an installer of solar panels? Can you be a subcontractor to a company that is in the middle of developing products for these innovations?

Effective and innovative marketing and sales distribution ideas are in demand by both new and existing companies. "Build a better mousetrap" has never been more relevant. We are looking for advancements in many new fields in health, energy, conservation, and technology.

The Secrets of Starting a Successful New Venture

The secrets of starting a successful new venture are the same today as they always have been:

- Creativity

- Focus

- Hard work

Although the convergence of easy money and exotic technology has muddied the waters a bit over the past few years, entrepreneurship has always had great draw. The media often portrays the Cinderella stories of grand success and shows little of those whose fate is less glamorous. You must remember that there are no guarantees, but you can up the odds of being successful if you work hard at it. Start with a well-thought-out idea—a concept that adds a new twist to what consumers or businesses need. And if this idea comes out of your personal interests or loves, so much the better. Your passion will always show.

Focus on how you will go about getting the company up and running; create a business plan that is complete and makes sense to you in terms of both available resources and your own ability. Do not plan on accessing capital you do not already have committed. Be sure that you have the knowledge to be a driver, not just a dreamer. Another option is to create a team or partnership where two of you bring all of the resources you require to get to the starting gate.

The need for hard work will never change, and I'm not talking about just physical labor. Hard work means that you will understand that the ultimate responsibility is yours and you will be there to do whatever it takes. If someone doesn't show up, you will be doing the work of two. You may have to come in early and stay late. Weekends are free unless there is work to do. Vacations are scheduled and sometimes not taken. Your business needs care and you are the one who will be expected to give it. It is this constant intensity that either energizes business owners or burns them out. I have seen and experienced both. My initial company was the one I grew up in, but there came a day when I wanted out. My latest venture into the world of social networking has been consuming at times, but I am always on the prowl for new ideas. I have never considered that a business startup involved anything but hard work. It must be embedded in your DNA.

Watching a New Idea and a New Owner Catch Fire—Or Not

It's interesting to watch new owners with new ideas and see which catch on and which don't. You can usually draw lessons from either scenario.

One That Worked

Carving fruit into flowers and making those shapes into centerpieces and gifts was a creative idea. People have formed franchises to promote the concept and other independent businesses have started to imitate them. I have watched one franchise operation grow from a small storefront with limited hours and a single (not new) delivery van to a much larger operation with three beautifully decorated vans running through the community.

The idea was creative and born from the thought that fresh fruit is both beautiful and healthy. The markup on the raw material was good, and the key would be in the marketing and the product satisfaction. One of the special features was in chocolate-covered fresh strawberries that anyone would love to receive. They could be a part of a centerpiece display or sold looking like a box of roses.

I have received these products as a gift, I have met the people who run the store, and I have transacted business as a buyer. The business was run flawlessly, whether it was in the middle of a quiet week in October or over a busy holiday weekend. There was a small staff that worked hard and shared their enthusiasm for their products, as well as their interest in customer service. One small delivery truck was parked in front. Some days, it did not seem to move much. Passing by in the early evening, you could see the owner herself dragging out garbage to the dumpster at the edge of the lot.

Today, this is a thriving business with three trucks, all brightly decorated and equipped with refrigeration for fuller and longer trips. This is clearly a thriving business. The reason is in the intent of the founder, a woman who was committed to building her own business to the level of success it has achieved.

One That Didn't

I have seen some fairly good ideas never make it out of the starting blocks. A Virginia business owner called me about an accounting program he was working on that would be a great management tool for other owners. He learned the process at a business seminar and worked with his office manager to perfect it on a spreadsheet. They were both so sure that the program had promise. So they started a new company with the owner's money and ultimately a substantial amount of credit. I agreed to look at the business plan, and it was truly impressive because it was professionally created, not by the actual owner. The projections of revenue and profit, however, stopped me in my tracks. They were overly optimistic.

They had decided on a name and already spent substantial money on a strong logo, a well-done Web site, and marketing material. But there was one small problem: The software had not been written. Now, the project was joined by two out-of-work software developers who were not writing in the current languages because they were experienced in COBOL. The software guys knew that they were working with rookies, so they made it sound like a major project. For more than six months, they spent several days a week onsite in Virginia, working on the program and running up expenses. The development cost grew to over $100,000 and there was still no product to take to market. Then one of them got sick and the work stopped.

I suggested that we convert it to a Web application and found people capable of doing the work. But too much time had passed and many low-priced accounting programs were capable of producing virtually the same effect. Three years and almost $200,000 had passed and no business was in place yet. The founder was too busy with other interests, including his original business, to focus on the new one. He had great dreams, but poor execution, and the results were less than satisfying. In the technology world, the window opens for a short time; and when it closes, there is no second look. Shelf life of new developments can be measured in months and not years.

Success Doesn't Take Rocket Science

The first time I heard this next idea, I was surprised. Surely this was too simple for others not to have tried it and failed. As a longtime business speaker, I have heard my share of ideas and I typically have an immediate reaction. This one took second consideration. A daycare center for dogs—were there really enough owners willing to pay for that service? I haven't had a pet for years, but I am aware of the devotion that most pet owners have for this special member of the family. There are animal portrait painters and animal cemeteries. But paying for daycare?

There was a boarding component that could be included, as well as grooming, so a revenue stream was clearly available. The first center I watched open was many times bigger than I ever anticipated, with the good news being that the property had been empty a long time and had few other uses. The dogs each had their own "room" and owners could watch them on closed-circuit TV from their computers at work. The occupancy soared to over 50 percent within a month, and the yield on the overhead is terrific. Staff needs are reasonable— this is not a dog hospital that requires highly trained professionals. Marketing has consisted of a large sign outside the building and discounts for referrals.

This business has been around long enough to now have franchise operations in the field. Camp Bow Wow is an available national business with locations throughout the country. Check out the Web site at www.campbowwowusa.com to see how cleverly the owners have positioned the company. Having a good idea and the focus and drive to see it through is not a sure shot to success, but it certainly increases the odds.

Using Technical Skills to Start a Business

University researchers have great opportunity to launch a successful project development into a business if it has commercial potential. Most medical and engineering schools have departments structured to help bring an innovative product full circle to private development, leading to a spinoff business opportunity. In fact, a federal technology transfer system provides non-confidential military research to be utilized by the private sector to find commercial applications. It was defense satellite systems that gave the thrust to the small GPS system now used in many cars and on cell phones. There are applications on the current generation of smartphones, as well, that came from government development.

Those with computer skills have a variety of opportunities, but the critical choice is when you begin by determining what market you will serve and what services you will provide. For example, there is a difference between a Web site designer and a Web site developer and customers are learning this. Designers are about the look and the message and developers are about the functionality of the site itself. Few people can do both.

Computer hardware sales and installation, including networking, is a different world than that of desktop application software. Both may be on the requirement list for a new system installation, but they are often purchased from two different sources. Why not create a strategic partnership with a firm that does the work that you do not? You can share leads and collaborate on successful implementations. There are any number of ways to enter into the world of technical entrepreneurship.

Becoming a Consultant or Coach

There are many formerly well-employed individuals who now have joined the world of consultants and coaches. The line between these two has become blurred to the general public because they have historically been self-defined descriptions. A consultant could be anyone who is an independent freelance worker in fields ranging from technology to marketing to business finance and stops in between. Although I have been one for the last 15 years of my working life, I still am not sure of what exactly this means. How does a client know where to go to find a consultant and test his or her credibility? And now my field has been joined by another group of independents known as coaches. I think of my work in those terms, as well.

But where is the licensing and certification coming from? There are few formal courses. The original professional association for coaches was the International Federation of Coaches, whose classes were online. Now many universities are also forming classes to teach this growing skill. Both consulting and coaching have an element of teaching in them. You need to be able to identify the problems or issues, suggest solutions, and encourage those who are responsible to act on your ideas. This is not as easy as it might seem. I am sure that the field will change over the next few years as it becomes more organized.

If you want to make a name for yourself in the area of consulting or coaching, you will have to make an extra effort to be known by your peers as well as your potential customers. You need to join professional organizations and become active in them. You will also want to include business networking groups so that you can become familiar to other members of the business community. If you are comfortable enough to give a speech, offer to do so at any organization that seems interested in having you. You are branding yourself because the service is, in essence, *you*.

Many consultants and coaches eventually consider writing their own books. Writing a book is always a good idea when you want to be thought of as an expert. Believe me, it is not as easy as it looks. You can have one ghostwritten if the thought of staring at empty paper scares you. You can turn out a small pamphlet or a workbook. But having your name in print can add zeros to your billing rate. Being self-employed as any type of a craftsman, technical guru, or expert can be the most interesting experience you may have. You spend all of your time immersed in what you love and are interested in. These days, many independent consultants are self-publishing their own books. Available services range from just the printing to the entire gamut, from cover design to editing and page layout. Choose from a variety of companies that provide information on the topic. Check out the extensive work of Dan Poynter (www.parapublishing.com/sites/para/) or try one of the offerings of Author Solutions (www.authorsolutions.com).

Business Ownership Does Not Work for Everyone

The best landscaper I ever had struggled from the first day I met him. He seemed to have new helpers with him every time he was at my home. Some of them were terrific and others were not very good. He always had great ideas and enormous pride in his work. I would walk around outside when he was done and marvel at the result. And then, the bill would not come for weeks and weeks and it was never exactly what he had quoted. I paid what I thought was due and sometimes I got a second bill and sometimes I did not.

I knew he wouldn't last very long, although from our talks I also knew that he loved his work and enjoyed having much of the winter months off. But in year three, the end came. Midsummer, he often came on Sunday with yet another helper and I could tell that being a business owner had become too much of a chore for him.

Any business has overhead; however, landscaping is particularly labor intensive. But there are also truck payments to make and worker payroll to cover. Working seven days a week will burn you out. The flip side of working 9 months of the year is that you have to earn 12 months worth of money in that time. So I was not surprised when Gerry knocked on my door to tell me that this was the last time he would be able to do any work. Since we had discussed the problems along the way, there were few questions to ask. I got into my car and drove around to find someone else who was servicing my neighborhood. I never received a final bill.

Not all of us are cut out to be independent and to do our own share of the work while managing others to do theirs and handle the finances and some of the marketing. You need to be able to multitask and exercise multiple skills. You may be able to find associates and partners to help, but they will move on and then it falls back on your shoulders. I have been through all of these ups and downs over 30 years. There have been highs and lows. But this is exactly what I was cut out to be.

The Joy of Having Your Own Business

I spend some of my time hosting a radio show about business. The man who owns the operation is the typical entrepreneur. Ron Morris has been starting business ventures since he was a young man, mostly in the world of high tech. But he has been involved in a magazine startup (a very high-risk venture) and now the radio shows as well. Ron made and lost substantial money over these years, but he did score big on one tech startup that sold for an excellent return. I suppose Ron could have gone to the beach or done a lot that is less stressful, but this is not the instinct of a real founder. Now he teaches entrepreneurship at Duquesne University and develops this radio time as the American Entrepreneur and Pittsburgh Business Radio. He works relentlessly, and you can almost see his enthusiasm.

This is something that I share with him. Over the past decade, I have been on his show many times and now I am a regular host. He sees the same thing in me as I do when I meet my clients for the first time. It is clear which ones love their independent work enough to do whatever it takes to save the business and have the chance to go on. And for many, including myself, the end of one business means another one is on the drawing board.

I sold the manufacturing company after more than 20 years and told anyone who would listen that I was glad to be out from under it. That lasted less than six months before I was starting a publishing company with an associate. An online database exchange came after, and I have had a few training and seminar ventures. Now I am the founder and chief blogger at WomenEtcetera.com. We are just gaining some traction with this site and organization for women over 50. We are branding for the purpose of marketing a variety of products and services. Who knows what's next.

I did not see this instinct in myself when I started. Like many of you, I needed a job. My father had passed suddenly and someone had to take the reins of the family business. Within a year, I was completely immersed in my own business and just the basics of how businesses work. I love it as much now as I did then.

Businesses are living things. The people who run them, as well as those they hire, give companies a face and a heart. When the owners and employees are happy, customers, vendors, and anyone who comes into contact with the company will know that. This attracts success and it is such a thrill to be a part of building this environment. I understand that the work is hard, the days are long, and sometimes the money is short, but the satisfaction of building a business from scratch is like no other. I believe that you can do it too if you are dedicated.

If I can help, or you want to tell me your stories, go to my site at www.suzannecaplan.com and send in a comment—good, bad, or in-between. I just might be able to help.

Suzanne Caplan
July 2009

GLOSSARY OF BUSINESS AND ACCOUNTING TERMS

accounts payable A list of the company's debts that are to be paid according to repayment terms established by the vendors. These payments may have a discount available if paid before a prescribed date, a penalty if not paid by a certain date, or both.

accounts payable turnover ratio A management tool used as a comparison with peer companies and with previous accounting periods to highlight trends. The ratio is calculated by dividing the total dollars of purchases by the total dollars of accounts payable. This can be further quantified by dividing 365 (days per year) by the ratio to arrive at accounts payable in terms of average days aging. You need to know whether you are paying customers more quickly now than before or if you are converting these short-term debts into long-term debts.

accounts receivable A list of customers who have purchased the company's goods, services, or both on a credit basis and the amount of credit they have outstanding. The seller establishes the timing of the expected payments and any discount incentives for early payment. Funding this credit is the major use of working capital for most businesses. The outstanding money will include part of the cost of inventory delivered, but not the markup for labor, overhead, and profit. The funds will be available to make cash payment for replacement inventory, labor, rent, utilities, and taxes when the receivable is actually paid or sold.

accrual-basis accounting　An accounting method that recognizes income and expense at the time they are incurred, not when cash is actually received or paid. The company assigns or matches the revenue and expense to a fixed accounting period based on the action that generated the income and the expense that was created. This allows you to make meaningful comparisons on the results of the actual operation of the business without them being arbitrarily skewed by the timing of the payment.

agings　The document that provides information as to how long a bill has been due to the company or due to be paid. This is typically measured in 30-day increments.

amortization　The process of allocating a portion of a total amount over a fixed period of time. In a loan situation, this is the allocation of a portion of the principal amount of the note over usually monthly periods. An amortization schedule shows the amount of the payment applied to interest expense and reduction of principal over the entire term of the loan or until a certain maturity date, where there may remain an amount of the principal that is unpaid: a balloon payment. In the context of an expense, amortization is the process of allocating the total cost of acquisition or development over the productive life of that expense. The useful life determination is based more on what the IRS will allow than any scientific approach because it is used as an offset on tax returns.

angel investors　Early-stage investors who put up cash in return for both equity and often the chance to be a part of the operation to provide management expertise.

asset value　The current value of all equipment and cash items (such as collectable receivables) and inventory that the company owns, not including the intangibles such as name, customer list, and goodwill.

assets　In a business entity, the total acquisition cost of the property and property rights owned, which may have been reduced in value by reserves for depreciation that may or may not actually reflect the reduction in value of the asset. Assets are not marked up to reflect any appreciation in value since that is more subject to estimate than conservative accounting permits, which has a premise that the cost value is more objective. In the case where there has been significant appreciation of assets, this market value and the method of determining this value can and should be placed in a footnote to the statements. Intangible assets such as brand names or customer lists do not appear on the balance sheet. When the assets are on an individual's financial statement, they can and should be reflected at the true value as of the date of the statement. The use of market valuation is a basis for a personal statement.

balance sheet   Compiles the list of all of the company's assets— whether short-term, as in cash and payables, or long-term, as in property and equipment. It also lists the liabilities, short- and long-term, that are used to reduce the net worth of the company. Assets minus liabilities gives you the owner's equity.

bartering   The exchange of goods and services with another company without any additional cash. One provides its service in exchange for the service of the other. This does have taxable consequence. There are also formal bartering companies that arrange these transactions for a fee.

break-even analysis   Determining the gross volume needed to be able to cover the overhead cost at the current gross profit margins.

business plan   A document that describes the business operation (usually prior to opening) in terms of the market, operating strategies, sources of revenue, and income projections. This document serves as a guide for the business owner.

cash-basis accounting   A method of accounting that recognizes revenue and expense at the time of receipt or payment. This method can be difficult to use as a management tool because the results of an action are not tied to the cause of the action. Thus, you cannot reliably compare periods to each other or to industry standards. Of more importance, this method can cause loss of financial controls in a business. For example, the misplacement of an invoice can result in an overstatement of earnings. The non-current payment of a large liability will not appear until it is paid, although this may have a major impact on operations.

cash flow   Technically, on an accounting basis, the difference between the cash on hand at the beginning of the period and the cash remaining at the ending of the period. Under this definition, cash flow can be increased by selling assets, lengthening the payment of payables, or acquiring new debt. These methods are in addition to the more desired increase by net profit and non-cash expenses such as depreciation and amortization. In the "summary of cash flows" section of the accounting statements, business owners should pay attention to the section marked "cash flow from operating activities," which is primarily net profit after tax, plus non-cash expenses. This is the best way to project the company's ability to meet future debt service, instead of having to rely on remedies such as the sale of assets.

cash-flow value   A company value based on a multiple of EBITDA based on the type of industry segment or type of business. The number typically runs from two to five times the company's annual earnings.

collateral   Assets of the company or assets of third parties, or both, pledged or encumbered for the payment of loans where there is a specific intent to pledge by way of a security agreement. Some collateral will be under the lender's control—such as securities or inventory under warehouse receipts financing—but most collateral, such as equipment, inventory, or receivables, will be in the possession of the borrower. The amount of the debt is not limited by the collateral pledged and any deficiency between the liquidated collateral. The balance on the note will remain the responsibility of the borrower or guarantors.

compensating balances   The borrower's deposit balances maintained with the lender; usually the borrower's operating accounts. They are rarely separate accounts unavailable for daily transactions. The lender will desire a certain amount of average daily balances to partially compensate for the rate of interest charged on the loan.

competitive analysis   The section of the business plan that presents and analyzes the business's competition.

confession of judgment clause   A clause in a note that permits the lender to record a lien in the county records against all assets of the borrower without having to bring suit against the borrower in court. Usually this is exercised only when there has been a default. Unless there are unusual circumstances, the judgment would normally be granted by the courts because there is evidence of the debt in the form of the note and the default should be provable, such as by a demand note not paid or a term note with past-due payments. Therefore, banks covet this clause in states where it is permissible because it saves them time and money. If the clause contains the phrase "as of any term," the bank can record the note without any default, much the same way it would record a mortgage.

confidentiality agreement   An agreement between parties that all information disclosed in the course of their negotiation will be kept confidential during that time and forever. This allows the parties to share business numbers and personal finance that would not otherwise be made available.

Corporation (S or C)   Tax treatments that determine how income is reported. With an S Corp, the income is a flow-through and goes directly to the tax return of the owner through a K-1. A C Corp pays tax on its own earnings and may carry forward losses to defer future earnings.

cosigner   Any signatory to a note, beyond the primary signatory. The cosigner is fully obligated to all of the responsibilities of the note, until it is paid, in the same manner as if that person were the sole borrower on the note. The obligations of a cosigner will appear on his or her individual credit report as if he or she were the primary signatory.

cost of goods sold   The products, raw material, and labor that are directly involved in the completion of a sale. These are the direct costs related completely to the volume of sale as the expense is tied to each transaction.

credit   The extension of time to pay for goods or services or the actual loan of money for operating capital in the company. Credit always has terms, which include time to pay and possibly interest for the use of the money.

current assets   Assets that are cash or fully expected to be turned into cash within one accounting period (usually one year), such as accounts receivable and inventory. When the assets are turned into cash, they are replaced with new similar assets. Few businesses bring these accounts to zero. Items such as notes receivable from officers of the company or others should not be included in this category unless they will be paid to zero within the accounting period. To do otherwise severely diminishes the credibility of the financial statements. Prepaid expenses for annually paid items, such as insurance, can be included in this category. Many bankers will move this item to the long-term category, based on conservatism, because prepaids are not normally turned into cash.

current liabilities   The mirror image of current assets. These are debts that are expected to be paid within one accounting period (usually one year). They include all accounts payables, unless on a multi-year payment schedule; all installment loans due within one year, including any balloon payments; taxes; and accrued but not paid items, such as benefits or withholding taxes. Lease payments—specifically, true operating leases—are not included here. They are included in footnotes to the financial statements because they are monthly expense items, just as utilities and payroll are.

current ratio   The numerical relationship of current assets divided by current liabilities. This ratio, and the trend of the ratio over several years, gives a quick indication of the company's liquidity—the ability to generate cash by the time it is needed to pay obligations. There are weaknesses in this ratio because slow receivables and dead inventory are included on the current asset side and may not turn into cash as expected, whereas current liabilities are always current.

debt   The amount of money owed to others on a formal or informal basis, but which has a definite repayment schedule, either amortizing or on a straight-line basis, by a certain period or on demand of the lender or creditor. Accounts payable are debt; however, in most financial statements, the amounts are shown as a separate category in the liability section. Those principal amounts owed within one year, or payable on demand, are shown as current liabilities. Debts may be unsecured or secured, as in encumbering certain assets as described in a security agreement or by the Uniform Commercial Code, or both, for inventory. Some debt may have a lower priority as opposed to all other debt, by its subordination feature, and may be convertible to equity, again by its own features. Debts are not reduced by the unilateral action of the debtor—except for payment—and thus represent a firm amount that could grow based on accrued interest and other penalties in the debt contract. Formal evidence of debt, such as notes, can be assigned or sold to others. But the debtor is just as obligated to the assignee as to the original creditor.

debt-to-equity ratio   A management tool for use in comparisons with peer companies and with previous accounting periods to highlight trends. It is the ratio on which banks will place a great deal of importance in analyzing financial statement trends. This ratio is calculated by dividing debt by equity. An increasing ratio—more debt in relation to equity—means that the growth of a company or the downturn of a company is being financed to a greater extent by creditors. Because most of these creditors will not enjoy higher rewards as their risk increases, they will, most likely, take some corrective action.

depreciation   The formula derived from the process of allocating the cost of a fixed asset over subsequent accounting periods as a way of matching the productivity of those fixed assets over the period of the useful life of the asset. This number is more determined by the IRS than by any scientific approach to this allocation. This expense allocation is irrespective of the actual timing of the payment for the fixed asset. Thus, the depreciation expense of each period is a return on investment, whether the investment was made in cash or a loan was taken to pay for the asset. The depreciation can be made in equal amounts over the useful life, known as straight-line depreciation; or taken more in the early years, known as accelerated depreciation, to allow for more maintenance and repair as the asset gets older.

due diligence   The required investigation of all documents which may have been referred to in a contract for sale that represent values of the company. All assets (including receivables) are checked, as are all liabilities stated or filed.

EBITDA   Earnings Before Interest, Taxes, Depreciation, and Amortization. This refers to pure cash flow.

equity   Often referred to as net worth, especially in the context of personal financial statements. This is the difference between the total assets of an entity and the total liabilities. It can be thought of as the amount owed to the owners because it is often shown on the liability side of the ledger. It is theoretically the amount available to be disbursed to the owners if the assets were sold and the liabilities paid. On a business statement, this represents the amount of original and subsequent investment, plus the cumulative amount of earning and losses retained in the business.

equity financing   A process that raises capital through any instruments that carry equity risk and reward. This can be stock, voting, or non-voting common shares (some of which, known as preferred stock, may have a superior claim on earnings). Debt instruments can carry some equity reward, such as convertible features or warrants to purchase a set amount of shares at a predetermined price. Because logical people will always require a higher return for taking a higher risk, equity financing is almost always more expensive—in terms of an unrestricted claim on the future earning of any enterprise—than debt financing.

exit strategy   A plan for the sale of the company or turning over the operation to an insider for financial payout. The owner's equity in the company is redeemed at this time.

franchise   A national corporation that creates products and process, which they develop into business units and sell licenses to operate units within a certain territory. The business concept as well as operating instructions and often product are purchased from the franchisor and a royalty for each unit sold is required to be paid in return.

gross profit   The recognized revenue from a sale, minus the cost of the inventory, labor, and variable costs associated with that sale, such as shipping, discounts, and sales commissions. Some statements net out the returns, allowances, and discounts to arrive at net revenue before deducting the cost of goods sold. The cost of goods sold includes items purchased for the sale or taken from inventory, plus the costs directly associated with generating the sale. The important point is to be consistent with other firms in the industry so that valid comparisons between periods and between industry averages can be made as a management tool.

guaranty (or guarantee)   An agreement by a third party to pay a specific portion of (or all of) the borrower's notes to a specifically named creditor. This pledge is a promise to pay any or all of the installments if not made in a timely manner or the total debt if accelerated, including principal, interest, and reasonable collection costs, if any. Under a guaranty, the primary debtor does not have to refuse to pay, nor does the lender have to exhaust its remedies against the debtor for the guarantor to be liable for the debt. The guarantor has the same responsibilities as a consigner on the note. Under a continuing guaranty, the guarantor continues to be responsible not only for existing debts of the maker of the note, but subsequent loans made by the lender, unless the guarantor specifically and formally limits the guaranty to the existing obligations of the maker of the note. Usually a subsequently executed guaranty will become the valid—and limiting—guaranty if accepted by the lender. All responsibilities for disclosure and recision (annulment) to the maker of the note are also the responsibilities of the lender to all guarantors. Under a joint and several guaranty, each of the parties signing the agreement is responsible for the entire amount of the debt.

income statement   See *profit-and-loss (P&L) statement.*

inventory   Assets held for resale, which may have value added from labor in the manufacturing or fabrication process, available to be sold as goods. The inventory may be raw materials, finished product purchased from others, work in progress, or finished manufactured goods ready for sale. It is important to understand that certain costs attach themselves to work in progress, such as direct labor, and are not released until value-added goods are sold. So expenses could be understated in a specific accounting period when sales are declining, which may signal a false reading or actual profitability.

inventory turnover ratio   A management tool for use as a comparison with peer companies and with previous accounting periods to highlight trends. This ratio is calculated by dividing the total cost of goods sold by current inventory. This number can be further simplified by dividing 365 (days per year) by this ratio to arrive at days on hand of inventory. A decreasing ratio—that is, less turns per year, thus increasing days on hand—could indicate that there are slow-selling items in inventory. This puts pressure on cash because this inventory does not turn to cash as quickly in the current asset cycle.

investment (vs. loan)   Capital at risk, whether provided by the owner or an outside investor. A loan carries a promise to pay and fixed interest as a return. An investment pays a return based on success.

landlord's waiver (of lien rights)   Either a general waiver or a specific subordination in favor of a specific party, usually a lender, of the claims a landlord has on the personal property, such as inventory, equipment, and fixtures, of a tenant who may owe unpaid rent. In many cases, this landlord's claim can result in a superior lien to that of the lending institution, even though the rent delinquency occurs after the date of the security agreement and filing of proper documents that secure in favor of the lender. Therefore, this is an important document to the lender. It is the responsibility of the borrower to obtain this properly executed waiver from any landlord when it is specifically requested by the bank.

letter of intent   The document that identifies the buyer and the seller and spells out the general terms that they are negotiating for completion of the transaction. This agreement is not binding to force a closing, but it may contain penalties for any delay or lack of good-faith negotiating.

Limited Liability Company   A business entity that is controlled by the members, who have management authority and financial responsibility but no liability for the actions or the debt of the company.

line of credit   A prearranged amount of credit, usually from a bank, to meet expected increases in inventory and receivables associated with peak volume, usually on a seasonal basis. These lines of credit could be non-revolving, but are usually revolving, with the ability to draw down on funds under the line, repay the funds on receipt of invoiced sales, and redraw the funds again when needed. These lines of credit are usually granted for one year with the ability to renew upon submission of current financial statements. A line of credit should be paid to zero balance with inflow of cash from collection of receivables, not from other borrowings or non-payment of existing payables. They should not be used for long-term capital purposes, especially to fund a continuing operating deficit.

liquidity   The ability to pay obligations when due from cash or the normal turnover of current assets into cash. A company can be bankrupt and still have balance-sheet assets that exceed liabilities, even if it cannot make payments when due. Thus, liquidity should be a prime management responsibility.

loan agreement   A document that accompanies a larger and longer-term loan, wherein the borrower and lender agree on certain rules, known as loan covenants, that will be used to determine whether the borrower is in compliance with the reasonable desires of the lender covenants. Failure to meet all of the loan covenants will subject the loan to being considered in default, even though installment payments are being made as agreed. Some typical covenants include the timely submission of financial information and statements; maintenance of a sound business condition, exemplified by payment of obligations and taxes when due; maintenance of insurance and the condition of the collateral; and restrictions on management salaries, dividends, and asset purchases.

loan proposal   A document closely related to the business plan but modified for the purpose of providing the bank items they require, such as the use of the proceeds, the security or collateral being provided, and the additional cash flow that will be used to retire the debt.

market value   The number that the buyer is willing to pay and the seller is willing to sell for; often based on multiples of the annual revenue according to industry norms.

markup   The amount added to the costs of goods that will cover both the overhead and the desired profit.

net (vs. gross)   Before-tax income, which is the result of deducting overhead costs from the gross profit.

network marketing   A selling strategy that involves finding more sub-sellers than product selling. The "director" puts together a team to sell products downstream; then a portion of that revenue is returned to the channel involved in the group. Organizations such as Mary Kay that have been around for a while and still have everyone selling product have tended to be more successful.

note   A document evidencing debt, including the amount, interest rate, maturity date, and the parties obligated to repay. Notes are quite simple, but will be accompanied by security agreements in the case of secured loans and loan agreements. The lender can assign notes to third parties; the borrower becomes obligated to the new note holder.

overhead   Fixed costs such as rent, utilities, and insurance as well as administrative salaries that are considered fixed as they occur regardless of the sales of the company; the cost of opening the doors.

partnership   A business created by two or more people that is unincorporated, provides income to both, and shares the liability between the two. Both partners pay taxes depending on percentage of ownership.

prime rate   Once the best rate available from an institution and given to its best customers for unsecured 90-day notes. Now primarily a benchmark number set arbitrarily by the bank at its discretion. In the bank's loan portfolio, there may be loans made under the prime rate or in excess of the prime rate. It is usually an index that variable-rate business loans are pegged against and it changes when the bank announces the change. Although all banks are free to set their own prime rates, most large institutions follow the same market rates, so rarely are there differences between the prime rates of larger institutions.

pro forma   On the business plan, a statement of profit and loss or cash flow for periods in the future. Anticipated new income or expense may be included. The numbers included in the pro forma require backup information as to how they were determined.

profit-and-loss (P&L) statement   Describes in detail all income and expense of the company as an operating unit that has resulted in profit or loss for a specific period of time. This is also described as the income statement.

profit margin   The difference between the selling price and the actual cost of the product or service plus the administrative costs.

rates of interest, fixed   Interest rates that will stay the same for the entire term of the loan. In business loans, it is unusual to see a fixed rate for more than a five-year period, when there may be repricing against an index. Fixed rates are still somewhat customary in residential mortgage loans because lending institutions sell off these loans through Fannie Mae or Freddie Mac to be securitized and sold as bonds, thus relieving them of the interest rate risk over a protracted period of time.

rates of interest, variable   Floating interest rates pegged to a certain index. Whereas most business loans are indexed to the prime rate and change when it changes, some are for fixed duration of one, two, three, or five years. The rates may then be changed by being indexed to the Treasury Bill index or some other widely publicized index. Some may have floors (the minimum rate to be charged) and ceilings (the maximum rate to be charged). These days, interest rates are the basis of much negotiation.

security   The same as collateral; the asset pledged to provide additional protection for the lender or creditor.

sole proprietorship   Ownership in the hands of a single individual who will pay tax on any income earned from the operation of the company.

succession planning   The strategy to bring in a member of the business owner's family and groom him or her for eventually taking over the company and redeeming the owner's equity.

Uniform Commercial Code financing statements (UCC-1)   The legal procedure for a lender to perfect its secured interest in certain assets. Perfection—the protection from the prior claims of others in these assets—is made through possession by the lender, as in the case of stocks and bonds; encumbrances on titles to equipment, where titles exist, such as over-the-road vehicles; and by the filing of the Uniform Commercial Code financing statement (at the office of the Secretary of State in the state where the debtor is located, as well as other areas) as specified by the code for untitled assets in the possession of the debtor. These are signed by the debtors. The borrower customarily pays a filing fee. Vendors or suppliers can retain a security interest in inventory of the purchaser until they are paid if they file a UCC-1, so certain inventory may already be encumbered and not free to be pledged or sold as free and clear of liens if these financing statements have been filed by a vendor.

vendor   A business that provides needed goods or services on a contract basis.

working capital   One of the most misused, overused, and misunderstood terms in the financial arena of small business. Working capital is the amount of the difference between current assets and current liabilities. Working capital is supposed to be an indication of liquidity and the ability of the company to meet current obligations when due from the current asset cycle of cash, to inventory, to receivables, and to cash. This presumes that current assets will turn to cash at the same rate that accounts payable and other current obligations become due. Unfortunately, although current obligations do come due on a timely basis, current assets do not turn to cash as predictably. Even though hard-to-collect receivables and slow-moving or obsolete inventory are still included on the current asset side of the equation, the cash may not present itself in a timely manner. Thus, a company may not be as liquid as its working capital position would indicate.

SAMPLE BUSINESS PLAN

Executive Summary

Liquidating excess inventory has long been a profitable business in the retail marketplace. Off-price outlets, catalogs, and TV shopping networks have been utilized to reach customers for disposition of available product, as have online stores and auction sites such as eBay.

Industrial products present a different scenario, however. Distributors of industrial goods, such as safety clothing and equipment, cannot easily merchandise their excess product in a cost-effective manner. Most initial sales are achieved without advertising and, in many cases, without utilization of a central store. Therefore, even the presentation of excess product is a problem. Returning excess inventory to a manufacturer for credit triggers a 25 percent restocking fee and, in some cases, the loss of future quantity discounts.

Safety Exchange has developed a unique method to address this market opportunity. Safety Exchange has designed a distinct online network to broker excess inventory to interested buyers. Listings of available excess inventory are e-mailed to subscribers on a periodic basis and members will have 24/7 access to the online listings. Additionally, Safety Exchange broker/salespersons actively pursue all sales opportunities. The integrity of Safety Exchange will be guaranteed to the industry by its promise of dealing only with the distributor, never the end user.

Safety Exchange initially will begin operations with three office locations: Western Pennsylvania, Maryland, and Connecticut. These initial offices will be located in existing offices of company officers in order to maintain a low-overhead operation. The financial resources of Safety Exchange will be primarily directed to maintaining a state-of-the-art online software system as well as to direct marketing efforts.

Extensive marketing and sales efforts will position Safety Exchange as a proactive player in the industry. Listings of available excess inventory will not be merely passively sent to subscribers. Safety Exchange broker/salespersons will maintain personal contact with subscribers and let them know when excess inventory that matches their needs becomes available. A marketing goal is to have distributors consider the Safety Exchange Information Network as a backup extension of their own normal in-house inventory. Distributors should consider the Safety Exchange Information Network a supply source capable of delivering product faster than original manufacturers.

The Safety Exchange concept can also be applied to other markets, thus providing natural opportunities for lateral business expansion. The basis of these markets will be smaller distribution companies that generate excess inventory based on customer requirements rather than efficacy of the material. This means that this process has little value in the traditional consumer markets.

The first logical extension of business will be to use the Safety Exchange Information Network to serve the safety clothing and equipment manufacturers themselves. Manufacturers can use the Safety Exchange Information Network to sell their excess and second-quality goods while maintaining their normal channels of distribution. When desired by the manufacturer, the origin of the goods can be kept confidential and not disclosed to the buyer.

An additional expansion opportunity will be to apply the Safety Exchange concept to general industrial suppliers. Almost any industrial marketplace is a logical target of opportunity for application of the Safety Exchange distribution concept.

The attraction of the concept for investors and stockholders is the absence of the problems associated with the production and distribution of a physical product. Safety Exchange is a pure service business, serving as a broker between buyer and seller. Expansion opportunities are extensive and will not require substantial capital investment. Low fixed costs will support increasing profits during the high-growth period. The initial startup costs will be invested in the enabling software.

Safety Exchange is well prepared to take advantage of the latest in software and telecommunications technologies to apply a revolutionary distribution concept to the safety industry. The movement of inventory of 30 to 50 companies to other sites can be managed as if it came from a single source. All listed products that are committed will immediately drop off the availability list. Online sales are anticipated within weeks of the start. Product information will also be included.

Market Analysis

The safety equipment and clothing business generates $2.2 billion in annual revenue through approximately 6,500 independent distributors nationwide. Virtually all distributors are forced to inventory far in advance of requirements by "just-in-time" delivery demands. With a constantly changing industrial environment, excess inventory has grown to 5 to 8 percent of total volume, or more than $90 million. Since most end users are very specific about their needs, liquidating unused inventory within a local market area is difficult to accomplish, although these same products may be in demand in another market area.

Safety Exchange was created to facilitate the sale and exchange of excess inventory between independent distributors in different parts of the country. Safety Exchange offers this service to the selling distributor at a cost less than the traditional 25 percent restocking fee charged by most suppliers for merchandise returns. The advantage to the purchasing distributor is immediate delivery of goods at below-market prices. The Safety Exchange Information Network is an ideal way for purchasing distributors to satisfy their customer requirements and for selling distributors to reduce their excess inventory burden.

The third year of operation, Safety Exchange forecasts a membership of 1,000 companies, or 15 percent of the market potential. Sales are projected at $3.5 million, or 5 percent of available inventory.

Additionally, Safety Exchange expects to introduce technical database services and custom software during the first year so that the excess on one company's inventory can be shown as available for all members without exposing the source of the inventory.

Sources of Revenue

1. Distributor registration fees.

2. Subscription fees, annually at three levels:

Level	Subscription Fee ($)	Expected User Distribution (%)
A	$1,500	20
B	$1,000	30
C	$300	50

3. Commission fees on sales, 5–10% based on value:

   a. Less than $10,000: 10%

   b. Between $10,000 and $25,000: 8%

   c. Greater than $25,000: 5%

4. Custom software sales will not come into play until year two, but they could exceed revenue of $500,000 depending on the lateral markets developed.

Operating Strategy

The initial marketing task for Safety Exchange is to register safety distributors as Information Network members. Distributors registered with the Safety Exchange Information Network can participate as both buyers and sellers of merchandise. Revenues will be obtained in this process by charging for registration and subscription access to the Safety Exchange Information Network.

Distributors will be charged a one-time processing fee to register their companies with the Safety Exchange Information Network database. Information such as company name, location, product lines, and type and quantities needed will assist Safety Exchange in effectively serving its customers' needs. Although a customer may not have a product to list for sale on the network at the time of registration, this process entitles the company to subscribe to Safety Exchange Information Network services for the purpose of both purchasing inventory and ensuring quick access if it wishes to list its excess inventory for sale at a future date.

When distributors join the Safety Exchange Information Network, their contract documents will include a copy of the current commission fee schedule. Commission rates range from 5 to 10 percent depending on the dollar amount of the transaction. Smaller transactions have a higher commission rate.

From information provided by the distributors, Safety Exchange creates a computerized inventory database that serves as the basis for periodic e-mails of an Inventory Bulletin to Information Network subscribers. The primary information supplied by the distributors for inclusion in the Inventory Bulletin is items such as type of product, condition of product (for example, whether it meets code specifications), and quantity of product available. Secondary information, when available, will include crucial industry information that could affect the distributor's business. Information such as tax laws and national and international events can be used to inform the distributors while also stimulating business for Safety Exchange. Availability of the Safety Exchange Inventory Bulletin is a function of the subscription level paid for by individual distributors.

Safety Exchange offers three levels of subscription service. Level A consists of online membership to the system and listing of up to 500 items at any one time. Level B consists of online membership and listing of up to 300 items at any one time. In addition, level B customers will receive special notification e-mails and/or telephone notification of new merchandise that becomes available between regularly scheduled mailings. Level C consists of an online subscription as a purchaser but no inventory on file.

Safety Exchange will focus on service and maintain constant contact with its Information Network members by including a locator service. This service will be organized in such a way that when new merchandise is entered into the Information Network database, a list of distributors looking for that merchandise will be automatically generated. For example, if XYZ distributor is looking for particular merchandise on a steady basis or in a particular situation, Safety Exchange will be able to provide the service of notifying that distributor when the merchandise becomes available for sale on the Information Network.

Financial dealing will be structured in such a way as to protect all parties involved. Safety Exchange will maintain an escrow account in which all sale proceeds will be deposited prior to the shipment of goods. Only after goods are shipped by the seller and checked and approved by the buyer will the funds be released to the seller, minus commissions payable to Safety Exchange. Our goal is to protect buyers by ensuring that they receive the correct goods and quantities in the stated condition before the funds are released to the sellers. Sellers are assured of payment in a completed and approved transaction because the funds are held in escrow for that purpose. Control of the funds will ensure receipt of commissions by Safety Exchange and minimize the need for accounts receivable.

Once a selling transaction has been completed, Safety Exchange will forward complete shipping documentation, including labels, to the selling distributor. Goods will then be drop-shipped to the buyer. On some occasions, Safety Exchange will take goods on a consignment basis; on rare occasions, Safety Exchange will consider outright purchase of goods.

Management

The four principals of Safety Exchange bring a unique blend of talent to this venture. The CEO has 20 years of experience as a safety clothing manufacturer and has extensive industry and product knowledge. The President has 20 years of experience as a systems engineer, having worked for the IBM Corporation, Westinghouse Electric Corporation, and Digital Equipment Corporation. The two other founders have both industry experience and substantial sales backgrounds.

Pro Forma Financials

	First Year	Second Year
Capital required (startup legal fees and software development)	$100,000	$60,000
Marketing material	$6,400	$4, 000
Office	$12,000	$15,000
Travel	$7,000	$7,200
Administrative expense	$4,800	$4,800
Salaries	$65,000	$100,000
Officer salaries	$0	$36,000
Commissions	$25,000	$50,000
Total	$220,200	$277,000

Officer Investment

Year one: 2,000 shares @ $50	$100,000
+ revenue of $187,200	
Year two: 1,200 shares @ $50	$60,000
+ revenue of $212,000	
First-year loss projected at $33,000.	
Second-year loss projected at $95,000.	
Third-year profit of $344,000.	

INDEX

SYSTEMATIC SOCIOLOGY

SYSTEMATIC SOCIOLOGY

An Introduction to the
Study of Society

by

Karl Mannheim

Edited by J. S. Erös
and W. A. C. Stewart

GROVE PRESS, INC. / NEW YORK

EDITORIAL ACKNOWLEDGEMENTS

We should like to express our gratitude to the University College of North Staffordshire for research grants awarded to us in connection with this work: to the Librarians of the College for the practical help and advice: and to Miss Mary Barraclough for her assistance in preparing the typescript of these pages.

Contents

CONTENTS

PART 2

THE MOST ELEMENTARY SOCIAL PROCESSES

Editorial Preface

When Karl Mannheim was proscribed by Hitler in 1933, like others on that first list he was at once offered academic posts in universities in different parts of the world. He came to London, and the book which follows is based on two of the courses of lectures that he gave in London: the first was given at the London School of Economics under the title *Systematic Sociology,* and the second elsewhere under the title *Social Structure.*

The first three parts of this book are based on the manuscript of Mannheim's lectures on systematic sociology, first delivered during the academic session 1934-35 and, in slightly modified form, during the following sessions. Part Four of this book is based on some of the lectures in a course on social structure delivered during the war years.

In editing the lectures on systematic sociology, we have considerably re-ordered the argument and re-phrased the text. A number of issues were raised as parentheses by Mannheim in giving the lectures, the relationship of which to the written text would not be easy to understand. We have in places omitted these comments so that the argument of the whole could be more clearly seen. Whatever the alterations and excisions we may have made, we have attempted to maintain the structural outline, the architecture of the argument.

In Part Four we have used Karl Mannheim's typescript without much alteration. However, we have not maintained the structural outline of the course of lectures on which this part of the book is based. The lectures covered a great variety of topics: the first lectures contained a shortened version of the topics dealt with in more detail in Part One of this book; several lectures dealt with what Mannheim himself called 'concrete issues' of modern society and thus do not fit into the frame-work of his systematic sociology, and finally there are a few lectures on 'problems of social stability and social change'—subjects which, according to the original syllabus of his lectures on systematic sociology, he wished to incorporate into his course on systematic sociology. It seems that considerations of time prevented Mannheim from analysing such problems as social control, social change, and social structure in his lectures at the London School of Economics, so that he decided to cover these problems within the framework of the other lecture course. We thought it fitting to restore Mannheim's original plan for a systematic sociology in this book and in doing this we have fulfilled a wish of Dr. Julia Mannheim.

We are grateful that Dr. Julia Mannheim allowed us the opportunity to undertake this work, and we are saddened by the thought that she did not live long enough to see it completed.

Karl Mannheim's Concept of a Systematic Sociology

In his introductory lecture to the systematic sociology lecture course (re-printed in this book as the Introduction) Karl Mannheim claims that the various forms of the 'living together of men' constitute the subject matter of analytical systematic sociology. This is, of course, only a preliminary definition, and a detailed study of this book shows that although an analysis of the different forms of human integration constitutes the central part of this systematic sociology, he also investigates psychological and cultural problems which may not at first sight seem directly connected with the problem of integration and with an analysis of the forms of the 'living together of men'.

Part One of this book deals with the problem of man and his psychic equipment. Here Karl Mannhein shows the unique plasticity of man's character and behaviour and analyses the processes which govern the distribution of his psychic energy. At the end of Part One a description of the main types of social attitudes and wishes forms a bridge between the psychological and sociological sections of the book, because a wish or an attitude is a more or less established response to an environment.

In Part Two, entitled 'The Most Elementary Social Processes', Mannheim analyses the social forms and processes which either bring people together or isolate them from one another or even induce them to act against one another. He deals here on the one hand with the processes which lead to the various forces of social integration and on the other hand with the phenomena of differentiation and individualism. Mannheim's interest in the human personality, as it appears to be on the one hand group-centred and on the other individualised, can be clearly seen throughout these chapters.

In Part Three of the book, 'The Sociology of Integration', however, he concentrates on the problems of human integration and attempts to give a systematic account of the different 'forms of human living together'. His description of human psychological development as it appears in Part One and his analysis of the integrating social processes in Part Two form an indispensable introduction to this third part of the book.

Finally in Part Four (which is based on the typescript of the lectures on social structure) the author analyses the social forces and institutions which create social stability, and discuss the theories relating to the factors of social change. His criticism of the Marxist theory of social change constitutes the central part of the concluding chapter.

We shall attempt here to give a brief analysis of the four main divisions into which this book, and Mannheim's systematic sociology, is divided, and shall begin with a discussion of the problems of man and his psychic equipment. Karl Mannheim attempted in these lectures a more systematic analysis of the psychological aspects of man and society than he had ever before essayed. Reading it at this distance of time, over twenty years after it was planned, it is not difficult to regard it as at least partly outmoded. The fashions have changed in psychology and in social philosophy. Where Mannheim describes personal development in the terms of transference of libido, the more recent work in America by Horney, Erikson, Sullivan or Alexander, or in this country the work of the Tavistock Clinic, has taken more account of social factors. Where Mannheim attempts to classify types of social integration or individualisation the tendency now in sociology is to undertake field work which relies for its methodology and verification on the case study method of social anthropology, the interview technique or on statistical analysis. Yet this section of the book should not be regarded as of historical interest only, but as a necessary chapter in the changing pattern of Mannheim's thought. It represents a synthesis of ideas and a method of analysis which can be indefinitely elaborated.

In considering man's psychic equipment Mannheim deals right at the start with the genetic bases of psychic energy and with the relationship between what may be termed instinct and what may be termed habit, with all the problems of learning attendant thereto. The emphasis on structure and relationism throughout Mannheim's writing ensures that he looks at the problems of perceiving, conceiving, experiencing, learning, knowing, as one interested in the dynamics of the processes, leaning to *gestalt* rather than connectionist or associationist interpretations. He says that associationism affords a descriptive model at a certain level of the processes of thought and behaviour, and such explicitness is to be welcomed for it represents a degree of conscious awareness of the process. However, such an account does not take into its reckoning the powerful basic experiences of life which become standards and give the personality a cohesion and unity which enable it to have 'initiative' in relation to learning and what the pragmatists call adjustment.

Mannheim's argument and methodology bring Freud and McDougall into the discussion; they also call in W. I. Thomas, who tried to meet the problem of the relationship between genetic enthe Marxian theory of social change. We are, equally, a long way away from the various positivistic and naturalistic sociologies which claimed that man and society should be studied as if these were nothing but parts of external nature, and that the methods of socio-logical investigation should be similar to those applied in the natural sciences.

Mannheim delegates the study of the impact of external factors, such as natural environment, upon social life to the specialised 'auxiliary' disciplines, human geography or demography. He claims that it is the analysis of the results of human interactions which con-stitutes the real subject matter of analytic sociology. He realises that situations may arise when the external factors, as studied by the statistician or geographer, might 'correspond' to real social bonds. This might happen, for example, in the case of certain lin-guistic groups or income brackets. Yet, even in these instances the methods used by the statistician cannot furnish an answer to the question whether the external factors have or have not turned into a genuinely uniting force between men. Economic or linguistic factors can become socially relevant group-forming links only if they are regarded by a sufficient number of men and women as playing a vital part in their life.

By stressing the internal, psychic character of social bonds, Mann-heim leads us towards a deeper understanding of social life. He stresses than in order to be effective all factors which link people in society must become constituent parts of the inner world of interacting persons through the mechanism of identification: sec-ondly, that the group-forming factors are integral parts of a wider social process. Consequently, the sociologist has to utilise the ana-lytic tool of a dynamic psychology as well as a systematic theory of society, and cannot rely upon quantitative methods or pure common sense. Mannheim's principle of group classification is in harmony with this theory.

Although Mannheim's analysis dissolves the group into its con-stituent elements, he denies that these elements are isolated and self-sufficient individuals. He analyses the social groups as the re-sultants of different social forces and processes, and although these processes are in fact different forms of interaction between indi-viduals they cannot be deduced from the deliberate, conscious de-cisions and purposes of single individuals. Having a structural character and being the constituent parts of a dynamic society, these forces and processes must be analysed and compared with one another within the frame-work of a systematic theory of society.

Mannheim begins his systematic investigation of social life with a description of the elementary processes which are found in most societies (see Part Two). According to him the elementary social processes differ from the social phenomena of 'Great Society', such as institutions and stratification. They belong to the minutiae of society and their importance lies in the fact that they take part in directly shaping the individual. When analysing the various group-forming processes he follows in the foot-steps of the pioneer of the German school of formal sociology, Georg Simmel, and of the American sociologist, Charles H. Cooley. But Mannheim goes one step further than his predecessors by applying the analytic tools of modern dynamic psychology. He investigates the psychological aspects of the intimate and frequent contacts within primary groups, such as the family, friendship groups or school classes which lead to the 'introjection of the impulses and sentiments' prevailing in such relationships. This psychological mechanism explains the fact that primary groups play such an important part in the shaping of the emotions, views and behaviour of man. Mannheim stresses that it is in these groups that the identification with others is first experienced by the growing person, and it is here that the feeling of social unity first emerges. Such capacity for identification normally returns later in life on a larger scale in the so-called secondary contact groups, like the church, the political party, the nation or the state. Mannheim shows here a keen interest in the problem of the transfer of emotions from the private to the public sphere, a problem which also fascinated Lasswell during the same period.

Beginning with the most simple and elementary social processes Mannheim proceeds with a step by step analysis of processes of increasing complexity. At each stage he contrasts the antithetical, yet complementary, processes. Thus, creating social contact is contrasted with creating social distance in society; the process of socialisation is compared with the individualisation of personalities. The various forms of struggle and social competition are set against the process of monopolisation on the one hand and co-operation on the other. He shows also that these processes are intimately linked with the different forms of social selection. Finally, Mannheim analyses the importance of the division of labour, and stresses the fact that this is one of the strongest integrating forces in modern society. He repeatedly points to the historical role played by the economic needs which induce men to co-operate systematically with each other and to set up permanent systems of integration. Yet he is not a defender of historical materialism and emphasises the importance of the non-economic factors in history and society. According to him, men co-operate to create stronger systems of military defence, more efficient forms of administration, but religious worship must also be considered as a focus of social integration.

By analysing the life and phenomena of society in terms of integrating and individualising processes, Mannheim encounters the following complication: elementary social processes affect not only the individual, the member of a group, but also the groups themselves. The integrating and separating forces act on two planes: firstly, within the groups, and secondly, between the groups, in the framework of 'Great Society'. The advantage of this view is that it enables us to analyse the structure of complex, modern society in terms of group relationships, subject to elementary social processes. Great Society is conceived by Mannheim as a society of groups, subject to largely the same forces and processes as the individual. The State is defined by Mannheim as the frame group of modern society, a special group which organises and regulates the relationship between the groups which constitute society.

In this group analysis of society and politics Mannheim goes even a step further when he raises the problem of international relations in terms of social processes which take place between conflicting and co-operating frame groups, the modern states. While outlining the conditions of setting up an effective international authority he draws our attention to the fact that mankind has not yet succeeded in setting up such a frame group to ensure co-operation between states and the peaceful solution of international conflicts.

The concluding chapters of the third part of this book, which deal with the dynamics of political groups, the sociology of classes and with a definition of the modern state, form a fascinating introduction to the basic problems of political sociology.

In Part Four ('Social Stability and Social Change') Mannheim turns to the problems of social structure and starts with the study of some of those forces which make for social cohesion and stability. According to him, social control is the sum of those methods by which society influences human behaviour in order to maintain a given order. Among a multitude of social controls, Mannheim picks out the most important ones such as custom and law, and analyses these both in isolation and also as mutually depending upon each other. He shows the displacement of custom by law, but also the new functions of customs in modern society.

He then undertakes a further step by describing the personal representatives of social control, the man in authority. This leads to an analysis of the situations in which leadership emerges, as well as to a sociological examination of prestige. Authority and prestige imply valuations and therefore Mannheim feels induced to conclude his analysis of social controls with a sociology of valuations. This is perhaps one of the most original and fascinating chapters of the book as Mannheim here applies the technique of analysis which he developed in his various contributions to the sociology of knowledge.

In the last chapter of this book Mannheim discusses the problem of the deeper causes of social change. He starts with an analysis of the Marxist theory of social change, 'historical materialism', and attempts to point out both the positive contributions of the theory to our knowledge of the mainsprings of social change and also the limitations of this theory. This is not the only place in this book where Mannheim, as we have seen, tries to overcome the limitations inherent in a purely economic interpretation of social and cultural dynamics.

The question arises whether Mannheim really succeeded in overcoming the limitations of a materialistic outlook or whether he only replaced 'economic determinism' by a less crude 'sociological determinism'. Only an analysis of the method applied by Mannheim in these lectures as well as a review of his ultimate aims as a sociologist can yield an answer to this question, and to these two questions we now turn.

The Method of Systematic Sociology

Mannheim's theory of man and society, as presented in this book, is full of contradictions and antithetical notions. This may be regarded as a re-emergence, as an attempt at a more general synthesis, of the dialectical views on culture which were characteristic of his early philosophical work. The synthesis is more general in the sense that Mannheim, during his London years, sought to weld together the speculative and empirical methods. The supporters of a rigidly empirical philosophy might question whether a synthesis between the speculative and empirical methods is possible or even desirable in the realm of the social sciences. Mannheim's results seem to show that the application of such a synthetic method can be fruitful and at the same time enables the scholar to avoid those pitfalls which, according to the spokesmen of the extreme empiricist school, are unavoidable, once the door is open to speculative methods. Mannheim was aware of the fact that theorising about the meaning of events would be empty talk without a specific and intimate knowledge of the always changing social realities, and urged that sociological interpretations and theories should be constantly checked in the light of practical experiences. Like Max Weber, he consequently rejected the claims of the intuitionists and the supporters of the morphological assessment as these showed little, if any, respect for empirical methods and renounced the quest for verifiable causal explanations. Further, Mannheim emphatically rejects the notion that social groups and institutions should be regarded as substantial units or mythical entities. He demands that the sociologist should be trained to analyse groups and other social relationships, regarded by many as mythical entities, as products of social forces and processes. On the other hand Mannheim does not follow the opponents of the Platonist and Hegelian view in their extreme individualism and atomism. In fact, he fought a two-front war on the one hand against the neo-Hegelians and morphologists of his time, such as Oswald Spengler, Othmar Spann and Hans Freyer, and on the other against extreme empiricists and individualists such as Bertrand Russell or F. A. Hayek. In this respect Mannheim can be regarded as a follower of Max Weber, who continually strove to improve upon Weber's procedure. The application of psychological analysis in the interpretation of social situations is one of Mannheim's most important contributions in this direction.[1]

In this book Mannheim tries to reach a genuine synthesis between the methods of modern dynamic psychology and those of sociology. As a sociologist he naturally stresses the role played by social factors in the forming of behaviour and thought patterns, and he claims that even the forms of individualisation originate in social processes. Yet, he takes into consideration not only the process of introjection of social situations into the psyche which itself is made up of interacting aspects of the self, but also the projection of inner tensions and mental concepts into the so-called external, social field. By analysing the role both of introjection and projection in the social process he escapes the one-sidedness of the extreme 'sociologistic' view, according to which it is the social situation alone which determines human development.

His description of the different processes which create social distance, such as the 'fear distance', the 'power distance' and the distance between different status groups, shows his virtuosity in fusing external, 'situational' and internal 'psychological' factors in the analysis of social and cultural phenomena. Another example of this can be found in his analysis of situations favouring the emergence of tyrannical rulers. He points out that specific forms of social and economic organisation and power distribution must coincide with certain cultural and psychic processes in order that a political leader should be permitted to turn into a tyrant, an isolated and domineering figure who, without incurring ridicule or revenge, can indulge in narcissistic notions of all-powerfulness and in orgies of self-glorification.

[1] In the original plan of the course of lectures on which a large part of this book is based, Mannheim had included a lecture on "Casualty, Function and Structure Dialectics." It was not in fact given, but in it he intended to show that social structures correspond to the network of interaction of single causes. He wrote on this topic in *Essays on the Sociology of Culture* (pp. 59-81) and Ernest Mannheim comments on it in his editorial introduction to that book.

The weighing of the various factors of social and cultural development and the rejection of any single-cause theory recalls the procedure of Max Weber who analysed a multiplicity of causal factors, such as the control of the physical means of coercion, and of administration, the ownership of economic goods, the development of science as well as of religious and ethical attitudes, when investigating the rise of economic and political structures and institutions. Yet, there is a significant difference between Weber and Mannheim. In Max Weber's system the relationship between the various factors is a much looser one, and their co-existence in a given situation seems incidental; he proceeds, as if believing in the rule of 'chance' in history. Mannheim, however, sees the various factors of social evolution as active within an all-embracing social and cultural process. He perceives the basic unity in the development of society, without losing sight of the various aspects of culture and the peculiarities of human activities. His procedure is characterised by a sort of speculative boldness which distinguishes his method from the pragmatism of Weber. The roots of this difference can be found in Mannheim's training in the application of a speculative, dialectical logic and his ceaseless search for synthesis and integration.

Anyone who has tried to think in this way can appreciate that what Mannheim has to say is not just intelligent sociologising, but interpretation based upon a massive knowledge. His attempts to reconcile apparently contradictory methods of research culminate in a *tour de force:* he applies both the generalising and the individualising method, resolving their conflict by allotting to each method different tasks in the various spheres of sociology. According to Mannheim, the study of elementary social processes and the study of social groups is most appropriate for the generalising and formal method. However, such phenomena of Great Society as social stratification and institutions of a given society can be best studied by applying the individualising or historical method. The formal generalising method should be applied in the study of social phenomena which are characteristic of *all* societies, whilst the structure of concrete societies succeeding each other in history should be analysed sociologically with the help of the individualising method. By this procedure Mannheim hoped to solve the conflict between those who wished to propound principles common to any society, and those who wished, following the historical method, to expose the principles characteristic of specific societies. This clash of aim and method had divided the social scientists of the Continent into two hostile camps ever since the romantic and historical reaction against the spirit of the 'enlightenment' had first begun to appear. Mannheim believed that he could reconcile the two approaches.

Although realising the usefulness of a formal and generalising method in the analysis of the recurrent phenomena of social life, Mannheim never accepted the thesis that a generalising method, akin to those of the natural sciences, should be applied to the study of social and cultural life. He disregarded the attempt to transform social facts, that is meaningful human relationships, into measurable quantities in order to study them as if they were physico-chemical processes. He was convinced that social and cultural processes have their own peculiar dynamics which cannot be studied with the help of the same methods as physico-chemical, or even biological processes.

In this book Mannheim applies mostly a generalising method, but adapts it to his subject. He claims that general sociology should deal systematically with such social phenomena as are characteristic of all societies. These are the so-called minutiae of social life which shape the individual and act as intimate links between the members of a group. Although Mannheim begins these lectures by emphasising the need for a study of the minutiae of social life, he is soon compelled to draw into the web of his analysis such phenomena of Great Society as authoritarian and democratic power structures, urbanisation and industrialisation, the modern state. He examines these and other phenomena of Great Society (like social classes and forces of social control and social change) by following a generalising method, but occasionally he refers to results which were obtained in other branches of sociology with the aid of historical and individualising methods.

Having considered the method appropriate to systematic sociology, it has become apparent that there are other questions of aims and assumptions implicit in the method which we should examine.

The Ultimate Aims of the Sociologist

Mannheim, when advocating the use of different methods of research, reminds his readers of the dangers of 'eclecticism' but claims that a real synthesis between the various methods hitherto applied in the different branches of the social sciences is possible. This optimism is based on his conviction that the sociologist is pre-eminently fitted to synthesise the results of the specialised social sciences which deal with the different aspects of human culture and society. The speculative philosophers of the nineteenth century had already attempted to break through the walls of specialisation and to create a central discipline dealing with the problems of man, but they did not realise that it was necessary to provide broad empirical foundations for such a discipline. Mannheim believed that twentieth-century sociology could succeed where nineteenth-century philosophy had failed. He might have been over-confident as to the great future tasks and achievements of the sociologist, but his virtuosity in the use of the various methods of social and cultural analysis cannot be denied.

Yet, in following Mannheim's argument the critic might feel that something valuable has been lost. The clear outlines of the picture of man and society, as constructed by scholars with a narrower but more coherent outlook, had to be sacrificed for the sake of inclusiveness. When denying the domination of a single factor over social and cultural evolution, the sociologist might lose, as it were, a key to some understanding of history and society. It seems that even to-day the attraction of simplified pictures of human evolution is considerable. This attraction might be explained by the fact that in the modern crisis man requires an interpretation of history which can serve as a guide for action in an otherwise obscure and disconcerting social situation. However, Mannheim also hoped that a true science of man and society could supply us with a guide for action and would function as a compass showing the way towards a better society and a more meaningful life. Yet he denied the virtues of simplification and believed that only a more comprehensive knowledge of man, even if it was at present necessarily vague, could lead to real progress both in the field of theoretical knowledge and in that of practical action.

Since the collapse of the Weimar Republic he incessantly studied the question: how could the sociologist contribute to a solution of the modern social and cultural crisis? In his theoretical work he tried to detect those economic, social, political and psychological determinants which, if correctly handled, would enable the social reformer to influence human development. The scientist's quest for hidden structural connections between the different spheres of man's activities was complemented by the moral reformer's search for the principles of social and cultural reconstruction. During his London years Mannheim's work as a social scientist shows increasingly active characteristics and he moved far away from the relativism and detachment amounting almost to fatalism which had dominated his outlook at the time of the Weimar Republic. His plans for social reform were always based upon sociological insight, as he never believed in the power of pure ideas and goodwill. He remained convinced that a comprehensive knowledge of all social factors was absolutely necessary. He believed that a sociologically trained educationalist and social administrator would be more likely to succeed where those who relied only on goodwill and on abstract principles had failed.

As a result, Mannheim's theoretical sociology is not a fatalistic one, nor are his suggestions of social reform, as they developed particularly in his later books, utopian in character. Already in this mainly theoretical work representing his earliest teaching after his arrival in England, the careful reader can detect the author's interest in the burning issues which were to be central in his later works dealing with the problems of social reconstruction and planning for freedom. In fact, the book which follows contains the theoretical and analytical spade work which prepared the field for his call to practical reform.

Those who believe that man is guided by 'enlightened reason', 'economic self-interest', 'biological instincts', or 'faith' alone, will repudiate Mannheim's claim that his complex theory could serve as the basis for a guide for social action. But if the motives of men are mixed, then a broadly based and inclusive theory of human behaviour and social development such as this is should fiurnish some opportunity of forming a reliable theoretical basis for social and cultural reform.

J. S. ERÖS
W. A. C. STEWART

Keele,
June, 1957

Introduction

The Scope of Sociology and of the Social Sciences

In the book which follows I have not covered the whole field of the social sciences, nor even the whole field of sociology. It would be wise at this point to give at least a survey of the whole field.

By the term 'social sciences' we understand, in contradistinction to the natural sciences, all those scientific disciplines which deal with man, not so much as a part of nature but as a being who builds up societies and cultures. All knowledge which helps us to a better understanding of this social and cultural process is either a part of or an auxiliary discipline to the social sciences

In this largest sense of the word all the cultural sciences belong to the field of the social sciences; for instance, philology, the history of literature, the history of art, the history of knowledge, economics, economic history, political science and anthropology. But this huge amount of material must be formed into some coherence by a central discipline which has both a point of view and a subject matter of its own. In the field of social sciences the central discipline is *sociology*. It is on the one hand a synthetic discipline, trying to unify from a central point of view the results of the separate disciplines; and it is on the other hand an analytic and specialised discipline with its own field of research. The specialised subject matter of sociology is the forms of living together of man, the sum of which we call society.

I shall consider some of the main forms of this living together, such as social contacts, social distance, isolation, individualisation, co-operation, competition, division of labour and social integration. The forms of this living together can be described and explained on two lines and therefore we have two main sections of sociology:

Systematic and general sociology which describes one by one the main factors of this living together as far as they may be found in every kind of society. It is called general sociology because the general forms and tendencies, as they may be found in every society, primitive as well as modern, are to be described in it. It is called systematic sociology because it does not deal with these factors of the living together of man in a haphazard way but in a systematic order, following the line from the simplest to the most complex and settled forms of integration—from transitory contacts up to the frame-group.

Besides general sociology we have *historical sociology*. This part of sociology deals with the historical variety and actuality of these general forms. Historical sociology falls into two sections: firstly comparative sociology and secondly social dynamics. These are not my concern in the discussions which follow.

Comparative sociology considers a transition from general sociology to dynamic sociology. It deals mainly with the historical variations of the same phenomenon and tries to find by comparison general features which are to be separated from individual features. Comparative studies on such institutions as marriage, family, law, education or government belong here.

By *social dynamics* we understand an historical study of society which deals with the interrelations between the various social factors and institutions in a certain given society; for instance, a primitive tribe, or the society of ancient Rome, of modern England or of modern Europe. This kind of sociology presumes knowledge both of general and of comparative sociology but it is more concerned with the unique setting of the phenomena implied (for instance the Roman family or the modern family of a certain social stratum) and is mainly interested in the problem of how the working of one social unit reacts upon the other (for instance, how the life of the tribe interacts with the life and forms of behaviour of the family within it). This kind of sociology is called dynamic because it has not only to answer how one social institution or social factor reacts upon others at a given moment—looking at an artificially static cross-section of history—but has also to answer the question as to where the driving force is to be found which brings about changes in the social structure in a given society. Sometimes the main changes may be due to the transformation of the technique of production but sometimes a new kind of power organisation or some other innovation is the starting point of social transformation and the related cultural changes.

So historical and dynamic sociology are two principal modes of inquiry in the study of the subject. They try to explain the changing life of society. In the discussions which follow in this book, I am not, however, concerned with historical and dynamic sociology but with the main problems of systematic and general sociology—that is, with the main factors of living together in any kind of society.

In order to be able to examine social facts the elements of sociological analysis have to be acquired. This means that one must first be a sociologist in order to become a specialist in one sphere later, for instance in education or in social work. In order to establish these requirements, the sociologist should first analyse the *psychological equipment of man*. In order to obtain a correct picture of this equipment we have to analyse the relationship of instincts to habits, the transformation of emotions and of the libido and the nature of interests and attitudes. This kind of analysis of human behaviour enables us to understand that social facts are never what they seem to be. For instance, the psychological assumptions apparent in stereotypes of masculinity or femininity, as well as of social habits, are usually mistaken for instincts. Nor will

3

the untrained observer notice behind ideologies the social guidance of emotions.

Secondly, the student of society should consider *the most elementary social processes*, such as contacts, distance, social hierarchy, isolation, competition, conflict, co-operation, division of labour and personality formation, as producing both conformity and individualisation. Thirdly, all these psychological and social factors must be related to *the nature of social integration* analysing such integrations as the crowd, the group and the social classes.

These, then, are the first three parts of this book—man and his psychic endowment, elementary social processes and the nature of social integration. In the fourth part we go a step further to examine some of the factors which make for social stability and for social change.

PART 1

MAN AND HIS
PSYCHIC EQUIPMENT

CHAPTER I

Man and His Psychic Equipment

I do not wish to attempt here a treatise on the biology and psychology of man. I shall enumerate only those results of these disciplines which explain the fact that man is capable of being shaped by society. By itself living in society would not have such far-reaching consequences if man had not a fundamental quality which lower animals lack; that quality is the flexibility of his behaviour. Ants and bees also live together, they too have a kind of division of labour and a kind of state, but, unlike man, there is no visible change in their psychic life—they still reproduce the same social and mental patterns, and in that sense they have no history.

In order to understand fully this statement it is necessary to work out the meaning of some fundamental notions, such as behaviour, behaviour pattern, situation and adjustment.

1. BEHAVIOUR, SITUATION AND ADJUSTMENT

As an introduction I would like to give an example. If you are at a party where you do not know anybody, and furthermore where the members of the group are either on a higher level in the social scale than you or your family, or on a lower level, then you are likely to become shy and not be sure how to act. The same might happen to you if you join a party in a foreign country with whose customs you are not familiar. Shyness is a symptom of a

7

lack of adjustment to a new situation, and is a consequence of the fact that you do not know how to behave. In order to avoid this embarrassment either you look for a kind of behaviour which fits the new situation or you ask somebody how to behave. In the latter case you are prepared to accept a traditional behaviour pattern, in the former you try to invent a new behaviour pattern.

Of course animals also look for right behaviour if they meet physical obstacles and they make adjustments to a newly emerging situation. In fact, adjustment is the most elementary process underlying all our activities. A behaviour pattern is a definite relationship between a stimulus and response, which causes the organism to behave in a characteristic and uniform manner whenever the specific stimulus occurs. A behaviour pattern may be either instinctive and thus inherited, or habitual and acquired.

But what is the difference between the adjustment made by an animal and our adjustments in society? An animal adapts itself as a rule to situations arising from natural surroundings with a very small scale of variability. Man, besides adapting himself to his natural surroundings, adapts himself also to the psycho-social-institutional environment, with a large variety in the situations demanding flexible responses. Thus great variability of behaviour and adaptation to surroundings of a social character is typical for man.

The child comes into the world endowed with mechanisms of neural action involving muscular movement. Respiration, circulation and digestion are the first physiological functions he carries out. The first movements of his limbs are random and spontaneous, but he soon acquires the power of muscular co-ordination, and repetition causes useful movements to become automatic. As time passes, inherited and acquired reflexes (such as choking, coughing, trembling, sneezing or crying from pain) can, up to a point, be consciously modified.

Animals inherit the mental pattern which they need for the performance of the few tasks they have to fulfil, and a newly born animal shows a mastery over the most important behaviour patterns immediately after its birth. An infant, however, is born helpless, with very few fixed behaviour patterns. He needs a long breeding period during which he acquires the most important of these. He obtains them from society, which stores for the individual those patterns of adjustment necessary for life in that society. On the other hand man can, during his lifetime, change his behaviour patterns and find new ones by the method of trial and error or by other means. Animals make the trial-and-error adjustments too, by being physically engaged in the trials and errors while man can make his adjustment in his mind, by searching for the right action in thought. An animal, having made an adjustment to an unusual physical environment, does not remember as a rule the behaviour which has brought the bad and the good result, it cannot communicate its experiences to other animals and it can seldom co-operate in making adjustments with others. Man can think out with the help of imagination more possibilities of action in a few minutes than even the evolved type of animal could acquire by trial-an-error action over a long period of its life.

The main difference between lower animals and man is that animals adapt themselves to situations by inherited behaviour patterns which we call instincts, whilst man has not only those fixed instincts which are adequate to the tasks which his environment lays upon him, but is forced to acquire new behaviour patterns during his lifetime. He has been able to make such great progress during the course of history because the most significant forms of adjustment for him are transmitted by the psycho-social-institutional medium which we call our social and cultural life, and not by biological inheritance. Such biological inheritance would necessitate the develops his leading idea that acts and experiences are the determining antecedents beyond which it is not profitable or even possible to seek any stable elements or absolutes.

Thus, to-day, instead of considering human life as governed either by reason or by instinct, the first two phases of development of modern psychology mentioned above, we speak of tendencies which come to be fixed by specific tasks presented by the changing situations. This is a dynamic concept of instincts, which leaves open the operation of social forces and actualities. As we shall see, it does not exclude the possibility of influence by unconscious aspects of experience.

ii. THE HABIT-MAKING MECHANISM

We have seen that behaviour patterns leading to good adjustments which become habitual are of the greatest importance to mankind, mainly because they save time and energy. However if the situations in which we act change fundamentally, nothing could be more disadvantageous than a rigid habit which does not fit in with new conditions. Since modern society is built up of a set of very rapidly changing situations, there is a great need to remake those of our adjustments which have become obsolete. For this reason we must turn our attention at this point to the problem of the habit-making mechanism.

Making behaviour patterns is accomplished through responses to stimuli, and new combinations of stimuli may bring about new combinations of responses. There are very simple stimuli which condition responses automatically. For instance, the hungry infant sucks instinctively, or the pupil of the eye contracts sharply in a bright light. In such cases we can speak of an instinctive response which is biologically adequate. That is the starting-point—but we have seen that human society is not constituted by responses to instinctive stimuli only.

There is a much larger range of possible responses than these.

What is the elementary mechanism which makes these more complex responses possible? The elementary mechanism, which creates responses that are not purely biological, is the conditioned, acquired reflex which was described for the first time by Pavlov. The experiments which Pavlov undertook with dogs have become famous. It was well known that hungry dogs normally respond to the presence of raw meat with a flow of saliva. In this case meat is an adequate biological stimulus provoking instinctive responses. Pavlov caused a bell to be rung a number of times simultaneously with the presentation of the meat. After a period of such training he experimented by ringing the bell without presenting the meat, with the result that the saliva of dogs exposed to the stimulus of the ringing bell only, flowed just the same. The bell, which was originally insufficient by itself to set off a response in dogs, acquired the power of conditioning the same reflex, which was formerly only conditioned by the biologically adequate stimulus, the presentation of meat.

Another experiment showing the same process can be made with bees: we put honey on red paper and a group of bees gets the habit of collecting the honey from the red paper. After a time the bees seek for honey on any red paper they notice, even if there is no honey on it. Similarly spiders to whom we have given flies to eat, previously plunged into turpentine, will in future show reluctance to catch any flies.

These simple experiments exemplify that elementary process which assists the creation of social life in general —the process of responses answering to stimuli which are not simply biologically adequate, as for instance when we learn to like foods which our parents like or if we learn to approve the religious and political views which they approve. In such cases we accept through sympathy conditioned responses which originally were not connected with the stimulus. In this way we may gradually take over most of the attitudes of those with whom we associate closely. If we blush when somebody says anything 'shocking' in conversation, this is the result of the fact that we were brought up in surroundings where the mentioning of such things was accompanied by appalled silence on the part of parents, teachers and others, so that we cannot hear these words without recapturing the painful emotions aroused in us during childhood. Education in the widest sense leans heavily on this kind of associated response.

It was the French sociologist Tarde who stressed very strongly the social role of the process of imitation. Imitation is a conditioned reflex, but it is not similar to the elementary process outlined above. It is a kind of system of combined conditioned responses. Imitation is the method by which the cultural content of society is transmitted from one generation to another. In the case of imitation it is the behaviour of another which is the efficient conditioning stimulus to the same behaviour in ourselves.

Thus we can distinguish two kinds of responses to stimuli: those made by ourselves as a consequence of our own experiences, and those which are accepted by imitation. In the second case we take someone as our model and learn to do as he does. For instance we take as our models people who have prestige, because we think that there is a functional relationship between their behaviour and their success.

3. EVOLUTION IN THE MODELS OF IMITATION

There is an evolution in the child's life from the more concrete to the more abstract forms of behaviour, and from proximate personalities to more distant ones. The child begins by imitating his mother or nurse, and later adds such models as the father, brothers and sisters, playmates and teachers, impressive figures like the postman or the members of the gang which he has joined. The first type of imitation takes as models the simpler acts and emotions of those persons near to the child. As the range of experience widens the process of imitation gradually becomes more extensive, more fundamental and more abstract. During the early teens there is a gradual transition from concrete personality models to ideal ones. For instance the personalities described in the stories which we tell children or which are presented to them in biographies, can be valuable assets in the process of influencing and integrating personality-responses. The danger of such models is that the sense of reality is absent. The disproportion in modern man's life sometimes becomes very painful. The small range of experiences afforded by the specialised work of a certain occupation or by narrow surroundings is often in blatant contradiction to the information and impressions which we obtain from newspapers, books and the cinema. Such a disproportion can help to produce a somewhat unbalanced personality, who possesses acquired behaviour patterns which neither correspond to the character and status of the person in question, nor to the field of his real activity. The danger for many intellectuals consists in the possibility that they may think and behave quite differently, without noticing consciously the discrepancy, or, more seriously, while noticing the discrepancy and experiencing only a crippling frustration thereby.

4. SOCIOLOGICAL AND PSYCHOANALYTIC DESCRIPTIONS OF MAN

When we were considering conditioned reflexes we raised the question of the relationship between the conditioning of reflexes and society. Man in society experiences the interplay of complex internal and external pressures, and his reaction to these has both an individual and a social significance. If we described society without previously analysing the psychic equipment and the mental forces of man, we would make the same mistake as a man who attempted to describe an electric motor without any knowledge of the nature and working of electric power. But if we limited ourselves to giving an account of the nature of the psychic energies of the individual, we would be acting like a man who explained the nature of electric power without giving a description of the machine which it drives, or the work it can be expected to do.

I started my analysis by outlining some of the most important notions of the behaviouristic approach in psychology. I now wish to consider some of the important ideas in Freudian psychology, selecting those notions which are necessary for a satisfactory explanation of the working of society. I am neither a behaviourist, nor a Freudian, nor a Marxist. Each of these schools, in my view, presents a partial analysis, while seeming to establish a whole system. I am trying to use the result of the investigations of all three, to obtain a more adequate picture of the working of society.

There is an essential difference between the Freudian and the behaviouristic approaches. The behaviouristic approach is entirely externalised, because for behaviourists it is overt behaviour that counts. The only accepted data are movements and bodily changes. Inner observation, introspection, sympathetic intuition are called by the behaviourist 'metaphysical' and are rejected. As a consequence he reduces the facts of consciousness to facts of overt behaviour. Behaviourism is furthermore entirely mechanistic. Reactions are always connected to stimuli, they are independent of the total personality and the personality is not a unitary configuration, but a mosaic-like agglomeration of reactions. On the other hand, the fruitful elements in behaviourism are to be found in the fact that there are partial and isolated mechanisms in animals and in man which are automatic and are independent of the personality.

Man's psychic equipment and his social character cannot be wholly defined in terms of behaviour patterns, habits, adjustments, imitations and ideologies. The development of a personality does not consist only in the process of conditioning new responses. The mechanical laws of association are not sufficient for the interpretation of man.

We must build into the pragmatist and behaviourist concept of man's psychology some fundamental notions worked out by psychoanalysts, without becoming totally committed to the Freudian view. These fundamental notions are: the unconscious, repression, and sublimation.

i. REPRESSION

When man makes his vital adjustments, such as co-operating with his fellow-men in society or doing his daily work, he disposes of psychic energy. In the process he uses and adapts forces called drives,. which were originally striving to fulfil the elementary needs of the organism, such as self-preservation and procreation. Both create impulses and wishes which strive for fulfilment and this has to be achieved in a social situation. Every real adjustment seems to be connected negatively with the repression of those quantities of energy which cannot be used in the social situation, and positively with the 'selection' of appropriate behaviour and states of mind and attitude. We mostly repress those impulses and the ideas connected with them, which are banned by society. The so-called 'censor' in personality structure postulated by the Freudians, is mostly composed of inhibitions which have been reinforced by living in society. Repression is one of the defence techniques the individual uses to protect his conscious life against wishes which could cause painful conflicts in his consciousness. That is to say we repress mainly those strivings which could not reach their goal in a given society. Primal repression refers to material which was never conscious, the so-called archaic repressions. Repression proper expels into the unconscious material which has been conscious or pre-conscious.

All our physical wishes, and those which derive from them, cannot be fulfilled at will, so repression is a normal process which accompanies every kind of response to given stimuli. It compels the individual at every moment to renounce the fulfilment of some of his wishes by apparently selecting others which he is usually satisfied at having chosen. On the other hand these drives and wishes, although repressed, still strive for satisfaction. Even systematic logical thought is built up upon a series of repressions. We always repress certain associations in order to attain a given end. Lasswell asserts that a careful scrutiny of individual behaviour over a twenty-four-hour period strikingly shows the extent to which the personality is controlled by very elementary psychological structures. Much of the energy of the personality is spent on blocking the entry of the maladjusted impulses of the self into consciousness and into overt responses.

According to Freud the repressed drive, the repressed energy, continues to work in our unconscious. The aim of repressions is to keep out of consciousness impulses which are repugnant to the moral standards of society. The process of repression, similarly to the process of imitation, is normally a time-and-energy saving mechanism which spares our conscious life from dealing again and again with tendencies and wishes which cannot be fulfilled in a given social situation, or which would raise a long series of inner and external conflicts which could in the end threaten the existence of the individual.

Although I acknowledge the permanent necessity of the existence of certain repressive mechanisms, I claim that the better a social organism works, the less repression it needs. Society can help its members to adjust themselves by furnishing outlets and channels for the superfluous energies of individuals.

In order to understand these assertions of the Freudian school, it is necessary to know what kinds of typical expression the repressed energies may take. The repressed drive can be either completely repressed or remain partly unrepressed. In the latter case it will try to find an indirect expression. Completely repressed drives will not at this point constitute a problem for us, but a problem is presented by those drives which have not been wholly repressed.

ii. NEUROSIS, REACTION FORMATION AND PROJECTION

The first outlet for a not quite adjusted repression is the so-called *neurosis*. This is a partial solution of a psychological dilemma. The well-known example is war neurosis. Some soldiers during wartime were tormented by the following conflict: either to rush into battle, in which case the fear and anxiety of death or mutilation terrified them, at any rate for a time; or to stay out of such danger, which produced the fear of being considered by others as cowards. An accidental wound provides a way out from the painful conflict. In the absence of such an accident some soldiers unconsciously developed such symptoms as blindness or paralysis, they sought refuge in illness. Such paralysis or blindness being of a purely psychic origin might be cured by analysis or hypnosis.

These are admittedly pathological symptoms of maladjustment in the process of repression, but similar kinds of maladjustment are working in the more normal processes of society, as, for example, in the extravagant behaviour of some adolescents, in hero worship, or in the passionate behaviour of many crowds at sporting events.

Another way of dealing with weak or inadequate repressions is by *reaction formation*. Prudery of a militant kind is very often nothing but the expression of the hidden wish to have some kind of concern with sexual matters. Many people who display a hostile interest in the sexual problems of others, do so in order to distract attention from their own hidden wishes and attempt in this way to strengthen their repressions. The whole development of over-strict moral codes can only be explained by this mechanism of reaction formation.

Another technique is called *projection*. We tend to project our thoughts and emotions on to others and criticise them for these unmercifully. In this way a forbidden stimulus—experienced as an inner enemy—is projected on the outer world. An example is to be found when we project our own unconscious doubts about our love for a person or of our fidelity to our partner on to that partner in expressions of distrust and jealousy. Doubt and jealousy may thus very often be a result of projection. These typical processes on a level of lesser intensity may be found in many people, and the mechanism has to be studied by us if we want to understand the typical origin of hatred by projection. We know that savages people the external world with evil spirits, but this technique is a well-known phenomenon of twentieth-century Europe as well.

iii. RATIONALISATION

Rationalisation is another way of escaping conflicts. We speak of rationalisation if we impute other motives for our own conduct than those which have really moved us. Its essence is the construction of an explanation which is more a justification of our acts than a real account of the motivation for them. This method is employed usually if there are conflicts between our habits of acting and our standards of conduct, and a person either tells a lie consciously, or succeeds in deceiving himself by some explanation satisfying to himself while evading the real issue. This happens if people do things which are out of harmony with their conscious standards, but by giving another reason for their deeds, they do not allow the discrepancies to disturb them any more.

Rationalisations are mostly used by people who live in two different, mutually incompatible environments. For instance, a child who was taught to be obedient to his parents and to be frank with them about everything he does, may come under the influence of a group of playmates who have elaborated a moral code quite different from that of the family. Consequently there will arise a conflict between 'gang behaviour' and 'family behaviour'. This leads to confusion of attitude and may lead towards repression. Much will be allowed in the gang that is forbidden in the family. There are three typical ways of reacting to this conflict. The first is by forgetting—the child speaking with his parents will really forget the behaviour which was disapproved of by his parents, and tell them what he has been doing, remembering his mistake too late. The second is by lying. The lies of small children should not be moralised about— they are often a symptom of a conflict. The third reaction is to rationalise. The child might try to justify his deeds by referring to the sanction of another authority— his teachers, 'what other people do', what the parents of other children let them do.

iv. SYMBOLISATION AND DAYDREAMING

The creation of symbols is yet a further way by which the human mind tries to find a discharge for repressed energies. A symbol helps us to obtain a fancied fulfilment of our wishes. We deceive ourselves by finding substitutes for our forbidden wants. By disguising, with the help of symbols, the real object of our wants we may be occupied in a hidden, latent way with it.

In this process of creating symbols, one object comes to represent another either by association or similarity, or by contrast. Mythology can be regarded as the system of primary symbols of humanity.

The role of symbols in political life is very great. Here collective symbols help the individual to overcome his private maladjustments. Lasswell has pointed out that political symbols like the flag, the monarchy, the proletariat, the fifth column, serve as targets for displaced personal emotional response. They are adapted to this because they are ambiguous and because they have a general circulation. The individual, says Lasswell, so to say, socialises his bodily symptoms and private obsessions 'by means of collective symbols in mass movements'.

Our dreams are full of symbols which, according to Freud, mostly represent wish-fulfilments which our conception of life would never permit. But even in our daily life we have periods when we lessen the strength of self-control and give an outlet to repressed experience or try to evade a difficult conflict. The essence of daydreaming is always the fanciful creation of a world that is more colourful, more appreciative of ourselves or in which our personality has a greater opportunity to be active, than is possible in our immediate surroundings. For instance, some children who are beginning to develop wants and desires, which cannot be adequately satisfied in their environment, react either by running away and seeking adventures elsewhere (these are the active types) or they turn inwards and seek to perform in their daydreaming a substitute for an unsatisfying reality. In both cases we see a manifestation of the expanding desire of the child for wider experiences and for new models of behaviour. Very often in such infantile situations the lineaments of future character formation in the individual appear. Once the child gets into the habit of solving his life conflicts by turning inwards, he becomes what is called an introverted personality. The active child finds new behaviour patterns to settle conflicts in changing his surroundings and adjusting himself to a real situation and may become an extravert personality.

Daydreaming is to a certain extent a helpful adjustment because it gives an outlet for energies by inducing the ego to tolerate what Healy calls 'fantasies of gratification' of an egoistic or of an erotic character. But if exaggerated, daydreaming may become an impediment to adjustments to real situations. The chronic daydreamer substitutes the easier method of imaginative achievements for the actual effort and realisation in the real world. Healy says of the daydreaming habit that in this case 'satisfaction is obtained entirely in a mental state'. He thinks that a growing individual should gradually bring the life of fantasy 'into closer relation with the facts of reality'. But he admits that fantasy is also 'a safety valve for the abreaction of strong affects'.

Daydreaming is correlated to the social situation where a large amount of leisure and a small range of activity compel the individual to use his superfluous energies in that way. Types whose activities do not absorb most of their energies, or people who work much but in a monotonous way, are predisposed to daydreaming; for instance, young girls, housewives who for various reasons are not absorbed by the duties of the household, employees in work which may have slack periods in the day, such as serving in shops, those in repetitive factory work, or wealthy idlers.

The cinema can be considered as a daydream-producing machine on the basis of large-scale industry. Modern mass-society produces more and more human beings with a very narrow scale of possibilities. They need a compensation and a substitute for lost activities—an outlet for their imagination. Formerly it was mainly the task of poetry, of the novel and of the theatre to give expression to these daydreaming tendencies. In earlier ages there were myths which had the same function. Psychoanalysts like Freud and Sachs have made comparisons between fantasy formation and artistic creation. The similarity can be found in the fact that both are free from the condition of reality, that both offer compensation for deficiencies and frustrations and both concern themselves frequently with pain, tragedy and happiness. The main difference—as Sachs has pointed out—is that the principal personage in a daydream is the self and it has a meaning only for the self, whereas the creations of art must have meaning for many. Further, daydreams are formless and without coherence except in terms of an individual's needs or wishes, whereas works of art must have form, unity and clarity.

V. SUBLIMATION AND IDEALISATION AND THEIR SOCIAL SIGNIFICANCE

There is much similarity between daydreaming and the process of idealisation and sublimation. The main difference is that in the latter case the superfluous emotional energy or libido is not used to create a second world besides the existing reality, but is used to spiritualise parts of real surroundings, to heighten the significance of real bits of environment. For instance, emotional energies of an erotic origin can be used—after having been transferred from their sexual origin—to idealise and spiritualise various persons and objects of our surroundings, such as the loved personality of the King or the Queen, of the political, religious or educational leader-personality, or the symbol of the fatherland, the party or the class.

Sublimation is a process that concerns the redirection of impulse, as when an earlier love of self-display becomes a generalised pleasure in achieving prominence in some career or calling. Idealisation concentrates upon the object and it represents a shift from the ego to the ego-ideal with the uncritical approbation which that implies. In the latter case the uncritical attitude refers to the object; in the former case, one is uncritical of oneself as one was in early childhood, in the period of feeling almighty. In psychoanalytic terms idealisation represents a displacement of early childhood self-love on to the superego and this process usually becomes particularly apparent during puberty.

The sociologist must note the importance, for personal and social integration, of the process of creating an ego-ideal. It offers a key to the way in which society, apart from the conditioning or encouragement of habits, can influence people. In fact, the ego-ideal is more important to the personality than all habit patterns, because habits and action patterns all become co-ordinated in the ego-ideal. This is the psychological side of the process. On the sociological side we see a point at which society can influence personality by means of ideas, myths, novels, and, of course, by religion.

Such social psychologists and sociologists as Emile Durkheim, Max Weber, G. H. Mead, J. F. Dashiell, M. Ginsberg and S. C. Pepper—to mention only a few— have stressed the importance of ideals in human society. According to Mead, social habits and customs are intimately connected with values. But values depend on social function. According to Pepper, human society is 'built around ideals'. Whilst societies co-operate in the service of certain purposes, 'these purposes are nothing other than ideals . . . ideals that actually function in morality. But for an ideal to function in morality, it must be more than a mere ideal. There must be co-operation of individuals about it, and that co-operation must be in some degree crystallised into a social structure. It is the action of the social structure that makes the obligation categorical. Until an ideal takes root in a social structure it can claim nothing, but hypothetical obligation. . . .'

Sloops again stresses the fact that ideals do not die when they are temporarily inhibited by the facts of the real world, which is unsympathetic to these ideas. Ideals, which are supported by love and by deeper instincts, but which are inhibited temporarily and deprived of expression in the objective world 'are forced down into the deeper unconscious levels of the mind'. If the hostility of the real world continues, the deeper self will use the intellect to 'transform the suppressed ideal into some form of dream, some form of imagery, in which it can survive temporary defeat'. The ideal of righteous social order, for instance, took, in the Hellenistic period of Attic civilisation, the form of inner life. Christianity transformed this ideal into an inner life in which God and man communicated in both immanent and transcendent experience.

The social function of ideals is different in different phases of psychic and social organisation. In the individual phase, the concept of a mutually helpful society becomes charged with emotional content, but it is ineffectual if kept within individuals. In the collective or social phase an ideal-concept and the emotion connected with it become the basis for action and interaction within groups. Finally, in the institutional phase the forms of the interaction remain, but are no longer charged with emotion because the embodied ideal works, so to say, by itself. This is a notion explored by G. W. Allport in relation to the part played by instincts in the development of human personality. He calls the process of detachment from emotional roots and the resultant operating of an ideal 'functional autonomy'.

This is the way in which new reality is created. Emotions are needed only when institutions are lacking. The breaking of an old habit and the establishing of a new one needs emotion—this is the social function of emotion. Consequently, if the founder of a religious or other emotionally charged social movement wants to preserve the original emotional content of the movement, he must be hostile to institutionalisation, as institutions and the rational doctrines they need may tend to kill the enthusiasm of the faith.

CHAPTER II

Man and His Psychic Equipment
(continued)

5. THE SOCIAL GUIDANCE OF PSYCHIC ENERGIES

Art, literature and all kinds of social and political idealism arise, according to the views of the psychoanalytic school, from the fact that psychic energies can be invested in socially approved objects, giving them a certain emphatic value. The great problem for the sociologist to-day is to find ways in which to use these energies in a socially valuable way.

We have seen that idealisation and sublimation, special forms of what we call, more generally, the displacement and transference of psychic energy, use the very same energy which is used with quite different results in the case of neurotic symptoms or rationalisations or reaction formations. Whether energies are to be invested in socially approved objects depends, of course, on the individual character, but perhaps even more on the nature of and the guiding forces at work in the society in which he lives.

We are living in a period in which the idea of social planning is not at all a strange conception. It is very probable that the guidance of our psychic energies will sooner or later be considered as an important social problem. Such guidance, of course, does not mean that we could or would want to regulate our individual development in a mechanical fashion or that we should try

27

to forecast the evolution of a given individual. This is neither possible nor desirable; but it is fairly possible that the general factors which tend to mould human behaviour and shape the utilisation of superfluous psychic energies may be so collected and guided as to influence the majority of the population to a certain degree and in certain directions. One should distinguish here between two entirely different things: the first is the shaping of a certain individual in a pre-determined way, enlisting the help of certain institutions to produce a specific type of individual. If anyone believes in the possibility of shaping a person in this way, he must assume a considerable degree of predictability and inevitability in society. This is not at all our view. We assume a second position in which certain conditioned causations will produce some effects with a given statistical probability. But the freedom for growth beyond the type is an essential to this much more tentative and flexible kind of development.

The guidance of emotional energy in earlier societies consisted firstly of adjustments of the active energies according to needs of the society, such as those arising from the process of the division of labour, and secondly in adjusting the superfluous energies by stimulating the growth of sublimation patterns, by influencing leisure activities and so on. We must study very carefully how in older types of societies sublimation and transference of psychic energies and emotions were guided.

6. OBJECT FIXATION AND TRANSFERENCE OF THE LIBIDO

The possibility of the guidance of emotional energies is provided by the fundamental fact that human emotions are not at birth all fixed on certain objects and it is very often the social situation which links them up with definite objectives. If an emotion is once linked up with an object, we speak about object-fixation or *kathexis*. Such fixations are, for instance, the love of children for parents and parents for children, of sisters and brothers, of teachers and pupils, of playmates, but they can include also certain non-personal objects like the home, or activities like work and games, and finally religious or political symbols or beliefs. Once the fixation has taken place, the bond may become firmly secured, but there is, nevertheless, usually a possibility of shifting the libido from one object to another.

In the same way as there is an evolution in the child's life in respect of the general models of imitation from persons near at hand to those more remote and from concrete to abstract models, there is also a transference of emotions, originally fixed on the mother and other members of the family, to members of the community outside the family and finally even to the abstract idea of community itself. Further, just as the basic situation for every kind of human sociability is founded on the fact that the human child is more dependent than the young animal, so the fate of the libido is determined by the same basic situation. During the period of suckling and protection, the child develops feelings of dependence which lead to the development of the libidinous tendencies and these emotional tendencies are integrated and fixed upon one person, usually the mother. As the first fixations occur during earliest childhood, the early family pattern will be critically important for the individual, in helping to create his fundamental attitudes. Lasswell stresses the fact that the adult mind is only partly adult and consequently introjected objects and models of early childhood may influence adult behaviour in social situations. One can very often observe that grown-up children in their behaviour reflect the attitudes of their mother. Feelings of anxiety, superstition patterns and taboos might be at work which were taken over from a parent and be at work even in adult life. Every family, therefore, exhibits many of those patterns of behaviour and attitude which the mother and the father might have brought from their own families. This partly explains the slowness of the development of society even in dynamic or revolutionary periods. This slowness is not due to the fact that the individual cannot be transformed, but rather to the fact that the fundamental moulding unit, the family, works for a long time in the same way, even if the social surroundings have changed. It is not the biological and the mental inheritance which is the reason why certain mental patterns are reproduced from generation to generation, but the fact that changes in public life penetrate only very slowly into the inner life of the family.

The child, once it has been moulded by the family, can only very gradually transform these primary patterns of action and of attitudes. Nevertheless, there is a period in the development of the child when the transference of an important part of libido fixation can take place. This is the period of puberty or adolescence. This phase of biological growth coincides with new social contacts and new social demands. A conflict of roles may emerge and the general, if not complete, displacement of emotional fixations may take place. There is a problem of adolescence in our society: youthful aspiration for autonomy and parental insistence upon dependence clash with each other. It is interesting that primitive societies have planned and institutionalised this transition in the customs connected with initiation rites.

In a symposium devoted to sociological research in adolescence M. Mead, E. B. Reuter, and R. G. Foster deal with different aspects of this problem. According to Reuter, adolescence should not be defined in terms of physical maturation. If we analyse it as a social experience, adolescence begins when society no longer looks upon the person as a child, but expects him to take over some adult responsibilities. The age at which this occurs depends on social and not on biological factors. Religious groups confer adult responsibilities—confirmation for instance—on children of 12 to 14 years. The age of consent in sexual matters in England is 16, for the serving of alcoholic drink is 18, for majority it is 21. Modern society tends to establish a long period of transition between childhood and maturity, while the adolescent usually considers himself an adult and urges in one way or another that family and society should no longer treat him as a child.

Sociologically, adolescence is a stage of social development and a state of mind; it represents an intermediate period of detachment of the young person from family control. There is a marked dependence upon his age-group, before he achieves the individual independence in making decisions, which is characteristic of the fully adult status. Many persons who are physiologically adult never really outgrow the attitudes and sentiments which we call adolescent.

Much depends upon the kind of patterns of behaviour and attitude which are offered to the young in the critical phase of growth. If a society could determine what it was appropriate to do in planning the vital influences and could decisively affect the two fundamental phases of development, infancy and puberty, individual difference would still arise but a greater guidance of society would be possible. Of course, even after puberty we constantly change our attitudes—mobile types do this more often than static types—but the common foundation would be greater. I believe that we are on the threshold of a situation in our society in which more guidance will be necessary.

That there is, even in later stages of social development, a continuous transformation and displacement of the libido can be shown by the fact that a revolutionary society is to a great extent characterised by a loosening of the previous fixations of the libido. The great tension in such a society arises from the fact that there are quantities of libidinous energies present, without any fixation, seeking for a new integration. In a conservative, traditionalistic society, emotional energy is fixed upon members of the family, on friends, on members and on membership of the traditional group into which one is born, on the ambitions which are cherished in such groups and, in some cases, urge the individual to attempt to rise in the given social scale. At the same time, the emotional value of religious ideas, of social customs and traditionally cultivated games is still very great.

But once there is a general shifting in the structure of society, many people lose their social and political ambitions, their religious ideals, their recreational habits and their emotional investments in personal ambitions. As a result there is an amount of displaced unattached psychic energy which can be utilised for new purposes.

The creation of a new religion only becomes possible in a situation in which a new generation has loosened its old emotional ties and when leading groups realise, perhaps not very explicitly, that they must create new common emotional fixations which can be linked up with loyalties toward the new social order. Libido fixation in revolutionary periods or in epochs of reformation is usually brought about by such a process.

The sociological significance of displacement and of transference must be regarded as very important, in just the same way as the displacement of private motives from family objects to public objects constitutes the normal form of development in the individual. Thus, feelings of admiration and loyalty felt by the child toward parents can be later transferred to figures of public authority and to the fatherland. On the other hand, repressed hatred of one or other parent may be turned later against kings, capitalists or other persons of authority. As Lasswell has pointed out, an adult who has the feeling that he cannot love his monarch any more, may feel that he can love 'mankind'. He cannot love God, but he can love the Nation. Or he may feel unable to love his country and makes instead out of his class or party an object of love and veneration.

The question arises here whether and how far psychology is useful in a political analysis. My view is that analysis of politics without psychology is quite inadequate. But on the other hand, psychology alone is insufficient because psychology has a very important limitation: it tends to cut out the social factors, such as the development of institutions and of the technical apparatus of society and it neglects economic pressures and the needs and influences arising from strategic and military factors to which a society is exposed.

7. THE SOCIOLOGY OF TYPES OF BEHAVIOUR:

i. ATTITUDES AND WISHES

So far we have spoken about the most elementary processes which integrate, dissolve, reintegrate, fix and shift the libidinous psychic energy.

These developments belong to general systematic sociology because every society, the most primitive as well as the most complicated, is based upon these mechanisms. Historical sociology, on the other hand, ought to deal with the more individualised forms of libido fixations and displacements, such as the character of family sentiments in a certain historical period or the concept of love in the period of chivalry, or the feeling of nationalism in a country like Germany in different social groups, or the history of libido displacement in the life of different groups.

Between these two levels of sociology—systematic general sociology and historical sociology—there is an intermediate level. Here we study certain general types of behaviour and types of attitudes which are sufficiently definite to characterise a whole mental type and which enable us to apply our general statement in more concrete historical settings.

An example of such an analysis is offered by W. I. Thomas, the American sociologist and social psychologist, who worked out a group of types and called them 'the four wishes'. Thomas recognised that if we have the task of describing a certain group of people and we wish to describe not only their activities and objective adjustments but also the changes of their inner life, their attitudes, wishes and feelings, then we need a classification into which most people can be fitted. This means either that they belong completely to one type—which occurs rarely—or it means that they represent a mixture of two or more of these types. Thomas recognises that human wishes have a great variety of forms, but he thinks that they can nevertheless be classified with some advantage into the following four types:

The desire for new experience.
The desire for security.
The desire for response.
The desire for recognition.

Thomas thinks, and I agree with him, that complex attitudes derive from very elementary tendencies, drives or so-called instincts. He tries to reduce the four types of wishes mentioned above to the most elementary attitude patterns which can already be found in the life of the infant and at a primitive level of social evolution. It is necessary here to recapitulate both his descriptions of the fundamental wishes and his attempt to reduce these to simpler urges.

The desire for new experience. All experiences which have something in common with pursuit, flight, capture, escape or death, are exciting experiences. Thomas speaks of experiences here which characterised the earlier life of mankind. There is a slow transformation from the original to the most complex and sublimated patterns.

34

Even to-day we can recognise such a thing as the 'hunting pattern' of interests. 'Adventure' is the first transposition of this pattern. Sensationalism in newspapers is another kind of transformation. Such individual activities and experiences as courtship have in them also an element of pursuit. There is a hunting pattern at work in every genuine scientific investigation and the same applies to the solution of puzzles or problems.

The desire for security. This desire is based mainly on fear which accompanies the possibility of physical injury or death and expresses itself in timidity and flight. The individual dominated by the desire for security is usually cautious and conservative, tends to regular habits, systematic work and to accumulate property. The social polarity between the rebel and the traditionalist corresponds to the first two types of wish.

The desire for response. This desire has evolved from the tendency to love, to seek and to give signs of appreciation. We see this tendency at work in the devotion of the mother to the child and in the response of the child. But we see it at work on another level also in the desire for responses between the sexes. An ardent courtship for instance is usually full of assurances and appeals for reassurance. Jealousy is an expression of fear that the response is directed towards another person. However, social success very often leads to a reduction of the wish for obtaining personal responses.

The desire for recognition. This wish is expressed in the struggle of personalities for positions of influence and prestige in their social group. We call this a desire for social status. An obvious example is found in the case of the politician or the captain of industry striving for success. A man or woman may provoke responses and gain recognition through a feigned illness; others may gain distinction by a display of feigned or genuine humility, self-sacrifice, saintliness and martyrdom. The same tendency may be socially useful in one case and noxious in others. The motives connected with an appeal for recognition through self-centred interest and ostentation we call vanity; whereas creative activities connected with the same wish are called ambition.

Some individuals are temperamentally predisposed towards certain classes of the above-mentioned wishes but the expression of the wishes is profoundly influenced by the approval or disapproval expressed by the person's immediate circle and by the general public or social environment.

Further, we must allow for the shifting from one category to another and also for the possibility of finding new objects for the same category. Finally, different wishes may be combined in the same individual's personality. An emigrant to America may wish to see a new world, to make a fortune, to obtain a higher standard of living, or any other of a number of possible examples of the working of each or all of these four wishes.

Character may be considered as an expression of the organisation of these basic wishes, resulting from the interplay of temperament and experience. The wishes are the starting points of activity and pressure is brought to bear on human behaviour by influencing human wishes.

ii. INTERESTS

So far we have considered the importance of the unconscious and irrational elements in human life. Although social life is undoubtedly guided to a large extent by unconscious and emotional factors, it would be a great mistake to overlook the role played by rational interest.

We shall distinguish two notions of 'interest': first, interest in a broader sense (e.g., 'I am interested in people . . . in art . . . in philosophy.'). This is interest in a purely psychological sense. The second notion we shall call rational interest.

Interest in the first, broader sense is the counterpart of attitudes. According to MacIver attitudes are subjective states of mind, involving the tendency to act in a characteristic way, whenever a stimulus is presented. Such attitudes are envy, abhorrence, contempt, worship, trust or distrust. All attitudes, of course, imply objects towards which they are directed; but it is the state of mind, not the object, which is denoted by the term 'attitude'.

When, on the other hand, we turn our attention from the subject to the object, we shall speak of an object of interest. A politician, for example, is an object of interest to many people although the attitudes of these people toward him may be very different.

We can start by considering an object of interest from the point of view of its subjective element. Once my interest has focussed on the object, however, the objective relationship between the object and me becomes more and more important. In this broader sense we can speak about interest in cultural objects, like a philosophy. In this case interest means objects which enlist our attention.

From interest, in the sense that I am 'interested in' a thing, we must distinguish interest which has the special implication of *personal advantage*, which we sometimes call self-interest. As an instance of this I may want to get the greatest amount possible in the fields of power, prestige or economic gain. It is principally the wish for advantage which urges me to purposive activities. This means that interest compels me to organise my behaviour to attain this given end of calculation, and in this case we can speak about the second sense of interest mentioned earlier, *rational interest*. This implies calculation and striving for a given end and is a complex form of adjustment, because calculation implies choosing the means which lead most effectively to that end in the shortest way with the greatest economy of effort. 'It implies a positive control over the sources necessary to carry purposes into effect and possession of the means to satisfy desires and the trained powers of mind and particularly of initiative and reflection required for free preference and for circumspect and farseeing desires.'

For instance, while the group based upon blood relationships (the family or the clan) prevails, the individual is so strongly bound to his family or his clan that he is unable to free himself from the common regulations and taboos. In this case he does not orientate his activities according to his personal interests, but according to the group interpretation of the situation, except that he realises his personal interests in those of the group. Tradition is decisive in such a situation, as Malinowski has shown us in his description of the economic life of the inhabitants of the Coral Islands, where prices do not follow the law of supply and demand, but follow tradition.

If I am striving for a certain good, which others also want to obtain, each for himself, we speak about *like interests*. If two or more persons pursue an aim, which remains a unit for them, which they think is a whole, we speak about a *common interest*. Whereas like interests lead to competition for the same good, common interests lead to co-operation. One of the most important problems for every harmonious society is how to turn like interests into common interests—how to turn competition into co-operation. This implies the guidance of libido-transference.

Another important distinction is that between *long run interest* and *short run interest*. If a man is in the habit of changing his wishes and interests, he will not be able to organise his behaviour in line with long term objectives. Examples for such behaviour are furnished by the spoilt child who always demands and receives fulfilment of immediate wishes, or the vagabond who has no definite aim in life.

One of the most important conditions for the growth of organised activities, and all self-organisation or life-organisation, is the creation of long run interests, and private property has been among the most significant forces in history creating a long run interest in the individual. Any complex system of production or social organisation needs long run activities and in the leading groups these activities were mostly created by private property. But they can also be created by organised common interest based on consciousness of common property, or by premiums given to the greatest common achievement. Examples can be found in the attitude of loyalty to a code or ideal found in Britain in, say, the soldier, the sportsman, the civil servant and also seen in the Soviets in successful cases of so-called 'socialist competition'. Compulsion gives poor results, and slaves are the poorest workers. Private property and efforts based on incentives of honour or advantage give better results.

Private property enforces long run calculation, which in turn reorganises the behaviour of the individual. The precise nature of the interest and of the organisation of behaviour varies according to the kind of property. Landed interest, for instance, creates a much greater libido fixation on the concrete object than money interest, which creates an abstract type of libido fixation on money *in abstracto*, that is, on the amount of money or the kind of goods. Landed interest, on the other hand, encourages a sense of belonging, of winning a living from the soil by personal striving and by 'understanding' the earth and the people who work it.

The creation of disinterested behaviour in society is a very important problem which will occupy us again and again. It is stimulated by the fact that there is a more or less long chain of intermediate links between the first and last steps of our activities. The man who belongs to a socialist party, for instance, has perhaps not ever the chance to see the aims of the movement to which he belongs attained during his lifetime. Thus, not only property, but every kind of co-operation and division of labour increases opportunities for abstract behaviour, develops the capacity to prolong the tension between wishes and their fulfilment.

The social integration of wishes and attitudes differs very largely from the integration of interests. The integration of interests is mostly performed by compromise, which means, for instance, that people with like interests, who compete for an advantage, resign one part of their advantage on the basis of a rationalised agreement. All barter consists in such a renunciation of expected advantages and every kind of association is the result of an integration of interests.

The integration of attitudes, on the other hand, is performed on the basis of direct identification. This implies that we identify ourselves with the other members of a community and also with the community as such. Modern society, establishing long-run interests, tends to repress the libidinous element from the field of public activities and from work, and this may be a serious handicap in certain social activities and situations.

PART 2

THE MOST ELEMENTARY
SOCIAL PROCESSES

CHAPTER III

A. Social Contact and Social Distance

We are not concerned any longer with the psychological equipment of the human individual, but with those elementary social processes which immediately affect his development. I shall only deal with a few of these, but they are of such fundamental importance that no individual and no social life can be fully understood without a certain knowledge of them. Such social processes are, for instance, social contact, social distance, and isolation.

Sociologists, who prefer to state only the phenomena of the so-called Great Society, such as social mobility, social stratification and social institutions, without linking up these studies with the observation of the minutiae of the elementary social processes are not likely to present an account which is as true as it might be.

1. PRIMARY AND SECONDARY CONTACTS

We must distinguish two kinds of contacts: the *primary* contacts, those developed in intimate, face to face associations, where visual and auditory sensations are always engaged; and *secondary* contacts, which are characterised by externality and greater distance. People who are mentally shaped by primary contacts, primary virtues and ideas, develop different characteristics from those who are shaped by secondary contacts. As an example compare the woman who is mainly a wife and a mother with the managing director of a factory or a

43

politician. There are, of course, connections between personality traits developed by primary and by secondary contacts. The wish for public recognition by the operation of psychological displacement is often, at least in part, a substitute for the lack of intimate responses within the family.

It is clear that the natural area of secondary contacts is the city. The Industrial Revolution by building cities and by breaking up small units of social life like the village, was the most important agency in creating a great number of abstract and impersonal relationships. The secondary contacts thus created operate in such a way that they promote the abstract attitude; they enable us to compare facts and to develop long-term interests and calculations, because 'trends' can be worked out and new systems of controlling people by emphasizing the different parts they play as taxpayers or workers, can be devised. The face to face situation, dominated by primary contacts, has thus been transformed.

2. SYMPATHETIC AND CATEGORIC CONTACTS

There is also another classification of contact which shows how the primary and secondary classifications come into being from a psychological and sociological point of view. People who do not belong to our group do not fall into the realm of our primary contacts. We do not consider them as real individuals, but we categorise about them. This means that we classify them in terms of different degrees of sympathy or antipathy. Here we find the social origin of prejudices. The feelings of sympathy connected with the different categories and groups create the so-called prejudices against persons whom we can classify, for instance, as Negroes, Germans, Jews, aliens, foreigners, 'them'.

The first phase of this process of categorisation is a

primitive kind of adjustment. We start by denoting or defining groups by convenient signs, because we are not able to deal with every object with which we come into contact, distinctly and separately. Further, if we meet an unknown fellow-being for the first time, we usually feel a sudden sympathy or antipathy. This is obviously an interpretation of the attitude, so common in animal life, where sympathy and antipathy are a kind of tool of selection for possible experiences. Our understanding is, further, in most cases determined by the notions and prejudices we have. The natural basis of prejudices is a propensity to fit new experiences into old categories by using early generalisations to cope with new experiences. Every real experience is based upon immediate contacts. Understanding is a battle between immediate readiness for new versions of experience and the propensity towards prejudice. People who are mobile, socially or geographically, are more critical and unbiased in judging others and less prejudiced, because they are used to getting into touch with various people. 'Rooted' people are, as we know, more inclined to prejudice. The mobile people may more easily move from categoric experiences into specific experiences.

The importance of the first impression you have in a great city stems from the fact that it reacts upon your self-consciousness and self-evaluation. The self-consciousness of the city dweller is unstable and flexible; whereas in the village, prestige is based on who your father is, to which family you belong and your position in the community, in the city prestige is based much more upon personal achievement. As a result, the city dweller is often more isolated and his self-evaluation is internalised.

A result of this is the flexibility, but also the instability, unsureness and scepticism in the character of the city dweller. Further, the relative anonymity of the individual in a great city increases the spheres of life within which we are able to turn over responsibility to somebody else.

As a result of this, more and more people get used to the situation of being spectators.

The categoric element in personal contacts disappears in real friendships. These are based on sympathetic contacts, which means a wish for identification of interests. The expression 'we' implies mutual identification and diffusion of personalities. Our 'neighbour' in some senses is essentially ourselves. The more individualised people are, the more difficult it is to attain identification. Instead, ambiguous feelings regularly arise within the medium of identification, and the feeling to be different is stronger. Friendship and marriage are relationships which channel more or less successfully this ambiguity.

The locus of earliest experience of social unity and identification are face to face groups such as families, self-governing play groups, neighbourhoods, clubs, fraternal societies or colleges. Sentiments of love, hero worship and courage but also of ambition, vanity and resentment are being shaped in these groups. According to Cooley, love, freedom and justice are primary ideas, they are at the root of Christianity, democracy and socialism, all three being based upon the ideas of primary groups.

Contacts within and without the group have been analysed by sociologists like Sumner, Cooley and Burgess. According to them internal sympathetic contacts and group egotism result in a double standard of feeling, thought and action : good-will, co-operation and trust between the members of the group, but hostility and suspicion toward the members of other groups. The relation of comradeship in the in-group and hostility towards others (the out-group) is correlative. The exigencies of struggle with outsiders strengthens the solidarity within the group so that internal discord should not weaken it.

Ethnocentrism is the technical term for this attitude. One's own group is everything and all others are rated in reference to it. Each ethnocentric group nourishes its own pride and vanity, its superiority, exalts its own divinities and looks with contempt on outsiders. This contempt is expressed by using terms of derogation to name and characterise other groups such as 'pig-eater', 'cow-eater', 'uncircumcised'. What underlies these judgments we may call gentile morality. Nationalism is obviously based on this attitude of prejudice and gentile morality.

3. SOCIAL DISTANCE

In every kind of social contact there is implied a social distance. Distance may signify an external or spatial distance, and an internal or mental distance. The whole variety and diversity of social and cultural life would be inexplicable without the category of social distance. Without it there would be objects and persons but not a social world. Distancing is, at the same time, one of the behaviour patterns which is essential to the persistence and continuity of an authoritarian civilisation. Democracy diminishes distances. Prestige (for instance that of an officer in the army) is thus largely a matter of 'distance'. Literally, distance means rendering something remote, transferring an object which is near to a position which is farther away from the point of reference. The word 'distance' originates from our direct experience of space. Its peculiarity is that spatial experience provides the pattern for mental experience too. That somebody is, for instance, at a distance of five feet from me is a spatial experience, but if I say that somebody is socially distant from me this means that I have either a higher or a lower social status than the other. There is a certain similarity between these two kinds of distances, although they are not identical. The sociologist speaks about creating artificial distance. What does he mean? Spatial distance, measurable in simple, physical terms, is being transmuted by a deliberate act of the human will into something which may be called mental distance. To create mental distance implies diminishing identification. It is to move from sympathising acts towards alienation, without, however, necessarily implying categoric or aggressive behaviour.

First let me give an example in the field of purely sensory experience of how the fundamental process of distancing can be observed. A seafarer, on approaching the port may at first enjoy a clear view of the town that lies ahead. Suddenly the whole prospect is rendered remote because of a mist. Actually the town is no farther off than before, but the mist has artificially created the illusion of remoteness. In this example distance was not created by the subject, but by the mist. All mental distances with which we shall be concerned emanate from the spontaneity of the subjects; in fact, they are created by the subjects.

The evolution of mental distancing from spatial distance can be clearly demonstrated in the case of fear. In fact, the fear distance is the simplest distance. If I keep a safe space between myself and the stranger who is stronger than me, then, in this spatial distance between us there is contained the mental distance of fear. Caged animals, in a certain situation, preserve a spatial distance from one another in direct proportion to their relative strength.

Schjelderup Ebbe established on the basis of careful observation that there exists a well-determined hierarchy among social animals, for instance among hens, cocks and chicks. He observed them in groups of from two up to twenty-five and later in groups containing twenty-five to one hundred. According to him, the first thing that struck the observer was that during the search for food, during eating out of the food-pot or going to the perch to rest or going to the nests to lay eggs, the birds observed an exact order: the dominant bird always came first and the second, the third and all the other places were taken always by the same birds. The question arises how this order was shaped. Observation showed that it was shaped by fighting. When two chickens meet, the first thing is to establish, so to say, their social rank by fighting. The bird which runs away first, becomes for ever subjected. Thus, a complete list can be worked out according to the fighting results and it seems that this hierarchy is strictly observed by the birds. There is always a first one who dominates all the others and a last one who is dominated by all the others. The observation further established that the order of rank does not follow strictly the differences in bodily strength, but that what may be called psychological superiority, such as courage, also plays a great rôle. But it is an established fact that the fear distance is always at work.

The next task was to establish the typical behaviour of the leading birds and of the subjected ones. It seems to be a general rule that those at the top of the hierarchy are more benevolent than those who are in the middle of the social scale. It seems that when the rank of the leading bird is once established, it does not need to fight any more to maintain its position. The psychological fear distance has been established and is stable. But the birds in the middle of the hierarchy are very aggressive, as they are anxious to maintain their position, which is permanently threatened on two fronts.

The next task which the observers had set themselves was to find out how the same bird behaves in changing conditions. If you take a cock which is the leader of one group and put it in a group where it becomes one of the 'middle class' individuals, it changes its behaviour. Instead of being benevolent it becomes aggressive. Obviously it is anxious to keep its position. On the other hand, if you take a leading animal of a big group and make it the leading animal of a small group, it behaves more benevolently than it did as leader of the big group. This observation seems to make it very likely that behaviour

49

depends more on social position than on inherent character.

The observers then tried to find the rule of social distance and social ranking among school children. They found that in a class of school children there is to be found a definite hierarchy, which does not coincide at all with the valuation of the school teacher, but is the outcome of the group life of the children.

If you take the leader of one group of children and put him into another group where he belongs to the 'middle class', his behaviour changes. Thus, amongst school children too, behaviour seems to depend on the social position of the individual as well as upon the so-called character, which seems to be to a great extent the result of varying social situations.

It is obvious that there are certain general tendencies inherent in group life as such, which work in the same direction, although they are altered by the mental equipment of the living beings composing the group. One of the main differences between animal behaviour and human behaviour in groups seems to consist in the fact that animals are incapable of organised action leading to revolutionary change. Only individual rebellion exists in animal groups. The subjected bird often improves its position by new fighting, mainly in cases in which the subjection was not due to bodily inferiority but to psychological fear which can be overcome. Observing such fights, one can see that the subjected animal is very excited, it attempts to overcome the traditional and established attitude of subjection, to overcome the fear distance. Révész, another student of animal sociology, observed the behaviour of caged monkeys. In the cage observed by him there were one leading animal, four weaker monkeys and one baby monkey. When food was brought to the cage there arose first an impulsive scramble, but this behaviour gave way very soon to a situation in which the strongest monkey was able to satisfy himself, without obstacle, as the first of the monkeys. The weaker monkeys driven by hunger made attempts to grab the food also, but suddenly seeming to remember the outcome of former fights and the beating to which they were subjected by the leading animal, they began to flee towards the opposite end of the cage. After this the baby monkey came forward and placing himself quite near to the leading animal started eating the bananas peacefully without being beaten by the tyrant. As long as the baby does not interfere with the competition of the other animals, he will be a privileged animal. But, the first time he participates in the competition he will be subjected to the same fate as the other competing animals. It seems that in every typical situation a certain distance again and again reproduces itself among the animals. The spatial distance contains here, at the same time, a distance of fear and respect; the objective space tends to be correlated to us with qualities of mental distancing.

The German expression *drei Schritt von Leib* (three steps from the body) used to characterise the attitude of keeping one's distance, expresses well a state of society in which spatial distance expresses at the same time fear and respect. One pace is the normal distance between members of a society. A distance of three paces is being imposed on persons outside the dominant 'group' as a mark of subordinate status in rigidly hierarchical societies. This is over-distancing and it can be opposed to under-distancing which is an expression of intimacy. Intimacy is correlated to a close, physical contact into which the individuals are brought—here again mere objective space tends to be correlated with qualities of mental distancing.

During the process of differentiation more complex types of distancing emerge from the fear distance; for instance, the power distance. The conventional distance which has grown up in a society strictly in response to the need for personal safety, has developed in many societies into a symbol of power relationships and into a fixed impression of the hierarchy of social rank.

We have to distinguish three kinds of distancing: distancing which guarantees the maintenance of a given social order and hierarchy; existential distancing, and self distancing, that is, creation of distance within a single personality.

4. MAINTAINING SOCIAL HIERARCHY

The hierarchical structure of a social order, the existence of social classes and estates is, in most cases, supported by a definite kind of distancing. The distancing apparent in social intercourse and in the selection of cultural objects belonging to that society, maintains a social stratification by mental means which tend to replace force. A very sophisticated system of dress and manners, speech, deportment and conventions can serve to keep up distance between the ruling groups and the subjected ones. The hidden task of this system is to create distance and thus to preserve the power of the ruling minority.

Distancing expresses itself by moulding social intercourse and by distancing certain objects in the cultural surroundings of a given society. Social intercourse can be moulded in two ways: first by limiting or excluding the co-operation between two groups (for instance, the prohibition of intermarriage, or of eating at one table), second by working out a sophisticated system of usages which accentuates distance between the different strata of society.

By a sudden integration of the subjected majority every ruling group could be overthrown. Therefore, the principle of divide and rule is usually followed by the ruling group and if successful it assures the stability of the system. But not only social intercourse within each social stratum and between the different social strata is guided by distancing; the objects of the social and cultural environment are distanced in the same way. If we look at different societies and ask ourselves what can be distanced, we find that both man (like the leader and the king) and objects (like relics) can be. In primitive societies, for instance, the divine character of the leader, of the chief or of the king is due largely to the elaborate ceremonial which surrounds him and separates him from his subjects. The figure of a saint, on the other hand, becomes a relic mainly by elevating it spatially and thus isolating it from the worshippers. Further, sentences, sayings and proverbs can be separated from common use by incantation, like sentences taken from a sacred text by a priest. One can isolate institutions and organisations or spheres of life and activity, like art or holidays.

There is a similarity between the distancing of social intercourse and the distancing of the objects of the cultural surroundings. The artificial heightening of certain values, and the distancing of certain everyday habits sustain the same system. The ideals of chivalry (such as heroism, courtesy, large-mindedness) elevate and isolate certain behaviour patterns and raise demands which cannot be satisfied by the average man. Thus they have the same social function as the distancing at work in social intercourse.

Democratic evolution is characterised by the tendency either to diminish distancing or to change the methods of distancing. Whilst in pre-democratic society strict rules determined the dresses which could be worn by different ranks, democratic society replaced the old system by 'fashion'. Deportment and intercourse became freer. A process of levelling up and levelling down developed and free self-expression replaced, to a great extent, the traditional regulated ceremonial.

The inhibition of free self-expression can also serve as a means of social distancing. Thus, the higher ranks can constrain themselves to preserve a certain kind of deportment or dignity.

5. EXISTENTIAL DISTANCING

This kind of distancing can be observed if we rule out all acts of distancing which have a social origin. That there exists a certain form of distancing other than the social kinds can be shown by the following example: if a woman of a humble social status visits a priest for the sake of confession, he is for her not a specific person but a personality representing an elevated social status. But, at the same time, she may be affected by her closeness to or remoteness from his purely personal self, the man as she experiences him. It is this last distance which we can call *existential distance*. But these two kinds of distance are usually confused. The social mask and the personal, existential character usually act simultaneously. The democratising process, as a rule, tends to diminish social distance and uncover the purely existential relationships between men.

Existential difference denotes a relationship between individuals which arises exclusively from the qualities of the inner spirit of man. It can be observed when somebody becomes suddenly aware of a sympathy with another human being and he establishes, so to say, an immediate contact with his innermost nature. This inevitable existential distance is that which remains after all social distancing has been forgotten. Existential distance was for a long time obscured in most societies by social distance, as for example in caste societies, and it is the rise of individualism which has torn the social mask finally from the person.

6. THE CREATING OF DISTANCE WITHIN A SINGLE PERSONALITY

An individual can be near or far from his own essential being, in the same way as he can be near or far from the essence of another person. We can observe within an individual the phenomenon of being far from one's self, suddenly gaining possession of one's self and being self-estranged. The democratic age has undermined the range of social distances but has thereby accentuated the existential distance to a greater extent. Self-estrangement, which in certain cultural climates is inescapable, restrains the self-expression of the individual. Sudden gaining possession of one's self is the experience of which religious mystics or inspired artists like Dostoievsky often give a moving description.

Distancing is a most important factor in the transmutation of the power structure into mental and cultural patterns. History shows that changes in the style of culture are closely linked with changes in the power structure. The sociology of culture has to deal with these problems in a more detailed way and has to find out how the various historical kinds of power organisation react upon the various forms of mental distance.

CHAPTER IV

B. Isolation

1. THE SOCIAL FUNCTIONS OF ISOLATION

Isolation is the marginal situation of social life. It is a situation deprived of social contacts. The simplest forms of isolation are created by barriers, like mountains, inland seas, oceans or deserts. Natural barriers create very often a protective kind of isolation. Both groups and individuals can be isolated and in both cases the most important consequences of isolation are individualisation and retardation.

Every individual and every group once excluded from connection with other individuals or other groups tends to develop into an individual or a community which deviates from the others. That is to say it goes its own way; it adjusts itself only to its peculiar conditions, without exchanging influences and impressions with other individuals or groups. In consequence of a lack of contacts with others, the individual or group does not know of the evolution of other persons or social units. A phenomenon which we call disproportionate evolution emerges in this way. Social contacts act rather like contacts between physical objects with a different degree of heat. The contact of materials equalises the respective heats of the objects and they all tend to get the same degree of heat. Something similar happens to social classes. Frequent contacts between the aristocracy and the middle classes tend to make them, in many respects, similar, or at least decreases the dissimilarity existing between them.

On the other hand, isolation and distancing increase their original differences and individualise them. You can see this happening in rural communities which are isolated by mountains or marshes, and also in individuals who withdraw from others and seclude themselves. They all become 'peculiar'.

One must recall at this point that isolation operates already within the process of zoological evolution, and contributes to the creation of the various species. Adaptation of species is intimately connected by specialised organic adaptation to varied geographic conditions. Something similar can be observed in group life and evolution. For instance, if a unified, wandering, nomadic group settles down on a given territory and the result of this settlement is that the various sub-groups separate from each other and remain without contact for a long time, both their habits and their speech will start to differentiate. That is how dialects arise, in a way which is very similar to the arising of species and variation in animal life. Thus, individualisation and specialisation are one of the possible consequences of isolation.

The other possible consequence is retardation. Obviously a certain amount of isolation is necessary to every kind of individualisation. The individual must sometimes withdraw from society, withdraw into himself, if his personality is to be preserved from dissolution and is to retain its wholeness, but if the individual completely separates himself from society, a retardation of his evolution can be expected.

Similarly, the establishment of a successful race or stock of animals requires an alternation of periods of inter-breeding (the so-called endogamy) in which periods the characters are fixed, and periods of outbreeding (exogamy) in which the fresh blood is being introduced.

Sects living for hundreds of years isolated among people of another culture are an example of the rule that isolation promotes the stability of types. On the other hand, the mixture of different stocks which takes place for instance in North America, shows that lack of a certain isolation creates a great variety and instability of types. As already mentioned the essence of social isolation is the diminution of contacts. In this section we have reduced the complex forms of isolation to elementary processes. Our next task is to discover what are the various causes which create isolation and to detect what consequences may arise from the various forms of isolation.

2. THE VARIOUS KINDS OF SOCIAL ISOLATION

We distinguish two main types of isolation: spatial isolation and organic isolation. *Spatial isolation* can be external, an enforced deprivation of contacts, as happens when somebody is banished from his community or imprisoned. As a result, the individual will be deprived of the protection of his group, or, in the case of an animal, his herd. It is very significant that the masculine leading animal, if detached from the herd, is known by hunters to be extremely dangerous. He becomes more easily aggressive and is then much more wild than animals which remain in contact with the herd. Somewhat similarly, the banished, the imprisoned and to some extent, also, the outsiders of society, show a greater propensity for anti-social behaviour. It is interesting that in German the word for 'miserable' and the word for living in a foreign country have a similar root. Anti-social behaviour, sometimes even thirst for vengeance, is the typical mental consequence of imprisonment in solitary confinement, which is an extreme form of enforced seclusion. Many well-meaning people, influenced exclusively by traditional, religious and moral views, hoped at the beginning of the nineteenth century, that solitary confinement and loneliness would improve the character of convicts and would facilitate their conversion. The consequences, however, were in most cases melancholic mental states, sexual abnormalities, sometimes even hallucinations and usually anti-social behaviour. The explanation for this is simple: the adjustment to the conditions of imprisonment imply, for most individuals, to become unaccustomed to society and social life and just this creates anti-social attitudes.

By *organic isolation* we mean symptoms of isolation which are caused not by externally imposed privation of contacts but by certain organic defects of the individual, such as blindness or deafness. The essential consequences of such defects are the lack of certain experiences common to all healthy men. Beethoven expressed this forcefully when he said: 'My deafness forces me to live in exile.' The consequences of the organic defects are very similar to social defects such as shyness, mistrust, inferiority or superiority feelings and pedantry. These social distortions are either the consequence and symptom of previous isolation, or they themselves create partial isolation. The consequence of such lack of experiences are that the deaf, the blind and the shy seldom get complete answers from normal people, that they are handicapped in every kind of public communication, that they become suspicious, distrustful and irritable and thus they have also less chance to choose their friends and comrades among those who are suited to them. We can then speak of 'lack of associations by choice' and the further result of this is a narrowed range of people with whom one can develop intellectual potentialities. All this may lead to resignation: the individual may give up the hope of obtaining a normal position and place in life or might even become a broken personality who accepts his role of imagined inferiority. Another frequent outcome of such a situation is compensation or even overcompensation for the disability, and a superiority complex might thus develop. Such a person might feel that 'nobody is good enough for me'.

Closely connected with these complexes is pedantry. The pedant is usually a person who only feels himself safe if he is under secure, reliable guidance, for instance under the harmonious shelter of home-like circumstances. Orderliness and cleanliness may mean for such people a protection against unforeseen frictions, collisions and criticism. Pedantry is mostly a symptom behind which there is a fear of coming into unexpected situations. So the pedant tries to define each situation in his own way. His precision has often been considered as a distorted form of scholarship. What distinguishes the pedant is the psychological compulsion, the inflexibility of mind and sympathy of which the exactitude is a fetish symptom.

Shyness is, in sociological terms, a kind of partial isolation which arises from an inability to make adequate responses in certain spheres of life. It is mostly a consequence of psychic shock suffered during childhood. This shock often occurs at the very moment when the child leaves the sphere of family and neighbourhood relationships and penetrates into the realm of secondary contacts. A kind of trauma, a psychic lesion, is the consequence of such a step, and chronic disturbance of the personality is observable. However, the seeds of shyness are to be sought in the familiar relationships during the first few years of life.

Shyness, arising at first only occasionally, tends to be later habitualised and can create all the symptoms of partial isolation. Early stages of such disturbances of the social abilities can be discovered in very young children, and later can appear as a general anxiety about meeting new situations. Such feelings arise, for instance, before examinations or even in the classroom when the child is afraid that he will be unable to answer unexpected questions. If this attitude becomes transferred to a later stage of development, it can hinder the normal decisiveness of the individual. An unbalanced personality very often attempts to compensate himself in some way or another, if the usual family support disappears, by outbursts of feelings, the seeking of tenderness, sudden strong attachments to other people, and by other similar intense expressions of emotion.

Another kind of partial isolation arises when a normal ability to make social contacts cannot find a suitable surrounding needed to elicit responses. As an example we can quote the situation of the spinster and the bachelor—celibacy is sometimes the consequence of shyness. Personalities in such situations will seek for some satisfaction for the losses which they may experience in their personal and social lives, by finding a career of social usefulness, by friendship, if they can face it, by spiritual discipline, or perhaps by keeping pets and preserving a general sentimentalism.

3. FORMS OF PRIVACY

Privacy itself also represents a certain type of partial isolation. Privacy implies that the sphere of our inner experience is protected from being affected by social contact. Modern man often attempts to withdraw part of his inner self from public control. Here we can speak of the privacy of our inner self.

We can see a similar development on the social and political plane when we observe how the modern liberal state refrains from interfering with the privacy of the individual, in so far as it abstains from regulating or controlling private conscience, private convictions and private feelings, or when, in the modern city, we see a protection of the private life of the citizens from the public view. The life of the village does not know either internal or external privacy. In a village, or a primitive community, personal intimacy and public life are not so strongly opposed to one another as in the modern city. With the home life and problems of a peasant usually the whole village is concerned. Public control penetrates into every hidden nook of the life of the families of the individual. Why is this so? Obviously because in primitive communities the range of activities of the single individual is connected with the scope of activities of the whole community. Social separation, the withdrawal of one's personality, is, in such groups, extremely difficult. The guild of the medieval cities was equally able to control most of the external and internal activities of its individual members, such as the expressions of religious belief, their professional activities, the forms of sociability, their artistic activities, their funeral ceremonies. Modern organisations, like professional associations or corporations, touch only certain limited spheres of the individual. The possibility of escape into privacy is here much greater and by escaping, modern man successfully isolates one part of his inner self. This isolation means a strengthening of individualisation.

The religious movements, Protestantism and Puritanism, represent a tendency to transform public religion into private religion and to keep certain parts of the inner self safe from external interference. Puritanism also reflects the tendency to deprecate publicity and to increase the estimation of our private inner experiences. This process of creating privacy starts—like most of the inner transformations—with external changes, such as the separation of the home from the workshop or of the home from the office. The burghers of the later Middle Ages and of the Renaissance, becoming richer, could provide for every member of the family a room for his own use. These are the main external circumstances which create a set of attitudes and feelings which we call private. This is one of the forms of individualisation.

We must, here, clearly distinguish between attitudes connected with primary contacts, sympathetic contacts (such as intimacy) and attitudes connected with privacy. Privacy is a kind of isolation within the realm of the family or within other primary groups. It is a way of escape in a social group where the group control is very near to the individual. Privacy is an important aid in the creation of individualisation; it nurtures the tendency to internal individualisation. One of the main consequences of privacy is the creation of a double standard of norms, both of legal norms and of the moral norms of the conscience. But another consequence is the emergence of a double standard in the experience of time. Speaking of time here we do not mean chronological time, which can be measured with the help of an objective scale, but the way we are *aware* of time in our inner experience.

Our inner experience of time is mostly orientated on collective experiences. As long as we are intimately and firmly connected with our fellow beings through common aims, the tension invested in these common strivings differentiates time in a collective way for every participant. People acting together in order to bring about the same collective result measure the time according to their common activities. The articulation of events, even of time, was orientated originally on these common purposes. But privacy separates certain experiences of the individual from the community and the inner experiences become separated from the outer world. As a consequence, inner time is separated from the time of the community. It must also be remembered that disproportionate evolution creates individualised and inward experiences. Because these are private and personal, they are not equalised or levelled. The careful discrimination of experiences, connected with introversion is the source of subjective poetry and of subjectivism generally.

The danger of an excessive privacy is that it may lead to a split in the personality. The inner world of privacy and the world of common activities lose their inner connection and the person then lives in two separate worlds. Kretschmer and Sheldon have this schizoid response as characteristic of one of their psychological 'types'.

Privacy has, of course, also a productive significance for

culture if it represents not an absolute but only a partial isolation. This valuable aspect of privacy was observed by the organisers of the religious monastic movement. The cell of the monk is a means of artificially creating external conditions which favour privacy. Those who live in such cells are 'cloistered'. The regulations of the monastic orders contain the advice to avoid external contacts. The cell and these regulations helped to create artificially homogeneous fields of experience. The same aim is being furthered by the monastic regulations relating to work and leisure. It is here that we must look for one of the origins of subjective religious feeling. Such feeling is one of the early forms of inner individualisation fostered by privacy.

CHAPTER V

C. Individualisation

Privacy is only one of the forms of individualisation. There is a great variety of social forces which operate in such a way that they foster individualisation, and there are according to these various and diverging external forces, many forms of individualisation, by which I mean those social processes which tend to make the individual more or less independent of his group and to create in him a self-consciousness of his own.

In analysing how the processes of individualisation work two misconceptions must be corrected. The first is that individualisation is a process carried through solely by the individual himself. This is based on the assumption that a man frees himself completely or less completely from the influence of his group by the exercise of mental qualities alone. The second misconception is based on the assumption that individualisation is primarily a mental or spiritual process which is being spread through the prevailing ideas of a time or place. If historians, for instance, deal with the Renaissance, they collect sentences which prove that a new estimation of individuality has arisen at a certain time and within certain circles, and then show that these ideas were successively accepted later by other groups and other individuals. The task of the sociologist is not merely to observe that such ideas exist at certain times but to investigate *how* these ideas came to exist. We ask ourselves what the social forces were which engendered them in a smaller circle and which set of social influences prepared a larger group of people to accept them.

Ideas do not by themselves create individualisation. They are usually merely the mental expressions of the process of individualisation for which ground was prepared by social changes which were tending in this direction. Within the medium of such a new social texture expressed ideas do strengthen and decisively mould the new situation, but they do not create it. When I say that in every social situation there is a set of social forces with an individualising tendency at work, I am aware that certain periods such as the Renaissance or the period of eighteenth-century rationalism and nineteenth-century liberalism favour individualisation to a much greater extent than others.

In order not to confuse the various kinds of individualisation, I shall start by distinguishing their different forms and shall try to discover those particular social forces which favour each of these forms of individualisation.

I distinguish four main aspects of individualisation. Each of them can be further sub-divided.

The four main aspects are:

1. individualisation as a process of becoming different from other people.

2. individualisation on the level of new forms of self-regarding attitudes: either by becoming aware of one's unique and specific character, or by a new kind of self-evaluation or organisation of the self.

3. individualised relationships through objects: individualisation of the wishes.

4. individualisation as a kind of deepening into ourselves, that is a kind of introversion, which implies receiving into our experience of ourselves and sublimating the individualising forces around and within us. This can also be described as the disclosure of an inner dimension in man's life.

The four main aspects are therefore: becoming different; the rise of a new kind of valuation of our specific

66

character; individualisation through objects; and the introduction of the individualising forces. These four processes are entirely different phenomena.

1. INDIVIDUALISATION AS A PROCESS OF BECOMING DIFFERENT

The external differentiation of types and individuals leads to the formation of new groups in which these new characteristics can be commonly expressed. The emergence of such groups is accelerated by the division of labour and by the division of functions, the latter leading to the development of professional characteristics. Such new groups permit more or less individuality in their members, according to the intensity and volume of internal organisation and regulation. Compare, for example, the difference between the labour of the craftsman and of the operative in the factory. In the former the artisan works with his own tools, and the labour is more individualised. In the factory there tends to be an impersonal régime of labour rules. A further social factor conducing to the external differentiation of types and of individuals results from lack of contacts, when people thus isolated have eventually to adapt to varied conditions.

In old Chinese society, regulated by Confucianism, the conduct of man in all his relations was fixed. In domestic life, for instance, the rules of behaviour of the son towards the father or of the wife towards the husband or of the younger brother towards the elder brother were fixed. This of course influences both the opportunities open to the members of the group and their reality sense. On the other hand, democratisation in the broadest sense, political, economic and pedagogic, works powerfully in the direction of making spontaneous and untraditional action necessary. Free competition also compels the individual to adapt himself to his own peculiar situation, to seize the initiative and not to wait for commands or refer to rules. It is especially the small social unit, if it is organised in a democratic way, which favours the growth of personality. Such small social units were the canton states of central Switzerland, the free medieval commune, the sect. Similarly, democratically organised educational groups like the medieval universities facilitated individual efforts and decisions.

An obvious example of the facing of an unpatterned situation can be seen in the case of pioneers or merchant adventurers, who leave their original group with the aim of conquering new territory or creating new markets, or even when a young man or woman leaves the protection of the family to earn a livelihood in a new place. But competition within the group compels each person to act according to his individual interest and to re-interpret his own situation.

The process of individualisation is further fostered by the increase of social mobility, especially of vertical mobility which enables a person to rise in the social scale as an individual and not only as a member of his group. In this situation it is necessary for his success to free himself from group prejudice, though maybe later he adopts the prejudice of another group. Horizontal mobility, to be seen for instance in the wandering individual, implies the need for him to give up the old small group viewpoint. However, in this case, it may be impossible for him to identify himself wholly with the new group and in this way he is forced to find his own independent view. If you join an opposition group, you lose your original viewpoint and seek to learn and adopt another.

The situation of being an outsider, whether relative or absolute, has a similar individualising effect. Examples of a relative outsider are the neglected son of a family or the leader of an oppositional minority within a group, whereas absolute outsiders are outcasts, unassimilated aliens, banished exiles. The early life of Hitler, Lenin, Trotsky or Stalin shows many outsider situations.

The last social situation to be mentioned in connection with individualisation as a process of becoming different, is the escape from the social control of one group to that of another. In each group there is something different contributed and learned by the same person in company with different people forming different kinds of group— a family, a play group, a club, a university class. Thus a widened circle of contact can offer a more varied experience on which individualisation may develop with greater flexibility.

2. INDIVIDUALISATION ON THE LEVEL OF SELF-REGARDING ATTITUDES

From one point of view an individualised personality consists in becoming aware of our specific character and in the rise of a new kind of self-evaluation. Thus, the organisation of the self proceeds as forms of self-evaluation arise. Striking examples of this process can be found in history where the worship of the mighty personality creates a certain type of individualisation. The pre-conditions of this process are: a strict differentiation and distance of the leading *élites*; the organisation of the group in such a way as to provide for certain circles a chance to become despotic; the existence of the isolated milieu of a court where the despot can have the illusion of being powerful if not almighty. These are the preconditions for the making of a tyrant, resting upon physical power and spiritual coercion (often based on an attitude to his putative magical qualities) together with power deriving from land, property or money, and finally from prestige and glory.

A similar process can be observed in a more moderate form and in a narrow circle if a child becomes the tyrant of a family. We see in both cases the domination of narcissistic impulses in the person of the despot, and this is accepted by his group.

A feeling of the uniqueness of one's life and character can be found at the origin of the cult of the autobiography. Its growth in the latest period of the Roman Empire is intimately connected with the emergence of the feeling that one's life and character are unique. But the origin of this feeling might be investigated even earlier in the death records of oriental despots. In this early stage of individualism, self-evaluation is founded on letting other people feed one's own sense of power by showing fear and respect. Examples of such self-glorification can be found in the annals of Assurbanipal (885–860 B.C.): 'I am the King. I am the Lord. I am the Sublime. I am the Great, the Strong; I am the Famous; I am the Prince, the Noble, the War Lord. I am a Lion. . . . I am God's own appointed. I am the unconquerable weapon, which lays the land of the enemies in ruins. I captured them alive and stuck them on poles; I coloured the mountain like wool with their blood. From many of them I tore off the skin and covered the walls with it. I built a pillar of still living bodies and another pillar of heads. And in the middle I hang their heads on vines. . . . I prepared a colossal picture of my royal personage, and inscribed my might and sublimity on it. . . . My face radiates on the ruins. In the service of my fury I find my satisfaction.'

Passing to the latest period of the Roman Empire and to the autobiography of stoic philosophers and statesmen we can point to the social situation favouring the strength of the feeling of uniqueness. We can point to the weakness of the organisation of the great society, and to the disrupted state of the empire, and connected with these the possibility for individuals to rise within the social scale. The weakness of the great organisation was such that its norms vanished away. We see here the dissolution of the ideals of the *polis*.

3. THE INDIVIDUALISATION OF THE WISHES THROUGH OBJECTS

In establishing the direction and constancy of feeling toward people and objects (what psychoanalysts call libido fixations or *kathexes*) the traditional attitudes and the durability of the primary groups are decisive. The peasant and the landed aristocrat are much more settled in their wishes than the rich mobile type of the city. The first seeks for a definite kind of wish fulfilment, whereas the second type has a standard in his attitude in so far as he wants to buy one thing or a certain kind of goods, but likes to vary the probabilities within these limits. His range of choice is likely to be wider and his actual choices more varied. Many factors increase the wish for sudden and individual choice—such as wealth, which creates the possibility of variations, or the process of modern production and distribution which favours individual competition and the man who is first in the field with a new idea; however, large scale industry which stimulates buying, also attempts to standardise consumer's choice. Besides these, there is social mobility, both horizontal (for instance, migration) and vertical (movements up and down the social scale), which tends to loosen the ties which bind the individual to specific wishes.

We might consider at this point some of the forms of the wish to possess. We can distinguish two: first, the attitude of possession toward single objects with definite libido fixation: second, libido fixation on abstract objects—for example, money, equality. Further, there are two kinds of wish attitudes to consider in connection with possessiveness—striving for a fixed object and striving for variety. In this latter case the libido fixed upon an object is, in a measure, shifted from the object to the choice itself. As examples of libido being fixed upon specific objects, we can quote the attachment of a peasant to his favourite pipe or to his favourite dishes at meal times, or to the landscape in which he moves. In all these cases the peasant is personally linked to his own property or to his personal situation. In the second case, where libido is fixed not so much upon objects but more upon the choice itself, we can quote the attitudes of those who follow fashion, of the liberal, or of the individualist in the competitive society. But even liberals and anarchists can have wishes for some anchorage in specific objects or people.

The strictly individualised libido fixation is shaped by the small family. For instance, libido fixation toward the mother and the father figures is greater in certain types of family than in others. In the primitive group-family, every child has several mothers and fathers, as in such families all mothers of the same age group are called mother by the child. In small monogamous families, the fixation is stronger and there is a deeply furrowed love of a mother observable in families with one child which is conspicuous if one compares it with families in which there are say ten children.

One of the main sources of individualised libido influencing notions of both unique personal and more general idealised love can be found here. Romantic love can only be explained in connection with introversion.

4. INDIVIDUALISATION AS A KIND OF INTROVERSION

By individualisation we understand a deepening of the personality; what could be called introjection. Its stages may be traced. The stage of estrangement, of becoming solitary, is characterised by the fact that the individual withdraws into himself his libidinous energy. We find this often in big cities where unfriendliness is felt and confusion is caused, and generally when the community loses its expressive force, when for instance forms of worship and ceremonies lose their collective and individual significance. The loss of the range of activities, the limitations of the possibilities of shared emotional expression, all contribute to estrangement, introjection and inwardness and to an introversion of the sublimating energies. This process combined with the emergence of individualised love makes romantic love possible.

There develops then an acceptance of privacy, partial isolation, as a means of escaping external control, as another form of individualisation connected with introversion. The predominance of introspection is also one of these forms. In the circumstances of social and cultural mobility when sudden inner readjustments become necessary, such introspective moods usually appear especially in personalities who have leisure time combined with privacy. Harmonious cultivation of the whole personality is the form of individualisation favoured by such people, who deal with things not specifically but as showing the variety and unity of experience at once. For such people, the social distance from the sphere of labour and social struggle results in a reduction of subservience to the power or finality of external facts. The great artists of the Renaissance, the writers and scientists of the seventeenth and eighteenth centuries, and some English thinkers of the nineteenth century, show these attitudes.

D. Individualisation and Socialisation

Where self-consciousness is dominant there is always a possibility of a predominance either of ourselves or of the self of the other person. If we say a person is selfish or self-centred, we think of him as being less able to see things and relations from someone else's viewpoint. Such a person has not wholly come through the first phase of social consciousness in which we see things only in their relationships to us. For example, children without brothers or sisters become very often especially self-centred. They are not socialised enough. By socialisation we understand a process which is the opposite of individualisation: it is a process of the expansion of the self. The expanding self follows certain lines which may be called the social access to the expansion of the self.

Sociologists have designated these various forms of expansion by symbolic terms such as the following:

The spheric self, which incorporates persons chiefly according to their propinquity. Persons in whom this aspect of self commonly appears care most for those they see most often, for instance their neighbours, and care little for those who are below their visual horizon. But reading, travel, city life and social stratification may stretch the radius of personality activities and thus are unfavourable for the development of this spheric self.

The linear self keeps to the family line, ranging back among ancestors and forward among anticipated descendants. It prompts a man to sacrifice much in order not to dishonour his forefathers or handicap his posterity. Family feeling is here a rival to wider social feeling.

The flat self emerges if social feelings are confined to the members of one's own social stratum. This horizontal socialisation weakens the barriers of jealousy which exist between neighbourhoods, parishes and provinces, but on the other hand creates new ones. Whilst hostile communities can avoid trouble by having little to do with one another, hostile social classes cannot avoid contacts and thus eliminate frictions in such a simple way.

The vein self. In big democratic cities, friendships and fellowships have a tendency to follow occupational lines. For instance, newspaper men identify themselves with and meet mostly other newspaper men. The fact that they are competitors is overshadowed by the community of interests they all possess. Those who do not love their own calling and profession overmuch may follow a non-professional line of private interest.

The star self. The expanding self will, in some cases, get into sympathy with various sorts of people following up several veins. Thus arises the star self which radiates into various planes. As examples, we can point to the personalities of Goethe, Albert Schweitzer and Bertrand Russell.

The functional differentiation and complexity of modern society favour the development of the star self. The great number of matters calling for team work put a premium on the spheric self.

It is a future task of sociologists and teachers to find out which social situations foster the expansion of the self according to these and various other social axes.

However, it is important to stress that these terms must not be hypostatised into separable 'selves'. They have a limited practical usefulness for the sociologist. The profound question exists behind all such analysis, what is the nature of the self to which the processes of individualisation and socialisation have contributed?

CHAPTER VI

E. Competition and Monopoly

One of the most important social forces is competition. We can classify social forces into two groups: those which foster co-operation and those which compel people to act against one another, opposing each other. The main social force aiding people to act against one another is struggle. Struggle can be defined as a social relationship in which we wish to compel another person or a group by force to act according to our will. Hereby the resistance of the latter is to be overcome. Competition on the other hand can be considered as a kind of peaceful struggle and can be defined as a peaceful striving of several individuals or groups for the same good.

Competition, like struggle, is a universal category of life—in biology we speak about a struggle for life—and it is a general category of social life. Many people believe that competition is a purely economic phenomenon mainly represented by barter. But nothing could be more wrong than this limitation of the meaning of the word. The principle of competition is equally at work when any kind of race takes place, the common end being for each of several competitors to try to reach the goal first. But there is also competition when two different scientific schools attempt to solve the same problem, or if two men wish to marry the same woman. It is important to see that these different things all belong together because competition is at work in all these fields. Economic competition belongs to the same field—and in this connection it again becomes clear that economics is bound up with sociology.

Looking into the history of the idea of competition, it is interesting to note that the principle of competition was first observed in economics and was later transferred to the sphere of biology. Adam Smith and the Physiocrats were the first to work out a systematic account of competition. For them freedom and competition were necessary elements in the harmony of interests. Malthus, in his *Essay on the Principle of Population*, published in 1798, stated the discouraging view that there is a general tendency for the human population to increase in geometrical progression and for the fruits of nature to grow only in an arithmetical progress. It was Charles Darwin who in 1859 transferred the idea of competition to the biological sphere. He considered the life of living beings as a struggle for existence and came to the conclusion that this struggle urges the individual living organism to adjust himself to his peculiar situation. Thus Darwin, who was impressed by Malthus's *Essay*, developed the principle of natural selection by struggle for life.

It must not be forgotten that the essay of Malthus in its turn was a pessimistic reaction against certain optimistic social theories propounded by Godwin and Condorcet, who believed in the endless perfectibility and natural equality of mankind.

1. THE FUNCTION OF COMPETITION

We distinguish between personal competition and group competition. Although competition is prompted by personal aims, it discharges the social function of selection, especially of assigning to each a place in the social system. The chief alternatives to competition as a means of assigning to each individual his place in the system are the following:

(*a*) The assignment of social status through inheritance. (*b*) The principle of seniority. (*c*) The measurement of ability by forms of graded tests. A planned society and all others which want to minimise competition might choose between these alternatives.

The amount of activity associated with the selection process in any society is an index of the intensity of competition. In a stationary society where, as a rule, children follow the occupation of their fathers, where certain positions are reserved for a limited number of castes; where the system of choice through a process of elections is unknown, a man expends a minimum of energy in finding a place in the social system. The intensity of competition varies with the degree of personal liberty, with the rate of social change and inversely with the nature of the selective agents.

The freer the individual in his choice of better paid or more highly esteemed occupations, the less often one encounters racial, religious or class discriminations, the higher will be the general level of achievement reached by a society.

Social change opens new opportunities to many who in other circumstances would believe themselves to be permanently and definitely settled. An impressive example of this process is the effect of the rising of the automobile industry in the U.S.A., which has in twenty-five years absorbed a million men, very few of whom might have inherited their jobs. The better the selective agencies are, the more economically and accurately are the competitors sifted.

2. SOME CONSEQUENCES OF COMPETITION

Every competitor tries to adjust himself as well as possible to his own peculiar conditions, in order to make the best of them and individualisation is a product of this adjustment in which the personal mentality of an individual reflects the structure of the situation and the peculiarities of the competitors whom he has to meet.

Competition heightens the versatility, the plasticity and the mobility of the individuals who take part in it. It is, in most cases, connected with social mobility. Only if I can move towards the best possible result is competition able to evolve its social potentialities. However, individual competition is an agency which tends to disintegrate group solidarity.

The place where competition originally arose was the market, which originated at the frontier of the tribe, that is, at the place where inter-tribal communication took place. The outlook engendered in this marginal situation penetrated later into the centre of society and the transformation into acquisitive society thus began.

Psychological competition tends to create inferiority feelings. This is a consequence of the means by which competition operates. I distinguish two kinds of inferiority feelings: those which make the individual active, urging him to adapt himself better to his situation (these feelings create new incentives and lead to reorganisation of the human personality); the second kind of inferiority feelings are those which paralyse the forces of the individual and compel him to accept his inferiority. The first kind of inferiority feelings are potential as well as actual, and in most cases are caused by a really free competition, whereas the second group of feelings are mainly fostered by the authoritarian behaviour of those who dominate an individual who is in a weak position.

The questions which emerge here are: Who is your competitor? How do you compensate for your inferiority feelings? Does competition increase your energies or are you meeting such situations by withdrawing yourself? Does competition encourage or discourage you in your efforts?

A minimum of inferiority feeling is often necessary for the discovery of new adjustments needed in new situations. It is the inferiority feeling which creates in the individual an urge to compensate for his inferiority. This mechanism turns a bad performance into a good one in school, in the workshop and so on. But an excessive amount of inferiority feelings paralyses the activity of the individual as it disturbs the balance of his personality and his self-estimation.

There are, of course, also discreditable methods of dealing with one's manageable inferiority feelings. For instance, if, instead of developing our own faculties, we try to handicap our competitors, as when a mediocre leader in a bureaucracy chooses his assistants from among the ungifted and so makes possible the rule of the inferior. Or, again, to denigrate the ideas or personalities of competitors. In this way resentment against heroism or achievement may arise and a less effective group might attempt to incite others against those who are more efficient and successful, as, for instance, when a landed aristocracy seeks to create hostile feelings against industrial 'money-making'. A third and not uncommon way of dealing with our inferiority feelings is to seek for a scapegoat.

3. RESTRICTIONS OF THE METHODS OF COMPETITION

As long as competition works in a constructive way it will urge the individual to increase his personal efforts and incite him to bring about the greatest possible achievement. When competition works most effectively the result can be the selection of the best, both as to the dominant human type and the best performance in work. But there is a possibility that the same principle of free competition can produce just the opposite results and become a tool of a negative selection. Free competition must, therefore, always be accompanied by certain binding rules and accepted standards. The phenomenon of fair play here enters into the plan.

Fair play means that either in a whole society or at

least in one of its strata a certain social control prevails in the form of a standard of behaviour which governs the mentality of the competing individuals. Fair-mindedness can be introduced into competition at school, at games, in business life and in the political struggle. The group accepts, or is at least admonished by some of its members and leaders to accept, a governing social standard, which assures fair play among the competitors. Cooley was one of the first who realised the great social significance of this principle.

Among business competitors it is generally regarded that factory espionage is unfair. Some business men often successfully urge that the practice of local price cutting should be avoided. In the professions, like those of medical practitioners or barristers, it is regarded as unfair to advertise. In the case of elections the buying of votes or the threatening of the voters with reprisals by powerful individuals would be a violation of the principles of fair play. In advanced society nepotism in the case of a public appointment is considered unfair.

The principle of fair play had, of course, an important part in the development of English society and also in the development of the dominant English personality, particularly that complex stereotype 'the English gentleman'.

It would be worthwhile to investigate which social factors bring about and sustain the rule of fair play, and which social forces counteract it. It is probable that both the inner conditions of the competition itself and the general social background in which competition takes place influence the effectiveness of the binding rules. As to the inner conditions of the competition itself, it is quite obvious that a great increase in the number of competitors may be one of the causes of a lowering of standards among the competitors and may induce them to use unfair methods more and more often. The general moral standard of the whole society or of a closed group in it might, on the other hand, act as an agency which puts a brake on the process of competition. Sometimes it may be useful to institutionalise this social control, that is, to set up institutions which might be independent of the competitors and are empowered to control their behaviour. Such institutions might be courts, administrative boards, professional councils, arbitration committees and so on.

The remarks of Davis and Barnes on this subject illustrate the dangers of socially uncontrolled competition. 'Perhaps the greatest objection to the profit motive is that it destroys higher values. There is a sort of Gresham's Law for motivation and for social standards. The worst competitor may drag down the good to his own level or force him to bankruptcy. For example, if southern mills use child labour, northern mills claim they cannot do without it. The bad standards drive out the good, as paper currency drives out gold. . . . . We will have to face the necessity of revolutionising the incentives of our business life away from profits and towards the service of all.'

4. SOCIAL MONOPOLY

One of the typical processes which follows in the wake of evolution of free competition is its turning into its opposite: the emergence of a closed group, possessing monopoly. In order to understand the significance of this very important social phenomenon we must introduce a distinction between the *open group* and the *closed group*. We say that a social relationship or a social group is an *open* one, when nobody is excluded from participation in its activities. We call it a *closed* one when the participation in these activities is bound to certain regulations and when not everybody is allowed to share in these activities. There are groups which are interested in seeing that as many people as possible should join their activities (for instance, political parties). On the other hand, it is more advantageous sometimes to the participants of a group that their membership should be limited. The guilds, at the time of their early beginnings, were interested in being an open group because an increase in their number increased their fighting capacities. Later, when the number of handicraft men seemed to increase to a dangerous degree and the supply of goods rose, they began to be interested in closing their doors to these newcomers.

A *monopoly* means the limiting of the chances of success prevailing in a given social scope of action to a certain limited number of people. The consequences of the closing of a group are immense, as far as the mentality of its members is concerned. People belonging to a closed group behave quite differently from people who are members of an open group. The members of a closed group tend to become narrow-minded, and may become intolerant and hostile to anything which does not fit into the framework of their prejudices. Another typical consequence of the closing of the group is the development of a strongly held *esprit de corps*. The reason for this prevalence of a narrow frame of mind is due mainly to the fact that the lack of fluctuation permits the mentality of a certain type to prevail. Both the individuals and their group tend to lose their faculty of adjustment and a strong traditionalism develops. However, there are cases when the closing of a group may have some advantage. For instance, when a sudden influx of elements of a lower standard threatens the morals and the acquired qualities of a group. The closing of the group may help to preserve these qualities.

The closed group can establish different types of inner organisation. It may either permit or rule out competition within the group. In the first case, a certain improvement of the personal achievement will usually be attained —but it must not surpass the limitations set by the group monopoly or else these must be re-adjusted. In the second case, when competition within the group has been ruled out, the existing chances will be distributed according to rigid rules. For instance, certain consumers will be consigned to certain producers and the profit will be guaranteed according to a certain fixed percentage. In this case, the closed group approaches the type of a bureaucracy.

CHAPTER VII

F. Selection

Every kind of competition and struggle among masses of people leads to a selection of those who have the abilities which are necessary for survival under the given conditions of a free competition. It would be wrong to believe that struggle and social competition always foster and select those who are the best according to an absolute standard of worth. Selection only fosters those qualities and human abilities which correspond to those social tasks and the social conditions in which competition takes place. In war the struggle may select those who are strongest in a physical sense, who are the most efficient among the cruel conditions of fighting. Competition in an election campaign may foster those who have the greatest ability in creating slogans and propagating them with a loud voice. Competition in a special market may select those who are most unscrupulous. Competition within a bureaucracy, or even within the artistic and scientific world, may put those at a premium who are best at pulling strings and discovering influential patrons.

It is very important, therefore, to distinguish between those faculties which are needed for the objective achievement necessary in a society, which may be called the *objective abilities,* and those capacities which are needed to get one's work or personality accepted and acknowledged: these we might call *social abilities.*

Every personal success is built upon the basis of these two kinds of abilities. The successful man who makes his way alone by objective achievement is very rare; he usually needs certain qualities which help him to convince and impress his fellow beings. On the other hand, it is very seldom that social qualities alone without any real achievement lead to success in a field where free social competition rules. It would be very interesting to map out those social abilities and those objective abilities which make for success in the various professions, the branches of business, or the different social strata. Cooley tried to discover those general qualities which are necessary for the attainment of success in any field. He stressed the importance of five qualities: self control, enterprise, perseverance, address and common sense.

Self control. This quality implies steadiness, the power to subordinate passing impulses to a rational rule. Steadiness is a prime command in every social career. It is also a condition of performing work of a standard quality.

Enterprise. By enterprise Cooley understands the disposition to make experiments on life, to try and try again, which, of course, implies a certain degree of aggressiveness. Enterprise means being in the habit of making, so to say, voyages of discovery in order to find out one's proper relations to the world and to find out where opportunities open.

Perseverance. In times of doubt, discouragement has to be overcome. If you overcome lassitude, depression and discouragement, you have perseverance. The inner ambition of reaching a high standard must be organically connected with social ambition. Mental ambitions wholly detached from social ambitions lead to resentment and feelings of frustration; social ambitions detached from the inner ambition of reaching high standards bring about a personality dominated by vanity.

Address. This quality, according to Cooley, is based on sympathetic insight into human nature, guided by intelligence and steadied by coolness. 'It is a faculty that is necessary to everyone in the early part of his career or at times of change in order to make his way through the social medium to the place where he can bring his special abilities into play.'

Common sense. This quality is based on a humanised and symmetrical intelligence and on a just equilibrium of the finer faculties.

Does competition function like a sieve or like a stamping machine? In the first case the individual himself would not be moulded by the selective process, he would only be selected by it and it would depend on the shape of the 'holes of the sieve' which individuals got through the selective agencies and which did not. But if the selective process is like a stamping machine, the selection actively transforms the individual, urges him to use his innate capacities in a definite way. For example, if you talk to a leading personality in a certain branch of industry or of politics in which forceful people are needed, you will notice that he had probably adapted himself to his job by systematically repressing his sympathetic tendencies, otherwise he would be in danger of being ruled out as being temperamentally unsuited to the work. This is an example where the selective agency acts as a stamping machine and not as a sieve. People who possess the qualities necessary for a ruling group are either moulded through 'the stamping machine process' or selected by 'the sieve process' for leading posts. Usually such people bear signs of having been affected by both 'processes', though one or the other is dominant.

G. The Main Effect of Competition and Selection on Mental Life

It is competition and selection that decide which human types, which standards, which thought patterns will be dominant in a given society.

After the victory of national socialism in Germany, many people were astonished that 'the Germans have changed their minds in such a short time'. People who speak in such terms are far from being able to make a proper sociological analysis. Not all Germans changed their minds between 1930 and 1933, but in the very same society different methods of social selection, brought about by competition and struggle, drew out different types of people. If types which were formerly at the bottom of society reach the top of social scales, their ways of thinking and behaving, formerly insignificant, pass for the new prototype of behaviour. Thereupon propaganda and social imitation help to spread this new type of behaviour and this mental pattern. That is the way in which new Germans were being shaped in a short time. Not the same Germans changed, but the selection favoured a new type which later reacted even upon the older type. It is the same mechanism which brings about a change both in mental patterns and in attitudes. It is not the ideas and the thought patterns which compete with one another, but the individuals. With the rise of a new type of individual, a new set of ideas comes to the top.

Competition and selection have two main effects on social life. First, they dissolve every type of isolation and close group-integration. The isolation and exclusiveness of local units (like farms or villages) change when they begin to participate in the great process of industrial, commercial and political competition. All the symptoms of isolation and many of the habits of stabilised traditional mentality are ruled out in a short time. Second, although competition dissolves the former stable stratification of a society, it tends at the same time to create a new stratification. One of the results of an intensive selection is the segregation of the weak. In the slums of great cities, for instance, we find those segregated who were the unfittest from the standpoint of a certain selection; for example, people lacking incentive and activity, the feeble-minded, but also those who were too soft-hearted and sentimental to maintain themselves in the struggle for existence; or those who were born there with an unequal chance in the social selection which is always in process.

The segregated group in turn again becomes isolated and soon unfolds its own mentality: the effects of isolation are again at work.

H. Co-operation and the Division of Labour

Whereas competition is a force which compels people to act against one another, co-operation is an integrating activity. Like-mindedness, sympathy, mutual helpfulness are the most important integrating forces. Like-mindedness alone does not integrate people for a long period. If you want to stabilise the integration you must have a common external purpose.

1. THE PURPOSES OF CO-OPERATION

The most ancient and frequent motive of union has been co-operation in fighting the enemy. Here two kinds of integration can be distinguished: fighting co-operation can be based on attack, but can also be based on defence. For instance, the predatory invasions of migrating nomads drew them into large loose unions. Somewhat similar was the union of the Israelites when they made their way into the land of Canaan. Such unions are, of course, temporary, because attack is usually optional. On the other hand, defence is imperative and creates therefore more lasting unions. The fear of being attacked by a powerful enemy is the master-builder of big, permanent unions. It was not the conquest of the land of Canaan which welded the tribes of Israel into a kingdom under Saul and David, but it was their wars with the neighbouring peoples. Another example is furnished by the rise of the Italian mercantile city states in medieval times. Genoa or Venice came into being chiefly in order to protect their trade from piracy and to maintain so-called consuls in the Levant who had the task of looking after their commercial interests.

A further important motive for co-operation was, in the early periods of history, the need to control the waters of great rivers. The early appearance of the despotic states of the Nile, of the Euphrates and of the Ganges, sprang from the necessity of maintaining irrigation ditches and reservoirs.

Another common enterprise is the construction of public works. The early city builders in Babylonia were tillers of the soil who provided themselves primarily with a stronghold and only secondarily with a market place. The essential instrument of such a sheltering stronghold was, of course, the wall.

Economic co-operation, particularly under primitive conditions, does not lead to large groups but gives rise to an infinity of small undertakings, such as the collective hunting of gregarious animals like the buffalo or the hunting of formidable animals like the elephant or the whale, or the providing of common protection for herds against predatory beasts, or the common mowing of the meadows owned by the village community.

Religious worship developed into a community affair rather early in history. It seems that the primitive agricultural tribes felt insecure unless the gods who were supposed to make their crops thrive became established as the permanent and principal members of the community. Hence, the covenant by which in return for the care of its interests, the tribe undertook to maintain for the gods, temples, and to organise regular sacrifices and worship. The domestication of their gods helped to train the primitive people for combined action.

That mutual aid is possible in certain circumstances without the help of sanctions based upon force, is shown by the voluntary establishment of tribunals for the settlement of disputes. The creation of the Icelandic republic in the tenth century is an instance of the possibility of settling disputes peacefully. The inhabitants of small settlements on this island organised a Republic in order to provide a machinery which would put an end to the feuds which raged among them. A government was established without an executive side. Only its judicial and legislative functions had developed. The League of Nations was in some respects a similar instrument: a voluntary, co-operative authority. The question can be asked, with some justification, whether it was not the absence of an international police force which was the main cause of the failure of the League. Further questions may be asked in connection with plans for a universal league of states. Can an international peaceful integration last for a long time, without the existence of an external opponent? Do we always need an external enemy in order to get a permanent peaceful internal integration? Is it necessary for a world wide integration to have an external enemy something like a threat coming from the inhabitants of Mars? Can the danger inherent in the huge accumulation of the instruments of war function as well as the threats of an external enemy as a lasting integrating force?

2. CO-OPERATION, COMPULSION AND MUTUAL AID

Co-operation cannot be effected without some kind of compulsion. The simplest forms of compulsion are needs arising from the dangers inherent in the forces of nature. The anarchists err in deriding coercive authority as the child of conquest or of personal ambition.

The most spontaneous co-operation between groups is the mutual aid between neighbours, which is a spontaneous combination of efforts without submission to authority. The characteristic of this spontaneous readiness to give mutual aid, is that it works better in hard times than in easy times. Many examples can be found for this: merchants band themselves into guilds when they are striving for recognition by kings or priests or when they are threatened by robbers; artisans organise themselves when they are struggling for legal rights; wage earners form unions to defend their economic rights and to improve conditions of work; settlers practise mutual aid, especially when they are poor and struggling. So, for instance, among the pioneers of North America it was customary that if a man was sick his neighbours would offer to harvest his crop. But also when all were well they used to 'exchange work' in harvest times. In a later period when most members of the pioneering communities were better off, these mutual aid customs became less usual.

Generally speaking the lower social classes are more in favour of mutual aid than the middle or the upper classes. The explanation for this is that in hard times most people realise how essential are the principles of co-operation, mutual aid, the principles of *do ut des*.

Mutual help is a response to social pressure which can often be observed in history. For example, the labouring folk of ancient Rome bound themselves together in so-called *collegia*. There was a union for each trade to protect its members against the upper classes, to assure security in work and to lend some dignity to existence. Each had its festivals and sacred banquets, its banners, its common fund, its elected head and its common property in building and land. Christianity, the religion of love and of brotherly aid, captured this class long before it won the high and proud.

According to Kropotkin, the Slavonic ideal has always been the group of small producers, the members of which were co-operating with one another, rather than the vast industrial concern, exercising an autocratic control over their personnel. There is some truth in the assertion that people who have but recently emerged from their old communal organisation, like the Slavs or the peoples of Asia, still preserve a set of spontaneous co-operative tendencies. In the bigger cities, on the other hand, the sense of mutual aid tends to disappear. The voluntary method of taking care of common needs is little used then—the community has become too large for its members to know each other personally and to act readily in concert. The community has become so differentiated that the sense of common needs to be cared for commonly has been dulled.

3. THE SOCIAL FUNCTION OF THE DIVISION OF LABOUR

We distinguish between simple collaboration, co-operation which is based upon a division of functions and co-operation which is based upon a division of professions.

As an example of simple collaboration we can mention common wood-cutting by the members of a village community. In such an operation, everybody can share in the performance of the common task without the need for a definite division of functions having to arise.

As a type of a definite division of functions but without professionalisation, the division of labour in primitive communities based upon sex itself can be cited. In this case men may go hunting and prepare for the task of fighting, whilst the women do agricultural work or prepare the meals.

Definite professions are formed when different groups of individuals deal with one task only. This is a higher form of specialization. Some individuals may become fishermen, living in the vicinity of rivers, others, living in the mountains, may become herdsmen, while the dwellers of the plain specialise in agriculture and become farmers. Miners and armourers or smiths are among the earliest specialists, making up the first professions.

The main factor responsible for the division of labour is obviously the greater efficiency of labour organised in this way. There is the familiar example given by Adam Smith of the needle manufacturing process. According to him, as an effect of the division of labour, eighteen workers were producing in one instance 200 times as much as they would have produced working separately without a division of labour. Adam Smith was convinced that the reason for the division of labour taking place was always an exchange of products undertaken between producers. He assumed that producers concentrated on the production of one part of a whole project in order to be able to exchange it. In his view, it was the utilitarian calculation of the single individual which urged him to differentiate his work. He was mistaken in that he considered as the main working incentive that which was dominant in a liberal society. To-day we know that the division of labour is older than profitable exchange. There is a division of labour in societies where there is no exchange at all. There are many tribes which know a system of division of labour but disdain bartering. Goods are never exchanged among them, they move from one man to another either as presents or by being stolen.

The different stages in the evolution of the division of labour can best be followed in connection with the different typical stages in the evolution and growth of the co-operative units.

The first stage in this evolution is the family or the family-like domestic and economic unit ('economics' derives from a root meaning 'the art of the house or the household'). This unit is a more or less self-sufficient autarkic community which produces most of the things which it needs. Everybody produces for the needs of all. Exchange may take place but is rare. Even the early medieval manor fits more or less into this type.

The second type is the economy of the small town, where the small workshops of the handicraft men were based upon a highly developed division of labour. This division of labour implies a product which can be split up into component parts, but the control of the final product remains, from beginning to end, in the hands of the same producer, who usually manufactures it for definite consumers. This system, although based upon professionalisation, is hostile to specialisation. It prevents a decomposition of the object so that parts might be made in different places, and it is also a check upon a rapid increase of personal wealth; whilst on the other hand it usually functions in such a way as to prevent pauperisation.

If the consumer or the merchant brings raw material directly to the artisan and gives orders to him, the process of decomposition has been pushed a step further. Under more developed circumstances the differentiation of labour may be guided more by market exchange. But differentiation by organisation is a permanent factor of the division of labour.

As a third type of economy Bücher contrasted with domestic economy and city economy, the system of national economy. In this system, the various branches of industry procure their raw materials themselves, they produce for an unknown buyer and do not wait for immediate orders; the commodities thus produced circulate in the whole society. Bücher also speaks of the stage of world economy where the market shows an extension over the whole surface of the globe and in which large scale industry concentrates production and organises the division of labour. The speculation of the capital owners driven by the profit incentive, decides upon capital investments and contributes to the development of trade cycles. Planned (or managed) economy seems to be the last stage in this picture of the evolution of the systems of production, division of labour and of exchange. However, this suggested sequence can only be regarded as a useful tool for investigating different types of economy, but not as a rigid system of development in the actual historical process.

4. THE SOCIAL VALUATION OF LABOUR

The distinction between 'noble' and 'ordinary' professions, reappears in social history again and again: in patriarchal societies, especially in the later stage of development, it is common to emphasise the noble character of the work of the warrior and of the hunter. Agricultural work is usually performed by slaves and women and this work is underestimated, although it may be much more difficult and harder work than hunting or taking part in war-like raids. This instance seems to prove that the social valuation of work does not coincide with its usefulness to the community, but hinges more upon the power structure of that society and on the fact that some functions are reserved for the ruling groups and others are allotted to the subjected ones. The work done by small artisans and handicraft men, being very similar to that of the work done by slaves, was not highly esteemed in the city states of Greece. Manual work was conceived in antiquity as corrupting both the body and the soul. Even the work of the sculptor and of the architect was looked down upon for many centuries, because the members of these professions originally came from the slave stratum and because the professions entailed manual work. The poet, on the other hand, who historically descended from the soothsayer or oracle, was held in high esteem.

On a higher stage of social differentiation, the nobles of the community connect the idea of noble work with the idea of leisure. According to their view only the man who has leisure and is able to contribute his share to the administration of the community, by taking over political or other communal functions without being paid for it, does 'noble' work. Both in Rome and in England administrative work was done for centuries on a voluntary basis by the members of the aristocracy—and only this unpaid work was considered to be worthy of a noble man.

In the rising democratic times, on the other hand, a counter-ideal was conceived: that of the nobility of *all* socially useful work. In Athens, in the democratic period, it was not regarded as shameful to be a descendant of a family of handicraft men, as was the case with such influential leaders as Cleon or Demosthenes.

In the early stages of our own European society, making war, hunting, the service of the king and voluntary service within the bureaucracy were considered as noble work. Later, leading functions in agriculture were also highly esteemed, but industrial and commercial functions were looked down upon. With the growth of the influence and wealth of the industrial and commercial middle classes, the so-called bourgeoisie, successful work in finance, commerce and industry began to be respected. Finally, during the nineteenth century, the century during which the ideals of democracy and socialism gained strong influence, the original scale of valuations was turned into its opposite, since sometimes there was a tendency to over-estimate manual work and to under-rate the significance of other kinds of work. For many members of our society, only manual work seems to be productive.

From this example we can observe clearly that social position, the rise and fall of various groups in a society, influences strongly the fundamental standards underlying our judgment of value.

5. THE INTEGRATING FUNCTION OF THE DIVISION OF LABOUR

Besides leading to greater productivity, division of labour has another very important effect—as an integrating factor. This was first described by the French sociologist Durkheim. At first sight, division of labour seems to be a separating agency. But if we realise that every division of labour divides the activities, which were formerly combined in a process of work performed by one man, into a great number of parts which are supplementary to each other, then we must realise that division of labour means that the work of one man or group seeks completion in that of another. Consequently, the division of labour must lead to the strongest kind of social integration. It is the strongest kind because it is a *functional* integration. The connection of functions and the exchange of services is the essence of the process.

Completing this observation, Durkheim distinguishes two kinds of social integration and two types of solidarity. First, *the mechanical solidarity of likeness* which rests upon the total subjection of the individual to the group. The group in question is called by Durkheim the unisegmentary or monosegmentary group. Second, *organic solidarity*, which rests upon social differentiation, a system in which one organ supplements the functions of the other. According to Durkheim the division of labour is due very often to the great density of population. If huge masses are concentrated in cities—as in the west—and not so widely spread as they were, for instance, in Russia and China in past centuries, the conditions are favourable for the developing of the process of the division of labour. It is interesting that the working of a similar law can be observed already in animal and plant life: homogeneous plants or animals cannot survive in some territories except in small numbers, but divergent races, if united on a similar territory, thrive in great numbers. The conditions urge them to a specialisation of functions. A similar result can be found in the fusion of small groups.

To the two kinds of solidarity, the mechanical and the organic, two kinds of morality seem to belong: (1) Uni-segmentary society is based upon mechanical imitation and rigid traditions. It does not tolerate deviations. (2) The more complex society of our day requires individual deviations because the various differentiated functions of this society can only be fulfilled by various individualised types.

PART 3

SOCIAL INTEGRATION

CHAPTER VIII

A. The Sociology of Groups

So far I have considered general social forces and processes which either bring people together (these are
the integrating forces) or urge them to act against
one another (these are the separating forces). But I have
not yet dealt with the end-products of these forces, with
the various possible forms of integration, with the groups
which are nothing but the more or less stabilised results
of the general social processes.

The great mistake of every kind of lay sociology is that
it considers such units as a political party, a family, a
business corporation, a church or state as a sort of
mythical entity, that is to say, as a substantial unit, and
fails to realise that these units are nothing but the integrations of diverse forces and tendencies. The reason
why the description of single forces has to precede in
sociology the theory of the group, is that without such a
description we cannot analyse and break up these mythical entities into their elements. It is our task now to
observe here, one by one, the different stages of social
integration and the different forms of more or less compact and stable social groups.

1. THE CROWD

I shall start with a marginal case, with that kind of social
integration which has the loosest structure. This is *the
crowd*.

If you observe people on a Sunday in Hyde Park, you

will have before you a mass possessing no integration whatsoever. But what happens if the attention of these people is focussed by an accident or if they begin to participate in a riot? The form of their integration is not then based so much on the fact that they react upon each other like members of a small group of friends, or a working group, as by the fact that they react to the same stimuli. One might say that they have similar interests and their responses are being made more or less uniform by being conditioned by the same stimuli. This is a description of a passive mass, but let a fire have to be put out by the members of this crowd—then the mass undergoes a change, it begins to become organised, though it is not easy for a random crowd to develop the disciplined and co-ordinated action of a purposive group, for such a group has a period of training and adaptation behind it. However, in so far as the crowd tries to deal with the fire an important change has occurred because there are now common activating interests.

The crowd may be defined as a physical, compact aggregation of human beings brought into direct, temporary and unorganised contact, reacting mostly to the same stimuli and in a similar way. It is always a transitory and unstable organisation, an incident, an eruption; therefore, integration based upon immediate suggestion plays an important part. All the inhibitions maintained by primary and organised groups tend to lose their strength in a crowd and the consequence is that a sudden regression to primary, primitive, uncontrolled reaction can occur very easily. Under such conditions, the sudden communication and accumulation of emotion creates a loss of the sense of responsibility and maybe even of identity. This loss leads to an overthrowing of the standards and habits which formerly were developed within the framework of enduring groups.

In the crowd the close physical contacts, the multitudinous swaying emotions, the gestures, the murmurs and shouts, stir deep-laid strivings and the symptoms of the crowd become intensified when a like interest is turned into a common interest. For instance, the group which at the beginning of the French Revolution stormed the Bastille was a like-interest group and not a crowd of passive observers. They were united by a revolutionary aim. In such a situation, such a very simple aim causes each to identify himself with all the rest. This sort of participation brings with it a social sanction for individual irresponsibility. It is here that the function of the leader enters the plan. The leader becomes a means of identification, he is henceforth the symbol of this group, of group identification, of group organisation. He is followed, not because he has social prestige or a certain status, as would happen in conservative societies or in times of a continuous evolution, but because the rank and file has faith in him.

The unorganised crowd is usually subjected to a process in which emotion increases and the capacity for reflection is lowered. In this stage nothing constructive can be done, because there is no common end. The crowd is then in a transitory stage, it preserves the material for integration, it is, so to say, susceptible to the reformation of new, consolidated groups, a solidarity which could replace the centrifugal tendencies potentially present.

The crowd often seeks for a victim, such as the aristocrats or the Jews. In such a crowd the personal censor is removed, and the primitive or infantile nature of man reappears. Emotion is prominent in such a crowd and it seems as if the repressed aggressive and sexual tendencies would take their revenge. The skilful politician, the evangelist, the patriot of our times, the tribal witch-doctor, all use methods which are within limits similar, directing the crowd by voice and gesture, by reiteration and the cumulation of images, by all the ingredients of the spell of the orator.

The crowd exhibits the underlying gregarious spirit in the processes of social integration, and modern techniques of communication create new avenues for that kind of spirit. The press or the radio thus may become agencies for the transmission of this gregariousness.

2. THE PUBLIC

The public is an integration of many people not based on personal interaction but on reaction to the same stimuli —a reaction arising without the members of the public necessarily being physically near to one another.

What are the significant features of an agglomeration of people who are attending a football match, watching the performance of a play or listening to an orator? The significant features here are that there is a great number of people assembled, that they are near to each other and that they make their responses not to one another but to the same stimuli. They are actually integrated only by the purpose of being affected by certain stimuli (in the game, the play, the speaker and his words) and reacting to these. Nevertheless, they are no longer a crowd but can be called a public, first of all because their integration is more or less purposive—they came in order to listen to the orator or to watch the game; secondly, a primary kind of organisation, an external routine of timetable and behaviour, stands behind them: they have certain seats, they occupy and leave their seats at definite times, etc. Finally, they play the definite role of being observers, of being an audience and they have the right to applaud or to criticise.

Observing a public, we can note from the common experience of their members that a certain kind of group spirit emerges spontaneously, based mainly on commonly experienced and expressed moods and emotions. These experiences and emotions are often guided and the climax, the integration and disintegration of these, takes place simultaneously in the whole agglomeration of people. As a result of these common experiences, we can even speak here of the development of a short, common tradition of the members of the public.

There is a further factor which distinguishes the public from the crowd. Namely, that certain elementary forms of public opinion also arise. Thus we see that during the pauses, small groups are formed by certain initiating personalities. Members of the public who go from one group to another influence the selection and launching of opinions. The public is for a time divided into active and passive elements. This is a differentiation of functions, but these functions are fluctuating and interchangeable. We can observe the transition from the public to a group if its members begin to react to one another, if reflectiveness arises in its members and if the individualised personality begins to play a greater role. The public is thus an intermediate type of integration between the crowd and the group.

3. ABSTRACT MASSES AND THE ABSTRACT PUBLIC

People who listen on the radio in various parts of the country to the same play or to the same speech or who look at the same advertisement in different streets or read the same leading article in their newspapers or read the same novel at home, form abstract masses or an abstract public. They form a mass because the unity of these people is formed only by the common reaction to the same stimuli; not the whole personality is engaged in listening to the wireless or reading a novel, but only a part of it. But the readers or the radio listeners do not form a crowd because all the reactions connected with physical, bodily presence are absent. They are a public because they follow the same experiences. The functions to approve or to reject, that is, to judge the value of the performance or of the novel, are maintained and these functions are fluctuating. The decisive fact is that as members of an abstract public we behave according to social integration. If we react to an advertisement, we react in some measure as the members of a crowd would react to a suggestion, we are thus members of an abstract crowd; if we react to the leading article of a newspaper, we react as members of an abstract public. The advertisement and the article are constructed with these factors in mind.

Every member of a society is in an ambiguous situation: as the member of a family or of a party he is influenced by certain definite types of motivation. Thus he has political attitudes, aesthetic attitudes, family feelings, sex attitudes, and so on. But if he becomes for a short time the member of a public in a real sense, he puts his traditionalised attitudes into brackets and lets himself be influenced by the impressions of the attitudes of a public. For instance, if a member of the Communist party is listening to the lecture of a Liberal on the problem of the freedom of the press, he must, if he wishes really to become a member of the listening public, put the traditional attitudes of his party into brackets. If he does not do so, he does not become a part of the new, momentary integration of the public except as a critical and separated member, and his fixed group attitude prevails. The public is the ever-present fluid element alongside the consolidated groupings.

On the other hand, as long as the fluctuating impulses of the public do not become organised and transformed into traditional group attitudes, they react upon the individual mind but do not transform the existing society. The totality of a society can only be explained in terms of both the fluid integrations and the group consolidations. We see here a balance between public spirit and group spirit. Fluid public opinion is the guarantee of the dynamic and flexible spirit of modern times as we can observe it in most parts of Europe since the time of the Renaissance.

Freedom of thought, sociologically, means that a person can think not only in terms of his organised group patterns but also in terms of the flexible reactions to the more fluid integrations of various abstract publics. The abolition of the freedom of thought in modern dictatorial society consists not simply in forbidding people to think, but in organising, and thereby making rigid, the public, which is in its essence an unorganised entity and can only function properly if it remains unorganised and fluid.

4. ORGANISED GROUPS

These are the more or less enduring forms of the social integration of a certain number of people who react according to a certain set of social forces. They react not only to external stimuli but to one another. The main characteristics of groups are:

(*a*) A relative persistence.

(*b*) Organisation, that is, a certain degree of division of functions.

(*c*) Social institutions based on certain traditional habits of the individuals composing the groups.

(*d*) Certain group norms or standards to which the members of the group adjust their activities.

(*e*) Certain ideas about the existence and the functions of the group and its relationships to other groups. Subjective ideas of the members of the group on its destiny and function do not, in many cases, coincide with its real functions in society. In such cases we can speak about the ideologies of the group members. The knowledge of these ideologies is very important because it helps to explain the activities of the groups. They can be regarded as parts of a defence mechanism, a kind of rationalisation or unwitting falsification, necessary for the successful functioning of the group. For instance, the members of a political party think that the purpose of their party is to help the economically weaker sections of the middle classes. Nevertheless, another function of the group, in realistic terms, may be to support and defend the ruling groups to retain their power and privileges. The criterion of the realistic functions can be found not in the words of the members of a group, or in the written programme but in the deeds.

(f) Every group has a collective interest and, at the same time, every member of the group has a personal and a collective interest in it.

(g) Every group has a more or less developed power organisation and a system of distribution of power.

(k) Every group produces specific situations, with typical tensions, repressions and conflicts, as well as typical repressive and discharging agencies.

Examples of groups are the family, the clan, the tribe, the neighbourhood community, the church, the sect, the political party, the bureaucracy and the state.

Observing the life of these groups in the course of history or their functioning in contemporary society, we see that they are knit together firstly by like responses, habits, social institutions; secondly, by complementary functions; thirdly, by fixed organisation and fourthly by conscious elements, such as norms, interests and ideologies.

The simplest forms of group integration are collective attitudes which fall into two groups: those which are relatively permanent—these we call institutional attitudes; and those which are comparatively ephemeral and change their character rapidly—the non-institutional attitudes.

Customs are examples of institutional attitudes, being uniformities of behaviour which tend to form habits in the individual. They come down from past generations, sometimes from periods so remote that it is impossible to trace their origin. The main holidays and festivals of any modern church have their origin in most cases in very ancient celebrations, and traditions are the psychic aspects of custom. However, practices are more easily imitated than ideas.

Folkways are uniform ways of doing things within a group; doing things for instance in the fields of recreation, social contacts or economic life. But the more settled forms of social contact, such as religion or public ceremonies, do not belong to this group. Conventions are simply present ways of doing things or contemporaneous beliefs about things. Conventional people are those who do not like to depart from the accepted forms of action and thought, and codes of conduct are laid down and formally sanctioned by some approving body which possesses authority for the sake of definiteness.

Non-institutional controls can be observed in connection with such social phenomena as the fad, the fashion or the craze. These are forms of behaviour which are not very widespread and which pass relatively quickly, a form of behaviour in the matter of speech, recreation, cooking, dress, or the like.

When we join a group, the process of becoming uniform starts at once. The consequence of this process of becoming uniform can best be observed in the case of professional groups in which professionalisation creates the same type again and again. It is partly the nature of the work but to a greater extent the imitation of and the adaptation to the standards of the profession which make members of a profession similar to one another. Groups consisting of two or three persons do not need group norms, as they represent purely personal relationships. The larger the group, the more must the personal attitudes be transformed into stereotyped standards and patterns. Group norms are, of course, not abstract rules but visible patterns or types of behaviour and attitude. Thus a living or a dead person can become the model for the members of a group.

CHAPTER IX

The Sociology of Groups *(continued)*

5. THE TYPES OF GROUPINGS

According to Simmel, very much depends in a group on the number of participants. There are basic differences in the nature of groups formed of two, three, four or a multitude of persons.

First, we must deal with small groups; these we may call quasi-groups. The smallest of these is the couple. We know sex couples formed by a man and a woman who may be lovers or married couples. But couples are also formed by members of different generations, like father and son or mother and daughter, and also by members of the same generation—brother and sister. We see couples based on friendship or based on subordination (employer and employee, teacher and student). Transitory contacts do not create groups, only constant relationship does so, and therefore we deal here with the latter only.

The couple relationship is the most intensive group relationship because the whole personality can enter into it. Most intensive relationships into which love and friendship enter seem to be correlated with the group termed couple. It is the social form most adapted to a specific intimacy. The personal quality of the members is more important in the couple than in large size groups. This is quite obvious in the case of friendship couples and the humanising of the couple relationship is the essential of friendship: in the couple the personal self becomes distinguishable from the social self.

The couple reacts on external stimuli differently from

the way in which individuals constituting the couple would act, separately. This is so because the members of the couple have a more or less permanent influence on each other. On the other hand, the less individualised the members of a couple are, the easier though not necessarily the richer is its functioning.

The next group with which we must deal is the group with three members. This group can be regarded as an extension of the couple but, of course, the appearance of a third member alters the whole balance between the members of the couple. The attitude of the original group, the couple, towards the third, who approaches the group, must also be taken into consideration when we analyse the nature of the new group. The consequence for the third member of the group may be temporary isolation, which lasts until he finds a new partner. A typical symptom of behaviour in a group of three is jealousy. The competition of two people for the favour of a third is very characteristic of many three-person relationships.

The layman usually tends to believe that the behaviour of man is more constant than it really is. The study of small groups shows very convincingly that he is wrong. The behaviour of persons changes according to changing circumstances. Thus, every meeting of two persons is influenced by such factors as what each feels about the other, what he seems to feel about me, the personal mood of myself but also of the other whom I meet, the occasion and purpose of our meeting and all the other factors conditioning this meeting.

There exists no definite and exclusive classification of social groups. All classifications depend on the nature of the point of view according to which way the variety of objects in question is considered. The usefulness or unfitness of a classification depends both on the purposes of the scientific observation and on the nature of the object itself. That is the reason why I offer various kinds of classifications of social groupings.

We have to distinguish purely statistical groups from sociological units. By a purely statistical group we understand a group of people having the same characteristics, who are united into a group in the mind of a scholar or statistician only, without being really integrated on the basis of these characteristics. Purely statistical groups are, for instance, 'males', 'females', 'newborns', 'redheads', '30-year-olds', 'agricultural labourers'. Our problem here is whether their common traits act as real group makers or not. The difficulty in applying statistics is that in statistics we need measurable units and therefore external characteristics have to be found. The nature of the real social bond on the other hand is mostly a psychological-spiritual one. People rarely act together on the basis of external features but very often on the basis of common psychological stimuli. When the statistical classification corresponds to a social or psychological bond, the data obtained may have considerable value in helping us to understand social processes, as can be seen when we consider income groups, ethnic or religious minority groups or the like.

Groups were classified by Tönnies into *communities* and *associations*. A community can be defined as any circle of people who live together and belong together in such a way that they do not share this or that particular interest only, but a whole set of interests. A community is a group which is wide enough to include, so to say, the whole life of its members. Such groups are the tribe, the village, the pioneer settlement, the city and the nation, but not the business firm, the professional organisation or the typical political party. The mark of a community is that one's life may be lived wholly within it.

A community is a social group occupying a territorial area and the common locality has an important part in creating its social coherence. But a purely spatial unit alone does not constitute the social bond: there must be common living. The fact that we belong to a small community (such as the village) of course does not exclude the possibility that we should adhere to a wider one such as the nation.

An association, on the other hand, is a group specifically organised for the pursuit of an interest or of a group of interests, in common. It is not a community, but an organisation within a community—such as a business firm or a club. If we observe various associations, we can always tell which are the particular interests around which these organisations are formed, but we cannot ask why communities exist, for what purpose, any more than we can ask why life exists.

We belong to an association only by virtue of the purposes of that association; some part of our life always escapes it. We are born into communities, but we choose our associations or are elected into them. Of course, there are many social groupings which are on the borderline between community and association. For instance, the family was formerly a community in the pure sense because it included the whole life of its members. Under modern conditions it tends to become more or less of an association. But, of course, it is still a community in the original sense, for the child.

Blood relationship and local groups. Which common factors act as group makers and which data and traits act as an impetus for common activities and for the emergence of a group consciousness? At different times and in different societies, and even within the same society, group integration often follows different lines. For instance, in nomadic times it was mostly the blood relationship which was the fundamental integrating influence. Family, kinship and tribe are, therefore, in such times and societies the basic factors of integration. All kinds of co-operative and ideological unification serve the aim of strengthening this classification. The totem expresses symbolically the form of this synthesis. But once a group of people gets settled, an element of space enters into the social relationship and local groupings become more important than blood relationship. Under settled circumstances people who live in the same village form a local community. It is significant that the immigrant, who settles down, or more significantly, is allowed to settle down, in the village, even if he does not belong to the kinship, may become a member of the local community.

At first, there is usually a struggle and competition between these two kinds of primary integrating principles and much depends on whether, during decisive periods of history, the tribal or the local integration prevails. In old Russia and in China the tribal organisation prevailed for a long time. The Russian peasant of the last century belonged to the *mir* and did not lose his adherence to it even when he went to town. If, however, the local unit prevails, the symptom of this change is usually that the tribal deity is replaced by a local deity, and there are instances of both forms of integration occurring together.

To-day, in our society, the principle of local unification still functions, although it is balanced by other principles of integration. The state is to-day the most impressive territorial community, based upon an integration bringing together many aspects of living together. But such primary groups, based on blood-relationship or local unification, as the family, the neighbourhood, the playground, also have their function, as Cooley has shown us. However, besides the principles of blood relationship and locality there are many other principles on which group integration may be based.

The principle of common activities gives rise to the professional groups. These arise because similar activities urge people to stand together. Here we have to distinguish two stages: in the first stage, groups are built upon spontaneous co-operation and in the second stage, there is set up an organisation with the purpose of knitting the different parts of the group together. By an organisation we mean a kind of co-operation in which the functions of every part of the group are definitely pre-arranged and stated and in which there is a guarantee that the planned activities and demands will be executed without major frictions. The best example of a group based upon common activities in connection with a strict organisation is a bureaucracy, that is, the executing organ of a state, of a business, of a party or of a trade union.

The principle of fighting for power within the state gives rise to political parties. There is always a process of re-distribution and re-organisation of power going on in the state and the agents in this conflict are the political parties. The nature and functioning of these can only be understood if we introduce the distinction between direct activities and representative activities. Under the latter we understand acting on behalf of somebody else. The necessity of introducing representatives gives rise to various difficulties. The representative may act in a manner not satisfactory to those whom he represents, he may go beyond his brief. It will, therefore, be necessary to build up a mechanism in order to readjust, if necessary, the personal will of the representative to the will of the mandating persons. The problem of what the common will of a group is and how it can be measured and ex-pressed, gives rise to further problems connected with such procedures as elections, the functioning of opposi-tions, the protection of the rights of minorities, and so on. Parliaments, councils, congresses, are means of organis-ing the will of a group for the sake both of giving initiative to and controlling the executive.

The principle of defending common interests gives rise to a grouping together of associations of employers, or of the trade unions, or the like. The membership of these associations is limited to a definite circle of persons. But the groupings based upon a general rather than a specific likeness and upon the free choice of companions have a different basis of recruitment. We have here selective associations founded on the principle of the free choice of companions and such are common experience groups or groups wishing to spend their leisure time together.

The principle of groups based upon free choice gives rise to innumerable free associations. There is no space to deal with all of them. I would like only to mention that many religious groups belong here although the religious aim (as all other aims) may be linked up with common interests and with the striving for common power.

6. THE STATE

One form of group must be discussed apart from the groups so far mentioned: this is the frame-group and in our epoch the frame-group is the state.

The frame-group is the power organisation which acquires the greatest control among existing groupings within a territory and is able to regulate the interrelations between all other fighting, competing or co-operating groups. The modern state has the power and claims the right to interfere more or less decisively in many of the relationships binding together all the other groups. The representatives of the state claim this right on the basis of the idea of legitimacy. The idea of legitimacy is a notion which governs the activities of the members of a state as long as the state is really acknowledged by them. The basis of legitimacy may differ in different states; it may be based upon traditional belief, upon established law or upon consent as expressed in plebiscites or elections. The idea of legitimacy differentiates the coercion as used by the state from the coercion used by a gang of robbers. The majority of people do not feel that the coercion exerted by robbers, even if one has to submit to it, is legitimate. The coercion of the state may be felt, subjectively, by many people as illegitimate, but as long as it succeeds in compelling people to act according to the rules laid down by the state, it has to be considered as legitimate *de facto*. The existence of a *de facto* legitimate state can be inferred from the fact that the orders of the state claiming legitimacy have, in fact, the chance of being executed.

The idea of legitimacy *de facto* can mean that a few groups may obtain and maintain power in order to suppress all others. As long as the majority of the population acts in such a way as to show its respect for or submission to the frame-group and thus acknowledges its authority and legitimacy, the frame-group, however oppressive, is the *de facto* state.

Even the individuals who do not acknowledge the legitimacy of the existing state show by their attitudes that they acknowledge the real existence of the state. For instance, the thief acts against the law, but acknowledges its real existence because he hides his activities. In the same way, the organisers of so-called illegal political activities involuntarily acknowledge the real existence of the state by being compelled to organise their activities with a keen eye to the legal regulations.

During a revolution there exists no such frame-group possessing the monopoly of legitimate coercion. The state disappears and partial bodies acquire parts of the power of the state to coerce. In stable times the power of the state is limited by the power of other states competing with it on the international scene. We have so far no world state. Bodies like the League of Nations or the United Nations may proclaim their right of being the source of supreme legitimacy but as long as such a body has not the coercive power guaranteeing the chance that its orders will be obeyed, it is not the real frame-group of international society.

CHAPTER X

B. The Class Problem

Having dealt with the nature and types of social groups we must now discuss the class problem. Class itself is more a layer than a group. Speaking of classes we must distinguish first social position; then the problem of the integrated class; and finally the political party as an organ of class activities.

1. SOCIAL POSITION

People who have similar positions in the social order have a greater chance of having certain experiences than others. For example, anybody who wears a worn-out coat and boots with holes (features which place him in the hierarchy of the social order) has a greater chance than others of being treated in an unfriendly way and without social reverence. Further, persons who have the same social position have a greater chance of responding to certain events and stimuli in a similar way. There is a chance that the philosophies of life of people having the same social position will correspond to some extent because of the experiences they have in common.

What is the difference between a class and a layer? The similarity of persons who belong to a given layer may be based upon various factors such as age, sex, education, etc. People who belong to the same layer have a chance to have similar experiences and may have also similar response patterns in certain fields. Persons belonging to the same generation, for instance, will have some similar experiences in their early childhood or during their adolescence, such as war, unemployment, prosperity, revolution or counter-revolution. Nevertheless, they do not form a class because the similarities which exist among the members of such a layer are not fundamental and consequently do not become integrated.

We can call fundamental such similarities as induce persons to feel alike and to act on the same lines. These similarities are, so to say, the breeding instances of common class activities, and of class consciousness. This set of characteristics can be found firstly in the similarity of chances of getting more or less of the goods which form the wealth of a nation, secondly in the similarity of chances of experiencing the same social respect (often called 'status') and thirdly in the similarity of chances of having comparable careers.

Economic class position, as mentioned above, can be differentiated as class according to possessions and income or class according to relationship to the means of production, as for example owner or employee.

If the *layer* is formed by people who can be characterised by chances of similar experiences, then *class* is the sum of people who find themselves in the same position concerning their fate in society.

Change from one social position, from one class to another, is called vertical mobility. If this vertical mobility is stopped by institutionalised regulations then we say that society is being divided into rigid ranks or castes.

An *integrated* class is the sum of people who are unified not only by these chances but by a class consciousness.

By class consciousness we understand the awareness of the similarity of social chances, the arising of a notion about similarity of interests, the growth of an emotional tie connected with this similarity of experiences and of a common striving towards a common social goal. This common striving is based on a compound of ideal and material interests. Class consciousness is the means by which the spiritual integration of persons possessing a similarity of social position and of life chances is transformed into a common group activity.

2. CLASS CONSCIOUSNESS AND POLITICAL PARTIES

Class consciousness alone does not bring about an acting class; it is only the soil for an easier growth of similar activities, a favourable soil for the development of certain social movements. In order to transform this common background of experiences, of emotional attitudes and of a uniting consciousness into long-term activities, certain social organs of the class must arise; among which the *political parties* are the most important. That is to say, the factor of organisation here enters the plan. We find class parties on the lines of the common activities which correspond to class interests, as defined above. But we find parties on various other lines if there is no definite correspondence between the class background and the rival political parties.

If the owners and the non-owners of the means of production are represented by definite and different parties, then we see the emergence of a party system based on economic class differences. But this does not always happen in the course of history. Which factors tend to bring about such integrations have to be studied in historical sociology. There we study the concrete structures of different societies and this may help us to understand the main trends of integration and their varying intensities.

PART 4

SOCIAL STABILITY AND SOCIAL CHANGE

CHAPTER XI

Factors of Social Stability

Turning to the problem of social structure, we must first study some of those forces which make for social cohesion and stability. These are the so-called social controls, such as custom and law. The problem of authority and of valuations has also to be analysed here and the personal representations of social control and authority have to be defined.

1. SOCIAL CONTROL AND AUTHORITY

What is it that guarantees stability to an existing system? Why do people obey certain rules for their activities? The orderliness and stability of a society is due to the existence of social controls. Social control is the sum of those methods by which a society tries to influence human behaviour to maintain a given order. There are hundreds of controls operating in society but usually their existence passes unnoticed. Every society has a different system of controls, or at least lays emphasis on different controls and controls can be exercised from different key positions. The simplest we may call mutual controls, as for instance when one member of a group rebuffs another for bad behaviour. The control is mutual because it is not yet transferred to an acknowledged agency which exercises control on behalf of the group, such as the police. The different controls are linked up with a system of sanctions, which vary from individual disapprobation on the part of one's fellows, which may be expressed by laughter, cold-shouldering and cutting in the street, to official punishment in the form of fines, imprisonment, etc.

The functioning of control is based upon the existence of authority. There are people of authority, there are statements of authority. There is no social order without authority, but the sources of this authority may be different. The source of authority may be procedure, tradition, established law, or the words of a prophet or a saint. Both anarchists and the supporters of brute force are mistaken, for social order cannot be built up without authority, and authority cannot rest on the threat of violence alone. Most societies are built up on an elaborate system of controls among which physical force is only a last resort. The existing controls are nearly all mutually dependent, and if one is relaxed another will at once replace it. Paternal authority was once the main focus of control, but to-day many of its functions are transferred to the state. To begin with a new kind of behaviour can often only be enforced by rigid control, but later this can be relaxed as habit systems take its place. Out of the many existing controls we will here discuss in detail only custom and law.

2. CUSTOM AS A FORM OF SOCIAL CONTROL

Custom is the earliest form of social control and whereas law is always made and always enforced by a definite power, according to MacIver custom is a group of procedures which has gradually emerged without any constituted authority to declare it and to impose it. In a simple group or in a primitive society mutual controls prevail and there custom is really democratic and totalitarian at the same time. It is democratic because it is made by the group, everybody contributes to its growth, anybody may act upon it and may re-interpret it according to any new situation. It is totalitarian because it affects every sphere of self-expression, private and public, it influences our thoughts, beliefs and manners. Sumner called these relatively durable standardised usages prevailing in a group 'folkways'—for example, the way of building houses, the worship of ancestors, the procedure of initiating members into a secret society, the wearing of clerical vestments and the mannerisms of speech and gesture. Although they vary from one tribe, nation or sect to another, as long as they are the ways of the folk they exert an immense pressure on behaviour. They are so powerful because in primitive groups, where face-to-face contacts prevail, no one can escape beyond the range of group opinion and group control. The authority of customs diminishes in complex society where impersonal relations largely replace personal contact and where individuals are further removed from the direct control of the group as a whole. But apart from the growth of society as such, there are other factors making for the disintegration of customs in modern society. Money economy disintegrates customs because they are too slow in their workings. In a society where production for the market and payment in money, not in kind, are dominant, legal rules expressly made for the situation and promptly enforceable are necessary. Any strong organisation of economic or military power works against custom. The reason is that customs tend to differ in different localities, whereas a strict organisation like the army needs homogeneous rules over all its spheres of action. Custom is obeyed more spontaneously because it grows slowly and can thus penetrate the whole web of human relationships, emotionally engaging all members of the group. Therefore as long as customs spontaneously prevail, they are the strongest ties in building up a social order and at this level they are equal to a moral order. The spontaneous conformity which results from them is an asset that should remain untouched as long as it prevails. In England the power of custom is greater than in any other industrial society, and here the laws have gradually developed out of the background of custom.

3. LAW AS A FORM OF SOCIAL CONTROL

Law is the code upheld by the State. It is a body of rules which is recognised, interpreted and applied to particular situations by the courts of the State. Whereas custom develops unconsciously, law is consciously created and put into force at the moment of its enactment. The transition from custom to law is just a part of the general rationalisation in modern society, a change which can be observed equally in all departments of life. Activities which were at one time performed unconsciously are now consciously formulated, their concepts defined and their principles set out. The former range of variation is reduced and hard and fast rules tend to prevail. This is one of the factors which makes a modern society a more exactly functioning machine, but on the other hand its vitality decreases. The disadvantage of law is also, as Sir Henry Maine pointed out, that it is only known by a privileged minority. According to him social necessities and social opinions are always in advance of law. Thus a continuous readjustment to changing conditions is necessary.

The functions of law vary to a certain extent in different societies. According to the philosophy of liberalism, law had two main tasks to fulfil, to maintain a fundamental order within which man should find security and opportunity and to adjust those conflicts and interests between individuals and groups which they cannot settle for themselves, or in the settling of which they encroach upon the interests of others.

Modern totalitarian methods would not be satisfied with such a definition because they are not usually satisfied with merely laying down the rules of the game, but aim at prescribing every action of individual play.

4. PRESTIGE AND LEADERSHIP

Social controls, custom and law, represent the objective aspect of authority. But authority is always exercised by individuals, and we speak of people with prestige and authority. There must be authority in every society, but the sources of authority may be different. It is wrong to identify authority with the application of brute force for authority based on force alone is exceptional and cannot be permanent. The sources and methods of exercising authority vary with time and with the structure of society. Among tradition-loving people authority is vested in certain families—the king, the hereditary nobility, the priesthood etc. Among peoples inclined to hero-worship authority is vested in the man of destiny—for instance in the hero of Homeric epics. Among religious people authority is vested in the intermediaries between the Divinity and man, for instance the hierarchy of the Church. Among war-like peoples it is vested in great warriors, in materialistic civilisation in business magnates, among democratic peoples in political leaders who claim to recreate the will of the people. In Russia, Marxism is worshipped as a scientific source of authority. The objection to this attitude is not that a society should not be built upon a scientific basis, but that it is contrary to the nature of science that any teaching should be taken as final truth. Many of the struggles in history are struggles between two types of authority—religious and political, democratic and totalitarian.

We must make a clear distinction between two basic types of authority. First, when authority is vested in office, and second when it is vested in a personal leader. An example of the first case is when we obey a policeman or other official; we do so not because of his personal qualities, but because he represents a social control, his authority is a borrowed authority. This kind of authority prevails in static societies and is strongest where there is least inclination for revolution or disorganisation. Authority based upon personal leadership is usually manifested in dynamic society when the leader is obeyed on account of his personal qualities. The prophets of Israel, Mahomet, Napoleon, Lenin, Hitler and Mussolini, are examples of personal leadership. Within the framework of analytic sociology the sociologist is deliberately unconcerned with the content of their doctrines and expresses no opinion as to the truth or falsity of their teaching, but interests himself primarily in the nature of their authority. In the contrast between the prophets and mystics on the one hand and the priesthood on the other, one can clearly see the two forms of authority at variance. The opportunity for the personal leader occurs when society is in a state of disorganisation and new norms of conduct must be found. The perturbed masses, seeking for new solutions, are prepared to accept the new valuations and patterns of conduct presented by the leader.

I agree with MacIver's definition of leadership as the power to direct men which is based on personal qualities and not on tenure of office. While authority bases its claims on facts and is respected for this reason, prestige may be gained by the mere appearance of power. Though this may be considered the accepted definition, Harold Nicolson draws attention to the fact that the word prestige means different things in England, France and Germany, and shows in a very illuminating way that the different interpretations of the word reflect different types of policy. He claims that it is the aim of traditional English policy to base power upon reputation rather than to base reputation upon power. To the French the word prestige has the connotation of glamour, romance, desire to deceive. To them prestige is not a political method but mainly an emotional effect. In German the nearest word to prestige may be translated as national honour. This term reflects a lack of self-confidence and is connected with the almost hysterical reaction which many Germans feel when their status in the world is in danger.

Mr. Nicolson then goes on to say that the traditional English attitude is that prestige cannot be acquired without power, yet it cannot be retained without reputation. The consequence of this attitude was that the English ruled gently and tried to avoid provocation but on the other hand tended to neglect defensive power whereby the offensive power of other nations has correspondingly increased. The value of Nicolson's analysis is that he shows that the different interpretations of the same words in different countries reflect the varying modes of action prevailing in these countries.

5. THE PHILOSOPHICAL AND SOCIOLOGICAL INTERPRETATION OF VALUES

In all the cases we have discussed, valuation has played a considerable part. Custom, law, leadership, prestige, represent phenomena in which valuation is inherent, though we do not yet know what valuations are nor how they come about and change. As we have seen, most of the struggles in history are due to the clash between two different forms of allegiance to authority, or to a change in valuations. What are values? To the idealist philosopher—even to the man in the street—they present themselves as eternal qualities, as gifts or commands from Heaven, as transcendental forces. To the sociologist they are part and parcel of the social process—functions of the social process. To him values are not abstract entities nor are they intrinsic qualities of an object. In the light of concrete analysis it is meaningless to speak of values as if they existed independent of the valuating subject or the group for which they are valid.

We have a deep resistance to this approach. It is rooted in our thought habits to imagine that we believe in values because they are eternal, presented by some superhuman or super-historical power. Further, we are reluctant to change this attitude because we are afraid of the relativism which may follow the realisation that values are created by society and vary in different societies, and that our own values are also dependent on our social system. However, just as science had to break the thought habit that the sun went round the earth, although the acceptance of this fact seemed to endanger the religious and moral order of the time, so we must accept the fact that values are socially generated—if this is the case. But on consideration we will realise that our sense of obligation to these values need not diminish because we accept the fact that they are not dictated by some transcendental command but by our rational insight into the needs of our social order. What will really happen will be that the theological and philosophical obligation will be replaced by a sociological one. The theological and to a large extent the philosophical justification of values appeals to the thought habits of men accustomed to act under authority, whilst the sociological approach appeals to the democratically educated man because the social obligation can be reasonably tested. Another advantage of the sociological concept is that it both explains the obligation and opens the door to reforms, whereas the old absolute conception rendered reform slower.

Let us take a very simple concrete situation in which valuation occurs. I wish to drive a nail into a piece of wood and I therefore look at everything in terms of its 'hammer value'—that is to say, measure its capacity to meet the special situation. I try out different objects; some of them are effective and become active factors in the context of my life. In this case, as in other cases, there is no abstract value, but certain things become valuable in the context of a certain activity, through performing a desired function. As a matter of fact the 'hammer value' corresponds to an emotionalisation of certain functions which become important in our lives. That is to say, the value is not inherent in any object or activity as such, but each may become valuable if it becomes necessary and therefore emphasised in the context of life. For instance, if through a war situation ambulance driving becomes an important occupation, all the activities connected with it will become emotionalised and valuable. If in the context of life it is important that I should learn shorthand, anything connected with this becomes emotionalised and valuable. In any value-generating situation therefore there are three factors: an organism, a situation and an object.

The organism is necessary to give meaning to the idea of value. It is not necessary to be conscious of the values that motivate us. The situation is the immediate occasion for action, in view of which the organism meets the situation, by an act of selection which is a step in its growth. According to Cooley, one can distinguish two kinds of values, human nature values and institutional values. To the first belong those which like the taste for salt and the pleasure in bright colours are fairly general in mankind. These human nature values are very few in number because most of our value attitudes are bred by institutions. For instance the values of the Roman Catholic Church, the values of the English, the values of the Nazi system, the values of a professional organisation or of an army. Institutional values are much greater in number and can only be studied with reference to their social antecedents —that is to say their history and the whole situation of the group. Because of this organic character, values vary with the time, the group and the social class. Within the frame of these group values each individual may have a value system of his own which is a variation of the institutional values within his reach. The individual approach to the problem of values leads us to believe that we ourselves are the original sources of our value systems. This is true to a certain extent—without the spontaneity of the individual no further development or value creation would be possible. But it is a delusion to think that the value system which we obey can be explained in terms of our personal life history. Most of the values which dominate our lives are linked up as we have seen with the institutions and groups in which we live, and very many changes in valuations can be traced back to the historical changes in the group and to changing functional needs. For example, H. M. Chadwick in his book *The Heroic Age* has shown how in a very short time during the great migration of the peoples, an opportunity was given to adventurous groups for easy conquest. This produced a division between the warrior groups and the peasant community in the Germanic tribes, to which the creation of a completely different scale of values corresponded. In the peasant community the former values of the community, conformity, mutual help, valuation of labour, were maintained. In the new warrior group the values of an heroic gang suddenly developed, individualism, bravery, readiness to pillage, personal allegiance to a leader; these values are, as it were, counter values. Whereas in the original group conformity and mutual help were virtues, here individualism and pillage prevail. The two sets of values are reflected in the gods worshipped by the Germanic tribes. The tribal ethics of the community are represented by Thor, an old peasant, and Wotan is the warrior god. As we see, society organised for labour produced a different set of values from that produced by a society organised for conflict.

To return to our original example, the warrior society tried to establish the new authority of a personal leader as against the established authority of the elders in the tribe. A kind of propaganda vaunting their new values in preference to the old community values was necessary. The new leaders with their small courts and retinues were a kind of *parvenu* power which needed justification and advertisement. This responsibility was given to the *scop*—

the poet. When we look at this poetry to-day, we see that it had two aims, first to establish the prestige and authority of the hero, who was present at its recital, and second to inculcate the values and patterns of life necessary to warrior society. Thus we see that in the making of new values an organic growth is at work. But the valuation is carried out by certain functionaries—as for instance the prestige lender, in this case the poet, who disseminates the value. The same basic situation can also be observed in the Renaissance where we have the rise of a new class out of traditional medieval society, the class of efficient bankers, industrialists and merchants who in contrast to the conventional values of the medieval community laid emphasis upon personality, extravagance, heroism, art. In this case it is again the poet and the artist who were the prestige lenders. Of course this does not mean that art and poetry are only a kind of advertisement, but we must realise two things. First that the sociologist must clearly understand that art and poetry did in fact have this function among others, and that prestige lenders have always existed; second that though the technique of advertisement has only lately been developed in detail, it has always existed in some form.

CHAPTER XII

Causes of Social Change

After having analysed the factors of social stability, we have to answer the question: what are the primary causes which make society dynamic, thus compelling both the groups and the individuals to remake their adjustments continually? As the Marxist theory of social change is the most consistent, and very widely discussed, it will prove useful to take it as a starting point for our discussion of the causes of social change.

1. THE MARXIST THEORY OF SOCIAL CHANGE

The Marxist theory of social change is the reflection of an age which witnessed the industrial revolution and realised the great significance of the change in economic technique. For this reason this theory is on the one hand highly sensitive to the technical factor, and on the other is apt to over-emphasise it. The right approach to this theory is to take it as a challenge.

The ultimate cause of social change according to the theory is 'the material forces of production'. These forces, as represented by economic technique, are subject to change, new inventions occur and these alter not only the machinery but the primary socio-economic relationships. By the latter is understood those human relationships which are directly determined by the changing division of labour which goes with the changed technique. Primary relations are the *paterfamilias* and his slave,

136

the craftsman and his apprentice, the entrepreneur and the wage-earning labourer. Primary socio-economic relationships connected to a society depending upon the hand mill, are other than those which are necessary to a society based upon steam and electricity. In Marx's words 'the sum total of these relations of production constitutes the economic structure of society, the real foundation on which rise legal and political superstructures, and to which correspond definite forms of social consciousness'. In this famous statement the idea is established that the basic organisation of society is expressed in its economic structure which to a large extent determines the legal and political organisations, and even the form of social consciousness; that is to say, the kind of thought and ideas people hold in any particular age. Whether one accepts this statement or not, its value consists in its hint that there is a correlation between the economic structure of a society and its legal and political organisation, and that even the world of our thought is affected by these relationships. One can interpret Marx's statement in a deterministic sense, as if the superstructure were definitely shaped by the basic structure. This is obviously going too far, but it is important to realise this point of view as a scientific hypothesis which induces us to study the legal and political setting of a society and its world of thought in a continuous relationship with the economic and social changes. It cannot be denied for instance that the legal organisation—the property system for instance—varies with the changing economic structure, or that the political and other ideas people hold are somehow connected with the social context in which they live.

How exactly does social change, according to this theory, come about and spread throughout the different spheres of society? Firstly, as we have seen, the material forces of production are subject to change through technical inventions, and thus a rift arises between the economic factors and the socio-economic relationships built upon them. The whole superstructure must change. For instance, our whole legal organisation, with its property system, was largely adjusted to meet the needs of a stage of industrialisation in which small economic units carried on production. To-day, as a consequence of inventions, large-scale industrial techniques dominate and the concentration of capital or state ownership should correspond to this. But this change does not come about easily, for the older order has created vested interests and ideologies which resist any alteration. Therefore the new forces of production are, as it were, fettered, and this leads to a strong tension and eventually to revolutionary outbursts. Who can break this spell of ideologies, of wrong habits of thought and vested interest? Only those who are, as it were, excluded from this order and are able to awaken to the consciousness of its decay. This is the proletariat, which is not interested in the maintenance of a superstructure which prevents the changed economic conditions from creating the social conditions under which it could work smoothly. So the Marxist theory runs and I now wish to make some critical comment.

In my view it is a useful approach to the problem to start with an analysis of society by focusing attention first on the technical foundations of its economic production. This is a sphere where change can be clearly observed and defined. Here I think one should go even further than Marx. He was only concerned with the changes in the techniques of economic production, the visible machinery which produces food, clothes, housing, and so on. But these are not the only techniques in which change influences society—for instance there are improvements in military technique which influence the shape of society equally. We have the opportunity of seeing that changes in military technique have made the domination of the army and of armed gangs more likely. In the same way we can see that the improvement of what I would call social techniques influences the course of events. For instance, modern methods of influencing human behaviour made propaganda a powerful agent, and those who have a grip on it may seek to influence society in any direction they please. In the same way improvement in the technique of organisation has brought about the power of bureaucracy, and it is a new managerial bureaucracy which is competing with the competitive class of captains of industry. All this shows that not only changed economic techniques influence the primary socio-economic relationships, and through them the whole of society, but improvements in the fields of other techniques supplement this influence. Whilst it is true that technological change influences what happens in societies, is there no scope for exercising the power of the mind in social affairs?

Some people think the mind is impotent to influence social affairs, others that it is omnipotent. Whilst I believe that technological factors are important, I should maintain that they may be manoeuvred according to human ends which are culturally agreed. Or, as Lewis Mumford puts it, 'our capacity to go beyond the machine rests in our power to assimilate the machine'. In our advanced technical age it would be impossible to destroy the machine but it is possible with intelligence to remove those institutions which do harm, or strengthen those tendencies which are already at work and useful but not yet fully developed. Social reform does not mean building society anew from the beginning, but observing the tendencies at work and through a definite strategy guiding it in the desired direction.

2. CLASS AND CASTE CONFLICT AS CAUSES OF SOCIAL CHANGE

Both class and caste refer to social position which means only that certain people have different chances in life according to the place they take in the social order. Caste or estate is a more rigid form of defining one's status in society and is based upon religious or legal regulations (taboos, laws, customs) limiting the scope of rise or fall in the social scale. Class is a more elastic definition of one's place in the social order. There are, in the main, no legal barriers, but only those of an economic and educational nature which make it difficult for certain classes to rise in the social scale. Modern society in the age of liberalism and democracy has transformed the system of estates into that of open classes. In medieval society, the society of estates, you were generally confined all your life to the social estate in which you were born. Modern capitalist society does not recognise such legal limitations but economic and educational handicaps may prove difficult to surmount. Although in everyday talk we think we are quite clear as to the meaning of class distinction, the more closely one examines its actual content the vaguer its form becomes. In considering the different definitions it may be useful to discriminate between the descriptive and the functional definition of class.

The descriptive definition of class is only concerned with the question of the distinguishing marks classifying people into classes. This definition does not attempt to give a deeper explanation of the dynamic causes bringing about class differentiation in connection with the changing social structure. This is the concern of the functional definition. Ginsberg attempted such a descriptive definition and found that in practice the basis of distinction into classes varies. We classify a person as lower class, middle class or upper class, according to his behaviour, speech, dress, habits of social intercourse, but we consider as more important distinguishing marks, economic status, which is defined by property and income, occupation, education, mode of life. All this means that our discriminating sense operates with a combination of points of view but these points of view vary in predominance. It is interesting that this distinction between higher and lower seems to develop in every social order whereas it cannot be made a general rule that either property or education or occupation or mode of life, are the main distinguishing marks in a given society.

The functional definition differs from the descriptive in that it groups those people together who have the same function in society, and therefore are expected to act in the same way and to develop a similar consciousness. Marx tries to define the position in society in terms of economic functions, and he therefore speaks of economic classes. According to this theory, persons who hold the same position in the process of production belong together, and so you have on the one hand the owners of the means of production and on the other the producing classes. As the forms of production affect the forms of distribution, a social class is also characterised by the source of income. Taking these two things together one arrives at the definition that a social class is an aggregate of persons who have the same functions in the productive process and who therefore have the same source of income.

The picture would be too simple if we were to distinguish only two classes, the owners of the means of production and the non-owners. Marx was aware of the fact that in addition to the basic classes there are found in every society intermediate classes, occupying a middle position between the commanding and the executing classes. There are for instance the transitional classes, resulting from the disintegration of the previous forms of industrial production—such as the small entrepreneurs and tradesmen. There are also the mixed classes, such as the corporate bureaucracy, the white collared workers, the professionals, the great army of the new distributive occupations, such as the employees of the big department stores, and the *déclassé* groups consisting of beggars, vagrants and the like. This functional definition enabled Marx to link up his theory of social change with the class structure of society. The classes play a certain role in the transformation of society, the original cause of which, according to Marx, is to be found in the changing economic technique. The dynamic process comes about in this way: those who carry out the physical work produce surplus profit—a certain amount of goods above their own consumption. Then there is a struggle for the distribution of the total national product and as this struggle becomes conscious it gives rise to class interests and class conflicts. Gradually class interests develop into a system which embraces all life and these interests are interwoven with political, religious and scientific interests, the result of which is the gradual development of class ideals and a definite class psychology. Each class tends to develop a frame of mind, a *Weltanschauung*.

The existence of class interests does not mean that they are always understood by a class itself. You may belong to a class, according to Marx, because you are a wage-earner, but if you are a white-collared worker, you are likely to conceal from yourself the fact that you are a wage-earner and share the interests and prejudices of the capitalist class. In this case, claims Marx, you have a 'false consciousness' and it is only through enlightenment and propaganda that you will understand your real position in society. It is difficult to show clearly the existence of class consciousness. For instance, a ruling class might try to diminish the awareness of class positions, or it may be that among members of a class temporary interests clash with general or long-range interests. According to Marx, class consciousness in the suppressed classes can be concealed for a long time, but sooner or later the antagonisms existing in the social order are bound to lead to a social revolution: 'Sooner or later when the productive forces of society reach a point when their further development is obstructed by existing social institutions, the class struggle becomes acute and it is then that it becomes the main driving force of social reorganisation.' In that revolution the proletariat has to capture the state and its whole machinery in order to remove those obsolete institutions which prevent the development of the productive forces and maintain the class structure.

3. CRITICISM OF THE MARXIST THEORY OF CLASS STRUGGLE. THE ROLE OF RELIGIOUS AND NATIONAL DIFFERENCES

Before putting forward my criticism of Marx's theory, I wish to emphasise its value even although in many ways it may be misleading. Its main virtue is that it tries to look at society as a coherent structure, as a mechanism, the rules of which, if they are found, can be consistently interpreted. This means that Marx replaces the piecemeal interpretation by a coherent hypothesis which helps us to reconstruct the working of the whole with the aid of imagination. In the natural sciences, if the variety and changes of factors are too great, we try to construct a model which reduces the variety to a simplified scheme in order to get away from the confusion and despondency. Without such a hypothetical simplification, the human mind could not grasp the whole. If we take the Marxian analysis of social change and class struggle as such a model and hypothesis, but not as a dogmatic statement of reality, then it will serve a useful purpose, all the more as we have no other coherent hypothesis and model of the structure of society. The physicist in trying to offer an interpretation of data will develop a model or a hypothesis. By this he will not mean that reality is bound to conform to his model, but he will only claim that his model approximates to what happens in reality. But if the variations in the data become too great for the hypothesis to explain, he will have to be ready to replace it by another model which takes into account the great number of changes which do not fit into the original theory. The trouble about the Marxists is that they do not take the Marxian hypothesis as a hypothesis, but as a dogmatic statement from which one is not allowed to deviate. This distorts the value of the whole approach. These preliminary remarks will help to show where the picture of reality deviates from the Marxist model.

For logical purposes it was quite useful to aim at a functional definition which artificially classifies society into two classes; the class of the owners of the means of production and the producing class. But if we look at reality and ask ourselves whether the people really act and behave according to these distinctions, we can only assert that there is a *tendency* towards the formation of economic and social groups and their stratification and stability vary from one society to another in accordance with general economic conditions. In a marginal situation it may be that people will act against each other according to this antagonism, but in most situations the dividing principle does not rise to the surface. The many other aspects enumerated in the descriptive definition of classes are continually at work modifying the functional division.

Marx originally saw the middle class as crushed between the millstones of the capitalist and the workers, and as a dwindling group. Actually the elaboration of capitalism has made it a growing group. He was right about the dwindling of the small entrepreneur and tradesman, but meanwhile a new middle class has developed. This class consists of technicians, white-collared groups, professional groups, those engaged in the marketing and distributive system, small business men, small investors, the housewives, the people with annuities and small founded incomes. A social theory which does not reckon with their special dynamics will be misleading. One of the reasons for the rise of Fascism is that the Italian and German working class parties alienated these groups by not realising their special psychology and lacking a constructive scheme which would have provided them with an active function in their movement.

In the same way, the statement that class struggles are inevitable is an unjustified generalisation, for it is only a tendency and not the only form of transformation of societies. There is no doubt that in modern society there is a latent struggle between economic and social groups, but this struggle is fragmentary and intermittent; often it may become completely latent, although it cannot be denied that if no other outlet is given to reform it may become the dominant feature.

If one takes it as a tendency, there will only be struggle if through reform we are unable to remove those institutions which hamper the evolution of the modern economic system, and thus cause continuous crises in it. But on principle revolution can always be avoided if these transformations are carried out gradually and in a peaceful way. If from the very beginning we state that the struggle is, and must be, inevitable, we sap reform. On the other hand, one has of course always to be alive to the possibility that through frustration revolution may become unavoidable.

Moreover, the formation of consciousness of the general interest of the class is slow and intermittent. It is inevitable that economic groups which are closely related should sometimes struggle against one another as well as against opposing groups. It is also inevitable that economic interests should be overshadowed from time to time by cultural, religious and ethnic factors. Nationalism both as an economic and as a cultural phenomenon, tends to offset the formation of classes. It would be more correct to say that the tendency to unite along the lines of class interests is one of the great tendencies in our modern societies, with which the tendency to unite along cultural, religious or national lines competes. The Second World War, for instance, is an example of class interests being over-ridden by national interests. The direction in which integration takes place very often depends on the situation, on where the challenge comes from. A Socialist

Catholic German miner in the Ruhr district, for instance, will react in terms of his *national* feelings if attack comes from an enemy to his country. The same man might be dominated by his *religious* traditions and emotions when he finds his Catholicism attacked. Finally, in a struggle in which he feels that his class allegiance is in jeopardy, his *socialist* feelings are uppermost. This approach prevents us from dealing with people as if they were to be put into separate drawers labelled 'Socialist', 'German', etc., for such classifications do not correspond to the dynamic nature of human motivations. Everybody is guided by a set of various motivations, and it depends, as we have seen, on the situation which comes to the fore.

With this more elastic theory, we are able to understand that this age is equally the scene of increased nationalism and increased class struggle, and it depends on the historical situation and the management of these situations, which tendencies will integrate. As an exclusive generalisation it is not true to say either that our age is one of class struggles or one of national differences. At the same time, the history of Europe from 1930 to 1945 has shown that, temporarily at least, class divisions can be over-ridden by the mobilisation of nationalist feelings. If we take the class struggle, not as a dogmatic necessity, but as a tendency, we are better able to understand the great structural changes in our society. We have to have both a comprehensive hypothesis and, at the same time, an elastic way of thinking which is always ready to adapt the hypothesis to the new realities.

Bibliography[1]

PART 1

CHAPTER I: MAN AND HIS PSYCHIC EQUIPMENT

1. *Behaviour, Situation and Adjustment*

Davis, J., and Barnes, H. E., et al.: *Introduction to Sociology.* Boston, 1927.
(Especially Book II, Part III.)

Folsom, J. K.: *Culture and the Social Process.* New York, 1928. (Especially Chapter IV.)

Healey, H., et al.: *Reconstructing Behaviour in Youth.* New York, 1929.

Parmelee, M.: *The Science of Human Behaviour.* New York, 1913.

Paton, S.: *Human Behaviour.* New York, 1921.

Sapir, E.: 'The Unconscious Patterning of Behaviour in Society'.
(See Child, C. M., Koffka, K., et al.: *The Unconscious: A Symposium.* New York, 1928.)

Thomas, W. I.: 'The Behaviour Patterns and the Situation'.
(See Burgess, E. W. (Ed.): *Personality and the Group.* Chicago, 1929.)

Zilsel, E.: 'Geschichte und Biologie, Überlieferung und Vererbung', *Archiv. f. Socialwissenschaft*, Vol. 65, 1931.

---

[1] In compiling the bibliography we have selected from the many titles gathered together in Mannheim's notes those which seemed to us especially relevant to his argument. As can be seen in some of his other books, Mannheim built up very large lists of titles in his bibliographies, and we thought that we should prefer to be selective. We have followed the principle of listing the titles in the same way as he did according to the chapter and subdivision headings to be found in the table of contents.

J. E.
W. A. C. S.

BIBLIOGRAPHY

2. i. *Habits and the Problem of 'Instincts'*

Dewey, J.: *Human Nature and Conduct*. New York, 1930.

Douglas, A. T.: 'Habits, Their Formation, Their Value, Their Danger', *Mental Hygiene*, Vol. 16, 1932.

Ellwood, C. H.: 'Mental Patterns in Social Evolution', *Publications of the American Sociological Society*, 1922.

James, W.: *Principles of Psychology*. New York, 1890.

McDougall, W.: *An Introduction to Social Psychology*. Boston, 1921.

McDougall, W.: *Energies of Men*. New York, 1933.

McDougall, W.: 'Organization of the Affective Life', *Acta Psychologica*, Vol. 2, 1937.

Mead, G. H.: 'Scientific Method and Social Sciences', *Journal of Ethics*, Vol. 29.

Murphy, G., Murphy, L. B., and Newcomb, T. M.: *Experimental Social Psychology*. New York, 1937. (Especially Chapter III.)

Park, E., and Burgess, E. W.: *Introduction to the Science of Sociology*. Chicago, 1928. (Especially Chapters IX, X and XI.)

Thouless, R. H.: *General and Social Psychology*. London, 1937.

Williams, G. M.: *Our Rural Heritage*. New York, 1925.

Znaniecki, F.: *The Laws of Social Psychology*. Chicago, 1925.

ii. *The Habit-making Mechanism*

Bernard, L. L.: *An Introduction to Social Psychology*. New York, 1926.

Bernard, L. L.: 'Neuro-Psychic Technique in Social Evolution', *Publications of the American Sociological Society*, Vol. 18, Chicago, 1924.

Davis, M. M.: *Psychological Interpretations of Society*. New York, 1929.

Douglas, A. T.: 'Habits, Their Formation, Their Value, Their Danger', *Mental Hygiene*, Vol. 16, 1932.

Jennings, H. S., Watson, J. B., Meyer, A., and Thomas, W. I.: *Suggestions of Modern Science Concerning Education*. New York, 1918.

Pavlov, I.: *Lectures on Conditioned Reflexes*. New York, 1928.

Tarde, G.: *The Laws of Imitation* (translated by E. C. Parsons). New York, 1903.

Watson, J. B.: *The Ways of Behaviourism*. New York, 1928.
Watson, J. B.: *Behaviourism*. London, 1931.
Watson, J. B., and McDougall, E.: *The Battle of Behaviourism*. Psyche Miniatures, General Series, No. 19.

3. *Evolution in the Models of Imitation*
> Burgess, E. W., et al.: *Environment and Education*. Chicago, 1942.
> Burgess, E. W.: 'The Cultural Approach to the Study of Personality', *Mental Hygiene*, Vol. 14, 1930.
> Burgess, E. W.: *Personality and the Social Group*. Chicago, 1929.
> Burrow, T.: 'Alternating Frames of Reference in the Sphere of Human Behaviour', *Journal of Social Philosophy*, Vol. 2, No. 2.
> Cooley, C. H.: *Human Nature and the Social Order*. New York, 1928.
> (Especially Chapter XIII.)
> Groves, E. R.: *Personality and Social Adjustment*. New York, 1931.
> Smith, W. R.: 'Social Education in the School through Group Activities', *Publications of the American Sociological Society*, Vol. 13, 1922.
> Smith, W. R.: *Principles of Educational Sociology*. Boston, 1929.
> Thrasher, F. N.: *The Gang*. Chicago, 1927.

4. *Sociological and Psychoanalytic Descriptions of Man*
> i. *Repression* ii. *Neurosis, Reaction Formation and Projection*
> iii. *Rationalisation*
> Alexander, A.: *The Psychoanalysis of the Total Personality* (translated by B. Glück and B. Lewin). New York, 1930.
> Allport, G. W.: *Personality. A Psychological Interpretation*. New York, 1937.
> Bain, R.: 'Sociology and Psychoanalysis', *American Sociological Review*, Vol. 1, No. 2, 1936.
> Burgess, E. W.: 'Freud and Sociology in the United States', *American Journal of Sociology*, Vol. 45, 1939–40.

Dashiell, J. F.: *Fundamentals of General Psychology*. Boston, 1937.

Dashiell, J. F.: 'Experimental Studies on the Influence of Social Situations upon the Behaviour of Individual Human Adults'.
(See Murchison, C. (Ed.): *A Handbook of Social Psychology*. Worcester, Mass., 1935.)

Folsom, J. K.: *Social Psychology*. New York, 1931.
(Especially Chapters II and III.)

Folsom, J. K.: *The Family*. London, 1944.

Freud, A.: *The Ego and the Mechanism of Defence*. London, 1937.

Freud, S.: *A General Introduction to Psychoanalysis* (translated by G. S. Hall). New York, 1922.

Freud, S.: *Basic Writings* (translated by A. A. Brill). New York, 1938.

Healy, W., Bronner, A., and Bowers, A. M.: *The Structure and Meaning of Psychoanalysis*. New York, 1931.

Healy, W.: *Personality in Formation and Action*. London, 1938.

Jones, E.: *Papers on Psychoanalysis*. London, 1923.

Jones, E.: *Social Aspects of Psychoanalysis*. Lectures delivered under the auspices of the Sociological Society, London, 1924.

Jones, E.: 'Abnormal Psychology and Social Psychology'.
(See MacFie Campbell, C., McDougall, W., et al.: *Problems of Personality. Studies presented to Morton Prince*. London, 1932.)

Lasswell, H. D.: *Psychopathology and Politics*. Chicago, 1930.

Schilder, P.: 'Psychoanalysis and Conditioned Reflexes', *The Psychoanalytic Review*, Vol. 29, No. 1, 1937.

Taylor, W. S.: 'Rationalization and its Social Significance', *Journal of Abnormal and Social Psychology*, Vol. 18, 1923.

iv. *Symbolisation and Daydreaming*

Blumer, M.: *Movies and Conduct*. New York, 1933.

Healy, W., et al.: *op. cit.*

Jones, E.: 'The Theory of Symbolism', *Papers on Psychoanalysis*. London, 1923.

Sachs, H.: *The Creative Unconscious*. Cambridge, Mass., 1951.

Schilder, P.: 'The Analysis of Ideologies as a Psychotherapeutic Method', *American Journal of Psychiatry*, Vol. 93, 1936.

v. *Sublimation and Idealisation and their Social Significance*

Bartlett, F. C.: 'The Psychological Process of Sublimation', *Scientia*, Vol. 43, 1928.

Dashiell, J. F.: 'The "Inner" Life as Suppressed Ideal of Conduct', *International Journal of Ethics*, Vol. 30, 1919–20.

Durkheim, E.: *Le Suicide*. Paris, 1897 (English translation, London, 1952).

Jones, E.: 'The Significance of Sublimation Processes for Education and Re-education', *Papers on Psychoanalysis*. London, 1923.

Lasswell, H. D.: 'The Triple Appeal Principle. A Contribution of Psychoanalysis to Political and Social Science', *American Journal of Sociology*, Vol. 37, 1931–32.

Lasswell, H. D.: 'What Psychiatrists and Political Scientists can learn from one another', *Psychiatry*, Vol. 1, 1938.

Mead, G. H.: *Mind, Self, and Society*. Chicago, 1934.

Pepper, S. C.: 'The Boundaries of Society', *International Journal of Ethics*, Vol. 32, 1921–22.

Taylor, W. S.: 'Alternative Response as a Form of Sublimation', *Psychological Review*, 1932.

Weber, Max: *Essays in Sociology From Max Weber* (translated and edited by H. H. Gerth and C. W. Mills). London, New York, 1947.

Znaniecki, F.: *The Laws of Social Psychology*. Chicago, 1925.

CHAPTER II: MAN AND HIS PSYCHIC EQUIPMENT (*Continued*)

5. *The Social Guidance of Psychic Energies*

Allport, F. H.: *Institutional Behaviour*. Chapell Hill, North Carolina, 1933.

Bernard, L. L.: *Social Control*. New York, 1937.

Dewey, J.: 'Social Science and Social Control', *New Republic*, Vol. 18, 1931.

Hart, H.: 'The Transmutation of Motivation', *American Journal of Sociology*, Vol. 35, 1929–30.

Jones, A. J.: *Principles of Guidance*. London, New York, 1934.

Mannheim, Karl: *Man and Society in an Age of Reconstruction*. London, 1940.

Merriam, C. E.: *The Making of Citizens: a Comparative Study of the Methods of Civic Training*. Chicago, 1931.

Osborn, R.: *Freud and Marx*. London, 1937.

Overstreet, H. A.: *Influencing Human Behaviour*. London, 1926.

6. *Object Fixation and the Transference of Libido*

Allport, G. W.: 'Attitudes'.
(See Murchison, C. (Ed.): *A Handbook of Social Psychology*. Worcester, Mass., 1935.)

Burrow, T.: *The Biology of Human Conflict. An Anatomy of Human Behaviour, Individual and Social*. New York, 1937.

Burrow, T.: 'Altering Frames of Reference in the Sphere of Human Behaviour', *Journal of Social Psychology*, Vol. 2, 1937.

Faris, E.: 'Attitudes and Behaviour', *American Journal oj Sociology*, Vol. 34, 1928–29.

Faris, E.: 'The Concept of Social Attitudes', *Journal of Applied Sociology*, Vol. 9, 1925.

Folsom, J. K.: *The Family: its Sociology and Social Psychiatry*, 1934.

Frank, L. K.: 'Physiological Tension and Social Structure', *Publications of the American Sociological Society*, Vol. 22, 1928.

French, T. M.: *Social Conflict and Psychic Conflict*. Chicago, 1939.

Freud, S.: *Reflections* (translated by A. A. Brill and B. Kuttner). New York, 1922.

Jones, A. J.: *Principles of Guidance*. New York, London, 1934.

Lasswell, H. D.: *Psychopathology and Politics*. Chicago, 1931.

Mead, M.: 'Adolescence in Primitive and Modern Society'. (See Calverton, V. F., and Schmalhausen, S. D. (Eds.): *The New Generation*. London and New York, 1930.)

Park, R.: 'Human Nature, Attitudes and the Mores'.
(See Young, K. (Ed.): *Social Attitudes*. New York, 1931.)

Reuter, E. B., Mead, M., and Foster, R. G.: 'Sociological Research in Adolescence', *American Journal of Sociology*, Vol. 42, 1936–37.

Wallas, G.: *Our Social Heritage*. London, 1921.

Waelder, R.: 'Aetiologie und Verlauf der Massenpsychose', *Imago*, Vol. 21, 1935.

7. *Sociology of Types of Behaviour*
  i. *Attitudes and Wishes*

Allport, G. W., and Schanck, R. L.: 'Are Attitudes Biological or Cultural in Origin?', *Character and Personality*, 1936.

Allport, G. W.: *Personality. A Psychological Interpretation*. New York, 1937.

Folsom, J. K.: *Social Psychology*. London and New York, 1931.

Frank, J. O.: 'Some Psychological Determinants of the Level of Aspiration', *American Journal of Psychology*, Vol. 47, 1935.

Thomas, W. I., and Znaniecki, F.: *The Polish Peasant in Europe and America*. New York, 1927.

Thomas, W. I.: *The Unadjusted Girl*. Boston, 1928.

Thomas, W. I.: 'The Persistence of Primary-Group Norms in Present-day Society'.
(See Jennings, H. S., Watson, J. B., et al.: *Suggestions of Modern Science Concerning Education*. New York, 1917.)

Thorndike, E. L.: *The Psychology of Wants, Interests and Attitudes*. London and New York, 1935.

Thorndike, E. L.: *Human Nature and the Social Order*. New York, 1940.

  ii. *Interests*

Beaglehole, E.: *Property: a Study in Social Psychology*. London, 1931.

MacIver, R. M.: *Society. A Textbook of Sociology*. New York, 1937.
(Especially Chapter II.)

Malinowski, B.: *Coral Gardens and their Magic*. New York, 1935.

Wallas, G.: *The Great Society. A Psychological Analysis.* London and New York, 1920.

Wright, H. W.: 'Rational Self-Interest and Social Adjustment', *International Journal of Ethics*, Vol. 30, 1919–20.

PART 2

THE MOST ELEMENTARY SOCIAL PROCESSES

CHAPTER III: A. SOCIAL CONTACT AND SOCIAL DISTANCE

1. *Primary and Secondary Contacts*

Burgess, E. W. (Ed.): 'The Urban Community', *Proceedings of the American Sociological Society*, Vol. 20, 1925.

Cooley, C. H.: *Social Organisation. A Study of the Larger Mind.* New York, 1924.

Ellwood, C. A.: *The Psychology of Human Society.* New York, 1925.

Kolb, J. H.: *Rural Primary Groups.* 1921.

Kolb, J. H., and Brunner, E.: *A Study of Rural Society.* Boston, 1935.

Park, R. E., and Burgess, E. W.: *Introduction to the Science of Sociology.* Chicago, 1928.
(Especially Chapter V.)

Simmel, G.: *Soziologie.* Leipzig, 1908.
(Especially Chapters 6, 9 and 10.)

Sorokin, P. A., and Zimmerman, C.: *Principles of Rural-Urban Sociology.* New York, 1929.

2. *Sympathetic and Categoric Contacts*

Eubank, E.: 'Errors of Sociology', *Social Forces.* 1937.

Lasswell, H. D.: *World Politics and Personal Insecurity.* New York, 1935.

Shaler, N. S.: *The Neighbour.* Boston, 1904.

Sumner, W. G.: *Folkways.* Boston, 1907.

Sperling, O.: 'Appersonierung und Excentrierung', *Internat. Zeitschrift f. Psychoanalyse*, Vol. 23, 1937.

Pilgrim Trust: *Men Without Work.* A Report. Cambridge, 1938.

3. *Social Distance*

Bogardus, E. S.: 'Measuring Social Distance', *Journal of Applied Sociology*, Vol. 9, 1925.

Bogardus, E. S.: 'Social Distance and its Implications', *ibid.*, Vol. 22, 1938.

Bogardus, E. S.: 'A Social Distance Scale', *Sociology and Social Research*, Vol. 17, 1932–33.

Bullough, E.: 'Psychological Distance as a Factor and an Aesthetic Principle', *British Journal of Psychology*, Vol. 5, 1912–13.

Park, R. E.: 'The Concept of Social Distance', *Journal of Applied Sociology*, Vol. 8, No. 6, 1924.

Révész, G.: 'Sozialpsychologische Betrachtungen an Affen', *Zeitschrift für Psychologie*, Vol. 118, 1930.

Schjelderup Ebbe, T.: 'Beiträge zur Sozialpsychologie des Haushuhns', *ibid.*, Vol. 88, 1922.

Schjelderup Ebbe, T.: 'Weitere Beiträge zur Sozial und Individualpsychologie des Haushuhns', *ibid.*, Vol. 92, 1923.

Sorokin, P.: *Social Mobility*. New York, 1927.

Wiese, L. v., and Becker, H.: *Systematic Sociology*. New York, 1932.

4. *Maintaining Social Hierarchy*

Pigors, P.: *Leadership or Domination*. London, 1936.

Raymond, E., and Kahn, E. E.: *The Craving for Superiority*. New Haven, 1931.

Simmel, G.: *Soziologie*. Leipzig, 1908.
(Especially Chapter 3.)

Thomas, W. I.: *Primitive Behaviour*. New York, 1937.

CHAPTER IV: B. ISOLATION

1. *The Social Functions of Isolation*

Park R. E., and Burgess, E. W.: *Introduction to the Science of Sociology*.
(Especially Chapter IV.)

Stock, W.: 'Isoliertheit und Verbundenheit', *Kölner Vierteljahrshefte für Soziologie*, Jg. 2, 1922.

Yarros, V. S.: 'Isolation and Social Conflict', *American Journal of Sociology*, Vol. 27, 1921–22.

2. *The Various Kinds of Social Isolation*

Fromm, E.: 'Die gesellschaftlich Bedingtheit der psycho-analytischen Therapie', *Zeitschrift für Sozialforschung,* Jg. IV, 1935.

Geiger, T.: 'Formen der Vereinsamung', *Kölner Vierteljahrshefte für Soziologie,* Jg. 10, 1919.

Ichheiser, G.: 'Die Vereinsamung des Individuums', *Archiv f. Angewandte Psychologie.* Bd. 3.

Park R. E.: 'Human Migration and the Marginal Man', *American Journal of Sociology,* Vol. 33, 1927–28.

Sorokin, P. A.: *Social Mobility.* London, New York, 1927.

Stonequist, E. V.: *The Marginal Man.* New York, 1937.

Wood, M. M.: *The Stranger. A Study in Social Relationship.*

Wirth, L.: *The Ghetto.* Chicago, 1929.

CHAPTER V: INDIVIDUALISATION AND SOCIALISATION

C. Individualisation

Allport, F. H.: 'Self-evaluation: a Problem in Personal Development', *Mental Hygiene.* New York, 1925.

Benn, G.: *Der Neue Staat und die Intellectuellen.* Stuttgart, 1933.

Burgess, E. W.: *Personality and the Social Group.* Chicago, 1929.

Flugel, J. C.: *The Psychology of Clothes.* London, 1931.

Folsom, J. K.: *The Family: its Sociology and Social Psychiatry.* New York, 1934.

Horney, K.: 'The Problem of the Monogamous Ideal', *International Journal of Psychoanalysis,* Vol. 9, 1928.

Lewis, E. H.: 'Some Definitions of Individualization', *American Journal of Sociology,* Vol. 18, 1912–13.

Martin, A. H.: 'An Empirical Study of the Factors and Types of Voluntary Choice', *Archives of Psychology,* Vol. 51, 1922.

Mead, G. H.: 'The Genesis of the Self and Social Control', *International Journal of Ethics,* Vol. 35, 1925.

Mead, M.: *Coming of Age in Samoa.* New York, 1928.

Mead, M.: *Growing Up in New Guinea.* New York, 1930.

Misch, G.: *History of Autobiography in Antiquity,* Vol. 1. London, 1950.

North, C. C.: *Social Differentiation*. Chapel Hill, N. Carolina, 1926.

Park, R. E.: 'Personality and Cultural Conflict', *'Social Conflict': Papers presented to the Twenty-Fifth Annual Meeting of the American Sociological Society held at Cleveland, December 1930*. Chicago, 1931.

Plant, J. S.: *Personality and the Culture Pattern*. New York, 1937.

Rothacker, E.: *Schichten der Persönlichkeit*. Leipzig, 1937.

Schiffer, H.: *Die Politische Schulung des Englischen Volkes*. Leipzig, 1931.

Simmel, G.: *Soziologie*. Leipzig, 1908.
(Especially Chapters 6 and 9.)

Sullivan, H. S.: 'Psychiatry. Introduction to the Study of Interpersonal Relations', *Psychiatry*, Vol. 1.

Thomas, W. I., and Thomas, D. S.: *The Child in America: Behaviour Problems and Programs*. New York, 1932.

Volkart, E. H. (Ed.): *Social Behaviour and Personality: Contributions of W. I. Thomas to Theory and Social Research*. New York, 1951.

D. Individualisation and Socialisation

Burgess, E. W.: *The Function of Socialisation in Social Evolution*. Chicago, 1916.

Cooley, C. H.: *Human Nature and the Social Order*. New York, Chicago, 1928.
(Especially Chapters III, IV, V, VI and X.)

Dewey, J.: *Human Nature and Conduct*. New York, 1930.

Mead, G. H.: *Mind, Self and Society*. Chicago, 1933.

Ross, E. A.: *The Outlines of Sociology*. London, New York, 1933.

Smith, W. R.: *Principles of Educational Sociology*. Boston, New York, 1929.

Spykman, N. J.: *The Social Theory of Georg Simmel*. Chicago, 1925.
(Especially Book I, Chapters I and VII.)

CHAPTER VI: E. COMPETITION AND MONOPOLY

Cooley, C. H.: *Sociological Theory and Social Research*. New York, 1930.

Cooley, C. H.: *The Social Process*. New York, 1927.
(Especially Chapters IV, V, VIII, XII and XXXII.)

Horney, K.: *The Neurotic Personality of Our Time*. London, 1937.

May, M. A., and Doob, L.: 'Competition and Co-operation', *Social Science Research Council Bulletin*, No. 25, 1937.

Oppenheimer, F.: *System der Soziologie*. Jena, 1922–27.

Reaney, M. J.: 'The Psychology of the Organised Group Game', *British Journal of Psychology*, Monograph Supplements, Vol. 4, Cambridge.

Schiffer, H.: *Die Politische Schulung des Englischen Volkes*. Leipzig, 1931.

Sombart, W.: *Das Wirtschaftsleben im Zeitalter des Kapitalismus. Hochkapitalismus: II Halbband*. Leipzig, 1924.

Tawney, R. H.: *The Acquisitive Society*. London, 1921.

Veblen, T.: 'Christian Morality and the Competitive System', *International Journal of Ethics*, Vol. 20, 1920.

Watson, G.: 'The Measurement of Fair Mindedness', *Teachers' College Contributions to Education*, No. 176, New York, 1925.

Wiese, L. v., and Becker, H.: *Systematic Sociology*. New York, 1932.
(Especially Chapters VIII and X.)

Whittemore, I. C.: 'The Competitive Consciousness', *Journal of Abnormal and Social Psychology*, Vol. 20, April 1925.

Wright, H. W.: 'Rational Self-Interest and Social Adjustment', *International Journal of Ethics*, Vol. 30, 1919–20.

CHAPTER VII: COMPETITION AND CO-OPERATION

F. Selection

G. The Main Effects of Competition and Selection on Mental Life

Cooley, C. H.: *Social Process*. New York, 1927
(Especially Part I, Chapter IV and Part V, Chapter XII.)

Hartshorne, E. J.: *German Youth and the Nazi Dream of Victory*. New York and Toronto, 1941.

Ichheiser, G.: *Die Kritik des Erfolges*. Leipzig, 1930.

Mannheim, K.: 'Competition as a Cultural Phenomenon'.
(See *Essays on the Sociology of Knowledge*. London, 1952.)

Pillsbury, W. B.: 'Selection—an Unnoticed Function of Education', *Scientific Monthly*. January 1921.

Sorokin, P. A.: *Social Mobility*. New York and London, 1927.

Thurnwald, R.: 'Führerschaft und Siebung', *Zeitschrift für Völkerpsychologie und Soziologie*, Jg. 2, 1926.

H. Co-operation and the Division of Labour

Bouglé, C.: 'Théories sur la Division du Travail', *L'Année Sociologique*, Vol. VI, Paris, 1903.

Bücher, K.: *Die Entstehung der Volkswirtschaft*. Tübingen, 1920.

Durkheim, E.: *De la Division du Travail Social*. Paris, 1922. (Especially Book I, Chapters II and III.)

Hughes, E. C.: 'Personality Types and the Division of Labour'.
(See Burgess, E. W. (Ed.): *Personality and the Social Group*. Chicago, 1929.)

Kropotkin, P.: *Mutual Aid a Factor of Evolution*. New York, 1922.

May, M., and Doob, L. W.: 'Competition and Cooperation', *Social Science Research Bulletin*. New York, 1937.

Mayo, E.: *Human Problems of Industrial Civilization*. New York, 1933.

Mead, M. (Ed.): *Coöperation and Competition among Primitive Peoples*. London, 1937.

Tylor, E. B.: *Primitive Culture*. New York, 1924.

Ward, H. F.: *The New Social Order*. New York, 1919.

Ward, H. F.: *In Place of Profits*. New York, 1933.

PART 3

SOCIAL INTEGRATION

CHAPTER VIII: A. THE SOCIOLOGY OF GROUPS

1. The Crowd. 2. The Public. 3. Abstract Masses and the Abstract Public. 4. Organised Groups

Blumer, H.: 'Collective Behaviour'.
(See Park, R. E. (Ed.): *Outline of the Principles of Sociology*. New York, 1939.)

Clark, C. D.: 'The Concept of the Public', *Southwestern Social Science Quarterly*. 1933.

Dewey, J.: *The Public and its Problems*. New York, 1927.

La Pierre, R. T.: *Collective Behaviour*. New York, 1938.

Le Bon, G.: *The Crowd*. New York, 1925.

MacIver, R. M.: *Society: a Textbook of Sociology*. New York, 1937.

(Especially Chapters X, XI and XII.)

Martin, E. D.: *The Behaviour of Crowds*. New York, 1920.

Ross, E. A.: *Social Psychology*. New York, 1909.

Sherif, M.: *The Psychology of Social Norms*. New York, 1936.

Simmel, G.: 'Persistence of Social Groups' (translated by A. Small), *American Journal of Sociology*, Volumes 3 and 4, 1897-8, 1898-9.

Young, K.: *Sourcebook for Social Psychology*. New York, 1933.

CHAPTER IX. THE SOCIOLOGY OF GROUPS
(*Continued*)

5. *The Types of Groupings*

Beaver, A. P.: 'The Initiation of Social Contacts by Pre-school Children', *Child Development Monographs*, No. 7, New York, 1932.

Bernard, L. L.: 'Conflict Between Primary Group Attitudes and Derivative Group Ideals in Modern Society', *American Journal of Sociology*, Vol. 41, 1935–36.

Burgess, E.: 'The Family and the Person'.

(See Burgess, E. W. (Ed.): *Personality and the Social Group*. Chicago, 1929.)

Dewey, J.: *School and Society*. Chicago, 1910.

Ellwood, C. A.: *The Psychology of Human Society*. New York, 1925.

Folsom, J. K.: *The Family and Democratic Society*. New York, 1932.

Hocking, W. E.: *Morale—Its Meaning*. New Haven, 1918.

Simmel, G.: *Soziologie*. Leipzig, 1908.

(Especially Chapters 2, 8 and 10.)

Simmel, G.: 'The Number of Members as Determining the Sociological Form of the Group' (translated by A. Small), *American Journal of Sociology*, Vol. 8, 1902–03.

Simmel, G : 'The Persistence of the Social Group' (translated by A. Small), *American Journal of Sociology*, Vol. 3, 1897–98 and Vol. 4, 1898–99.

Smith, W. R.: *An Introduction to Educational Sociology.* Boston and New York, 1929.

Spykman, N. J.: *The Social Theory of Georg Simmel.* Chicago, 1925.
(Especially Chapters I, III and VII in Book II.)

Sumner, G. W.: *Folkways.* Boston, 1907.

Thrasher, F. M.: *The Gang.* Chicago, 1925.

Tönnies, F.: *Community and Association* (translated by C. P. Loomis). London, 1955.

Wiese, L. v., and Becker, H.: *Systematic Sociology.* New York, 1932.
(Especially Chapters XXXIV–XLI.)

6. *The State*

Lowie, R. H.: *The Origin of the State.* New York, 1927.

MacIver, R. M.: *The Modern State.* Oxford, 1926.

Oppenheimer, F.: *The State* (translated by J. M. Gittermann). Indianapolis, 1914.

Sumner, W. G., and Keller, A. G.: *The Science of Society.* New Haven, 1927.
(Especially Vol. I, Part III, Chapter XVI.)

Weber, Max: *Essays in Sociology From Max Weber* (translated and ed. by H. H. Gerth and C. W. Mills). London, New York, 1947.

Weber, Max: *The Theory of Social and Economic Organisation.* Being Part I of *Wirtschaft und Gesellschaft* (translated by A. R. Henderson and T. Parsons). London, 1947.
(Especially Chapters I and III.)

CHAPTER X. B. THE CLASS PROBLEM

Beard, C. and M. R.: *The Rise of American Civilisation.* New York, 1936.

Briefs, G.: 'Das Gewerbliche Proletariat', *Grundriss der Sozialökonomik*. Part IX/1. Tübingen, 1925.

Carr-Saunders, A. M., and Caradoc Jones, D.: *A Survey of the Social Structure of England and Wales.* London, 1927.

Cooley, C. H.: *Social Organisation.* New York, 1922.

Dollard, J.: *Caste and Class in a Southern Town*. New Haven, 1937.

Ginsberg, M.: *Sociology*. London, 1934.

Hobhouse, L. T.: *Morals in Evolution*. London, 1915.

Hobhouse, L. T.: *The Making of Man*. New York, 1931.

Klineberg, O.: *Race Differences*. New York, 1935.

Laski, H.: *The Modern State in Theory and Practice*. London, 1935.

Marshall, T. H.: 'Social Class—A Preliminary Analysis', *Sociological Review*, Vol. 26, 1934.

Marshall, T. H. (Ed.): *Class Conflict and Social Stratification*. London, 1939.

Marx, K.: *Das Kapital*. Vol. III, Chicago, 1909.

Marx, K., and Engels, F.: *The Communist Manifesto*. London, 1883.

Mosca, G.: *The Ruling Class*. New York, 1939.

Mukerji, D. G.: *Caste and Outcaste*. New York, 1923.

Sorokin, P.: *Social Mobility*. London and New York, 1927.

Speier, H.: 'Social Stratification in the Urban Community', *American Sociological Review*, Vol. 1, 1936.

Veblen, T. B.: *The Theory of the Leisure Class*. New York, 1925.

Weber, Max: *The Theory of Social and Economic Organisation*. Being Part I of *Wirtschaft und Gesellschaft* (translated by A. R. Henderson and T. Parsons). London, 1947. (Especially Chapter IV.)

Warner, W. L.: 'American Caste and Class', *American Journal of Sociology*, Vol. 42, 1936–37.

PART 4

SOCIAL STABILITY AND SOCIAL CHANGE

CHAPTER XI: FACTORS OF SOCIAL STABILITY

1. Social Control and Authority

Benne, K. D.: 'A Conception of Authority. An Introductory Study', Teachers College, Columbia University, *Contributions to Education*. New York, 1943.

BIBLIOGRAPHY

Cooley, C. H.: *The Social Process*. New York, 1927.
(Especially Parts I and II.)

Davis, J., and Barnes, H. E., et al.: *An Introduction to Sociology*. New York, 1927.
(Especially Book II, Part IV.)

Ross, E. A.: *Social Control*. New York, 1901.
(Especially Chapters X–XIX.)

Stern, L.: 'The Sociology of Authority', *Publications of the American Sociological Society*, Vol. 18.

Wallas, G.: *Our Social Heritage*. London, 1921.

Wooddy, C. H., and Stouffer, S. A.: 'Local Opinion and Public Opinion', *American Journal of Sociology*, Vol. 36, 1930–31.

2. Custom. 3. Law as a Form of Social Control

Ginsberg, M.: *Sociology*. London, 1934.
(Especially Chapter V.)

Maine, H.: *Ancient Law*. London, 1907.

Sumner, W. G.: *Folkways*. Boston, 1907.

4. Prestige and Leadership

Bogardus, E. S.: *Leaders and Leadership*. New York, 1934.

Gerth, H.: 'The Nazi Party: Its Leadership and Composition', *American Journal of Sociology*, Vol. 45, 1940.

MacIver, R. M.: *The Modern State*. Oxford, 1926.

Nicolson, H.: *The Meaning of Prestige*. Cambridge, 1937.

Pigors, P.: *Leadership and Domination*. London, 1936.

Waller, W.: *The Sociology of Teaching*. New York, 1932.
(Especially Chapter 16.)

Whitehead, T. N.: *Leadership in a Free Society*. Cambridge, 1937.

Speier, H.: 'Honor and Social Structure', *Social Research*, Vol. 2, 1935.

5. The Philosophical and Sociological Interpretation of Values

Burrow, T.: 'Social Images vs. Reality', *Journal of Abnormal and Social Psychology*, Vol. 19.

Chadwick, H. M.: *The Heroic Age*. Cambridge, 1926.

Cooley, C. H.: *Social Process*. New York, 1927.
(Especially Part VI.)

Mannheim, K.: 'Sociology of Human Valuations'.
(See Dugdale, J. E. (Ed.): *Further Papers on the Social Sciences*. London, 1937.)
Weber, Max: *Religionssoziologie*, Vol. I, Tübingen, 1925.
Weber, Max: *The Protestant Ethic and the Spirit of Capitalism* (translated by T. Parsons). London, 1930.

CHAPTER XII: CAUSES OF SOCIAL CHANGE

Berthe, E.: *Du 'Capital' aux 'Réflexions sur la Violence'*. Paris, 1932.
Buber, M. M.: *Karl Marx's Interpretation of History*. Cambridge, Mass., 1927.
Dewey, J.: 'Authority and Resistance to Social Change', *School and Society*, Vol. 44, 1936.
Hobhouse, L. T.: *Social Evolution and Political Theory*. New York, 1922.
MacIver, R. M.: *Society: a Textbook of Sociology*. New York, 1937.
(Especially Book III.)
Mannheim, K.: *Man and Society in an Age of Reconstruction*. London, 1941.
Marx, Karl: *Zur Kritik der Politischen Ökonomie*. Berlin, 1859. Translated by N. Y. Stone, New York, 1904.
Ogburn, W. F.: *Social Change*. New York, 1929.
Ogburn, W. F.: 'Stationary and Changing Societies', *American Journal of Sociology*, Vol. 42, 1936–37.
Thornton, J. E. (Ed.): *Science and Social Change*. Washington, 1930.

Index of Names

Index of Subjects